The End of a Tradition

INSTITUTE OF LATIN AMERICAN STUDIES

COLUMBIA UNIVERSITY

The End of a Tradition

CULTURE CHANGE AND DEVELOPMENT

IN THE MUNICÍPIO OF CUNHA

SÃO PAULO, BRAZIL

by Robert W. Shirley

 *1971*

Columbia University Press

NEW YORK AND LONDON

ROBERT W. SHIRLEY is Assistant Professor
in the Department of Anthropology,
The University of Toronto

Copyright © 1971 Columbia University Press
ISBN: 0-231-03193-9
Library of Congress Catalog Card Number: 76-129535
Printed in the United States of America

TO MY FAMILY

THE INSTITUTE OF LATIN AMERICAN STUDIES of Columbia University was established in 1961 in response to a national, public, and educational need for a better understanding of the nations of Latin America and a more knowledgeable basis for inter-American relations. The major objectives of the Institute are to prepare a limited number of North Americans for scholarly and professorial careers in the field of Latin American studies, to advance our knowledge of Latin America through an active program of research by faculty, by graduate students, and by visiting scholars, and to improve public knowledge through publication of a series of books on Latin America. Some of these studies are the result of research by the faculty, by graduate students, and by visiting scholars. It was decided to include in this series translations from Portuguese and Spanish of important contemporary books in the social sciences and humanities.

When Dr. Robert Shirley undertook the field research for the present book, he was a graduate student in the Department of Anthropology and he was closely associated with the Institute of Latin American Studies. His study of the community of Cunha in the State of São Paulo, Brazil, which was first presented as a doctoral dissertation in anthropology, was later revised for publication in its present form. It represents an important and original contribution to the field of community studies in complex developing nations and more specifically to our understanding of Brazil. It has particular interest in that Cunha, which is described in this book, in the late 1960s was perhaps the first Brazilian community to be studied by modern social anthropological and sociological techniques. It was studied in the early 1940s by Professor Emilio Willems, then of the University of São Paulo, and his students. While Dr. Shirley's book is not essentially a "re-study" of Cunha, he did have a baseline in this earlier research against which to measure socio-cultural change. We are proud to include this book in our series of books on Latin America. The publication program of the Institute of Latin American Studies is made possible by the financial assistance of the Ford Foundation.

Preface

The effects of growing industry upon an agrarian nation are complex and profound. Economics, demography, politics, society, and culture, all are changed by the growth of industrial cities and the extension of metropolitan mass culture. Because of the importance of these changes, a great deal of research has recently been done on social dynamics within cities, often with special emphasis upon rural-urban migration. The rural zones themselves, and the small towns linked to them, however, have been largely neglected in these studies, the assumption being made, perhaps, that they remain static and for the most part untouched by the changes taking place in the national metropolitan centers.

In late 1964 I went to Brazil to do a study of social change in one of the oldest communities in that country, the *município* of Cunha in the upper Paraíba Valley. Because of the distinctive and conservative culture which existed there, Cunha had been the focus of considerable research on Brazilian rural "folk" society, and was the actual site of the first community study made in Brazil, by Emilio Willems in 1945. Yet Cunha lies in São Paulo State, the major center of industry in Latin America, and I was interested in investigating the effect the growth of this great industrial metropolis had had on this historical region. This book, then, is an account of change: of the disorganization of an old agrarian society, planters and peasants alike, and the multifold effect which an industrial center has on its dependent zones.

I have not attempted to change the name of the community

since it is already well established in the literature. To protect
the many people who helped me in the town, and some who
did not, the names of all individuals have been changed and
sufficient events and facts scrambled in my descriptions so as to
avoid embarrassment to any specific families.

The research upon which this paper is based was carried out
during eighteen months in Brazil under a training grant from
the Foreign Area Fellowship Program. I am grateful to the
program and its staff for their continued support and encour-
agement. I am greatly indebted to Dr. Charles Wagley, Director
of the Latin American Institute of Columbia University. Without his support and recommendations this research could never
have adequately developed.

In Brazil, the Universidade de São Paulo has given me considerable help and advice. I wish especially to thank Professors
Floristan Fernandes, Octavio Ianni, Oracy Nogueira, and their
student, José de Souza Martins. I am indebted to the Instituto
Brasileiro de Geografia e Estatística for aid, information and
advice. In addition, the Departamento de Estatística do Estado
de São Paulo, with its director Waldemir Pereira, has been
most helpful.

I wish to thank Dona Maria Julia Pourchet for invaluable
assistance. I am also grateful to Dr. Alceu Maynard Araújo,
Professor Emilio Willems, and Professor Donald Curry for important ideas and information. I am also indebted to Professor
Peter Carstens of the University of Toronto, who read the completed manuscript, and to Mrs. McCullough and the staff at
Scarborough College for typing it.

In Cunha itself I wish especially to thank the judge, Dr.
Francisco Cesar Pinheiro Rodrigues; the mayor, Sr. Francisco
Macedo Rodrigues; and the Chairman of the City Council, Sr.
Osmar Felipe. In addition my thanks go to Sr. Antonio Accacio
Cursino, Cônego Francisco de Assís Carvalho, Dr. João Sebe
Hajar, Dr. Lescar Ferreira Mendes, Sr. Sylvio Mendes de
Souza, and Dr. Fued Seraphim. My special gratitude is to the

Rev. Nelson Luís de Campos Leite, and my chief field assistant, Sr. Antonio Geraldo da Silva.

Most of all, I am indebted to all the people of Cunha, whose unfailing courtesy and good humor, despite my inquisitiveness and inadequate Portuguese, made my stay there profoundly rewarding. To my field assistants and friends in the town and *município*, I can truthfully say that the strength of this study is due to them. I will take the responsibility for any errors of interpretation.

ROBERT W. SHIRLEY

May 18, 1970

Contents

The End of a Tradition

Chapter I

The Setting

"Brazil," says the historian João Camillo de Oliveira Tôrres, "offers the social scientist one especially valuable condition, travels in space are also travels in time . . ." (1965:11). While major Brazilian cities are among the most modern and cosmopolitan in the world, poor transportation and communication have left many isolated little communities apparently unaffected by the passage of time. The "Two Brazils" noted by so many students of the country (Lambert, 1967) refers not just to agriculture but to whole communities and ways of life. Almost anything can be found in this enormous country, from the most modern of factories to aboriginal Indians and colonial plantations. These are pockets of history left by the tides of Portuguese expansion.

Few places can this be demonstrated more dramatically than in the state of São Paulo. São Paulo is both Brazil's largest city and Latin America's largest industrial center. For those who expect Latin American cities to be sleepy tropical towns, the Paulista capital comes as a shock, with mile after mile of skyscrapers, huge avenues and viaducts, and the most modern of architecture. It is a city that is transforming itself year by year, and even minute by minute, from an old coffee town to the industrial and financial heartland of a nation. Yet the change has been very rapid and the influence of this great industrial urban center has not been felt equally in all parts of the state of São Paulo. Here the importance of transportation and geography in economic development can be shown with great clarity.

The city of São Paulo lies at the edge of the Brazilian *Planalto*, the high tableland which makes up much of the interior of Brazil. This highland rises spectacularly from the sea in the rugged escarpment of the Serra do Mar, but the crest of the Serra lies only a few kilometers inland and thereafter the land slopes gently to the north and east.

Transportation across the Serra is very difficult but on the *Planalto* it is relatively easy. Thus the city of São Paulo is located beyond the mountains above its own port of Santos, at a point where communication with the interior in several different directions is possible: north to the interior of its own state, west to the Sorocaba region, and east to Rio de Janeiro. On the other hand, with the exception of Santos, there is little communication across the Serras. Thus, it is in the mountains to the south and east of the metropolis that one still finds the poorest, as well as the most conservative regions of the state. Here one can find old colonial port cities such as Paratí and Angra dos Reis, preserved as they were built, hundreds of years ago. Here also are imperial coffee cities such as Areias and Bananal, unchanged since the end of slavery in the last century.

To the east and running slightly north of the urban center of São Paulo lies a great valley through which flows the Rio Paraíba do Sul. This broad and flat valley, some 10 to 20 kilometers wide, was caused by extensive block faulting and collapse of the mountains of the highlands (Rich, 1951:15; Long, 1949:16). The Paraíba valley forms a natural corridor between Brazil's two largest cities, São Paulo and Rio de Janeiro, and thus is one of the historically richest and most important areas in the country. The significance of the valley for transportation is enhanced by the fact that the mountains on either side, formed by other blocks thrust upward, are some of the highest in Brazil, reaching altitudes of nearly 3,000 meters.

The Rio Paraíba do Sul is not large, as Brazilian rivers go.

Its watershed is limited to the mountains on either side of the valley, rising in the mountains to the south, flowing toward the city of São Paulo, and then abruptly reversing itself to flow east-northeast into the collapsed valley away from the city for 600 kilometers until it meets the sea in the state of Rio de Janeiro. On its way it flows by many cities of great importance in the past and present of Brazil, São José dos Campos, Taubeté, Guaratinguetá, the religious shrine of Nossa Senhora da Aparecida, patron saint of Brazil, and the huge steel complex at Volta Redonda.

The region is exceptionally beautiful. The floor of the valley is largely flat and excellent agricultural land, and some extremely prosperous ranches can be found here. To the north looms the Serra da Mantiquera, a large serrated massif some 2,700 meters high. Soaring over a mile above the valley floor, this area has become the mountain resort region for wealthy Paulistas. This is the "Switzerland of Brazil," though without snow. Two other crystalline mountain blocks form the southern wall of the valley, the Serra da Bocaina to the east, some 2,100 meters high, and the Serra da Quebra Cangalha ("packsaddle breaker") in the west, about 1,200 meters in altitude.

The major cities of the Paraíba Valley maintain much of São Paulo's hustle. São José dos Campos is the site of General Motors do Brasil, and Taubeté, with a population of some 200,000, sponsors its own university. The importance of transportation is demonstrated most dramatically in the valley. Brazil's major highway, the Via Dutra, and the railroad *Central do Brasil*, pass along the valley between Rio de Janeiro and São Paulo. Cities on these routes have prospered greatly with the development of industry in the south, but those cities not connected with the major centers have remained agrarian and poor—they are, in the words of Monteiro Lobato (1959) Brazil's "Dead Cities" (*Cidades Mortas*).

Of all these isolated regions in São Paulo State, the oldest, the largest, and in academic circles the most famous, is the *município* of Cunha, which lies in the region south of the valley, in the *Alta Paraíba* (upper Paraíba). Because of a combination of historical and geographical factors, Cunha until very recently remained one of the most isolated and conservative regions of the state, and one of the last remaining centers of the old rural folk culture of São Paulo, the so-called *Caipira Paulista*. The *município* has thus been the focus of considerable attention on the part of social scientists and folklorists from São Paulo, who, stimulated by the works of Robert Redfield in Mexico (1930 and 1941), sought a simple "folk" society within their own state. Cunha was thus the site of the first community study ever made in Brazil: Emilio Willems' *Cunha: Tradição e Transição em uma Cultura Rural do Brazil* (1947). In addition, at least five other Brazilian and French scholars have visited and published on the *município*.* As author of this study, however, I was less interested in the content of the *caipira* culture, ably described by Willems and others, than in the forces and changes which had taken place in the region under the impact of the industrial cities of the state. Thus I lived and studied in the *município* for a year, in 1965–1966.

Guaratinguetá, with a population approaching 80,000 and a number of light industries, is far from being a "*cidade morte.*" It is a sophisticated, though highly class-conscious town, aware of its historical importance and a bit snobbish about other regions. Some of the residents found it incredible that an American (and from New York City!) should want to visit Cunha, let alone live there. This despite the fact that many of the residents of Guaratinguetá have relatives in the *município*. Transportation, however, is no problem, as there is a regular bus service, and it is a sign of the changes taking place in the region that this service was recently purchased from Guaratinguetá by one of Cunha's own entrepreneurs.

The foothills of the Quebra Cangalha begin at the edge of

---

* See Appendix A for an account of the literature on Cunha and the *caipira* culture.

the city of Guaratinguetá and the road winds around them for
several miles before reaching the steep escarpment of the
valley wall. The city itself is soon lost to sight but the traveler
can see the jagged peaks of the Serra da Mantiquera appear
to the north with increasing clarity, purple above the haze of
the populous and industrialized Paraíba Valley. To the American observer the dominant impression is made by the color
green, the lush green of tropical forest vegetation struggling
back in thick tangled clumps from its losing battle with the
axe and fire of man. But there is green even where the forest
has lost, the green of pastures and brilliant green of fields of
sugar cane, corn fields are rarely seen along the main roads
of Cunha these days. The earth, when it is exposed, stands out
sharply since, as in much of Brazil, the soil is rich in iron
and brick red in color. The earth roads stand out as do regions
where erosion has stripped away the vegetation. Here and
there also can be seen the red mud walls and tile roofs of the
traditional *caipira* house, made of *pau-au-pique,* a framework
of sticks plastered with mud. Frequently now, however, the
houses are made of brick and are painted in the bright colors
of Portugal, pink, blue, and yellow.

In the *Alta Paraíba* region, above and to the southeast of
the valley cities of Guaratinguetá and Lorena, lies a gently
depressed plateau which extends about 35 kilometers between
the crests of the Quebra Cangalha and the Serra do Mar. The
plateau is not flat, however, but instead is made up of an ex-
traordinary confusion of little hills and valleys in a complex
dendritic pattern which has been aptly called by Brazilian
geographers the *"Mar dos Morros,"* "The Sea of Hills" (Ab'
Sáber, 1950). The major part of this plateau, bounded by the
heights of Bocaina to the northeast, is included in the *município* of Cunha. The *município* totals some 1,333 square
kilometers (by official estimates) and contains the headwaters
of both the Paraitinga and Paraíbuna rivers. These eventually
join to form the Paraíba River itself.

In the center of this hilly plateau stands the town of Cunha, the *sede* (center) of the *município*. It lies on a small hill and can be seen from quite a distance, appearing as a collection of small white towers above the green during the day, and forming a long string of lights at night. Emilio Willems described the town in 1945 as "resembling a compact edifice condensed on the height of a hill, crowned by the towers of the *matriz* church" (1947: 8–9). The edifice is still there, but it has thrown long wings along the crest of the hill in phenomenal growth during the past few years.

Geography has critically affected Cunha's history and is basic to understanding its past as well as its future. The mountains of the Serra do Mar, and of the whole *Alta Paraíba* region, although not exceptionally high, are exceedingly rugged. The hundreds of valleys in the region are small, but steep-sided, so that transportation across the mountains is very difficult. This is especially true to the north around the great block of Bocaina. In the southern part of the *município*, however, there extends a belt of granitic rock where the hills are lower and not as rough (map, I.G.G.E.S.P., 1963). This region, therefore, was chosen as the route for one of the very first roads built by the colonial Portuguese into the interior of Brazil from the port of Paratí. The base rock of the ancient Brazilian Shield, moreover, decomposes into soils which are relatively rich, and thus this section contains some of the best agricultural lands in the area. To the north, however, in the highlands of Bocaina and the crest of the Serra do Mar, the sides of the mountains are so steep that the dangers of rapid erosion make the land unsuitable for agriculture, and even in some cases for grazing (Rich, 1951; also map and publications by the Serviço Nacional de Pesquisas Agronômicas, 1965).

Climate also has played a major part in the region's development. Most of Cunha is over 800 meters high and the *sede* itself has an altitude of nearly 1,000 meters. Thus the region receives frost every winter. This fact has prevented the planting of coffee in the region as coffee trees are instantly killed by

Map of the Município of Cunha

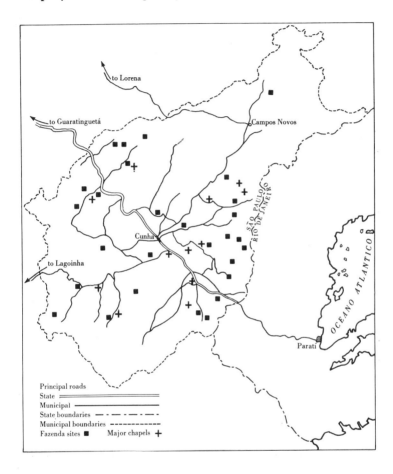

to Lorena

to Guaratinguetá

Campos Novos

to Lagoinha

Cunha

SÃO PAULO
RIO DE JANEIRO

OCEANO ATLANTICO

Parati

Principal roads
State ═══════════
Municipal ─────────
State boundaries ─ · ─ · ─ · ─ ·
Municipal boundaries ------------
Fazenda sites ■   Major chapels ✚

temperatures below freezing. On the positive side, the frost also kills many of the insects which serve as vectors for malaria and other diseases and the region is by tropical standards very healthy. Aside from the frost the region has a good climate for agriculture. The yearly rainfall averages 1,470 millimeters with nearly half of that total falling during the warm and wet summer months of December, January, and February. In the winter, June, July, and August, on the other hand, it is common for weeks to pass with no rain whatsoever and this *sêca* presents a problem for ranchers since the fields on the hillslopes dry up and for a few months the animals must be fed by hand (all data from Setzer, 1943).

The coastal escarpment receives a much greater rainfall, sometimes up to 2,000 millimeters a year, which permits the growth of luxuriant vegetation and insures rapid erosion when this is removed.

The northeastern part of the *município* of Cunha, forming a subdistrict, Campos Novos de Cunha, is isolated and very sparsely populated. It is beautiful, wild country, much of it completely uninhabited and even unexplored. In fact, in Cunha —only 15 to 20 kilometers from the municipal center and just a day's travel from the metropolis of São Paulo—it is still possible to find virgin Brazilian rain forest untouched by man since the Portuguese rounded up and enslaved the Indians hundreds of years ago. Legends of lost treasures and hidden gemstones—legends which lured the Portuguese into the interior in the first place—are still very much alive among the rural people of Cunha, accompanied by Indian and Portuguese stories of ghosts and forest monsters. To travel in Cunha is to travel back in time 400 years, to the very opening of the country, to the original *sertão*, the rain forest. The enormous trees of this forest, many of them in flower, make an unforgettable sight. The famous hardwoods which were Brazil's first product: *peroba, canjarana, ipé, guatambú, jacarandá, canela preta, canela vermelha, cedro do campo;* still grow here in abundance, a fact which is not lost on commercial interests in São Paulo. Because of the beauty of the region and its fine climate the region has considerable potential for tourism. People do, now and again, come up from São Paulo for hunting or fishing. *Onças* (jaguars) can still be found in the forest as can many other animals. No description, moreover, can do justice to the spectacular escarpment of the Serra do Mar. The high, steep, rounded domes characteristic of Rio de Janeiro can be found here as well, surrounded by their original deep forest. At their foot, at the bottom of an escarpment 1,200 meters high, lies not a city of three million people, but a tiny colonial port. Paratí is a town so ancient yet so well preserved, that it has been declared a national historical monument and is only now being "discovered" by the tourist industry.

The paradox of Cunha, therefore, is a microcosm of the paradox of Brazil, great age together with raw frontier. Here the new and the old exist side by side. But the old is feeling the impact of the new, and is changing.

Chapter II

History

The history of Cunha goes back almost as far as the very earliest Portuguese settlement in Southern Brazil. Its history, as Mario Wagner da Cunha has stated (1944:641), is intimately tied up with the history of transportation, the history of roads, of migration of peoples and of the shipping of many kinds of products. Cunha is, and has always been, a peripheral region. It has always been secondary to, and dependent upon, the great social and economic movements which occurred in the nearby Paraíba Valley and the vast interior of São Paulo and Minas Gerais.

Brazil, writes Celso Furtado, was occupied as an "aftermath of commercial expansion in Europe" (1963:1). This is a fundamental point. The Portuguese in the New World did not find in the lowlands the dense, organized, semi-urbanized populations, such as the Inca and Aztec, which the Spanish conquered in the highlands. The Brazilian Indians were said to be a fierce people, and probably more numerous than most modern ethnographers seem to think (see Staden, 1874). On the other hand, they were weakly organized and apparently devoted to continual internecine warfare. They were, in the long run, no match for the rapacious Portuguese warrior-merchants, who brought their firearms—and diseases—from the Old World. The Indians were soon exterminated, driven into the interior, or enslaved and absorbed into the Portuguese-speaking population. The new possessors, however, were businessmen as well as adventurers and were for the most part interested in obtaining the things which were scarce, and hence

Location Map 1: South America

B R A Z I L

SAO
PAULO

had value, in the international trading economy of Europe. This commercial-exploitative aspect was to color all of Brazilian history, society, and culture.

The economic links which traditionally bound Brazil to the urban industrial centers of Europe, and later of the United States, have always been, however, of the most tenuous kind. *"Produtos da sobremesa"* (dessert products) the Brazilians scornfully call their main export crops: sugar, cacao, coffee, bananas, etc. Brazil has suffered the added disadvantages in that her enormous natural wealth meant that she was often the first country to develop any tropical commodity, and thus other nations frequently profited from her early mistakes.

In reading Brazilian economic history, one sees the same pattern thus endlessly repeat itself. The market for a given commodity grows rapidly and local entrepreneurs move in and expand production precipitously. A brief period of opulence opens for these small commercially active groups, followed by stagnation and economic collapse. Anthony Leeds has explicitly compared the various cycles (1957) and several excellent studies exist on specific cycles (Stein, 1957a on coffee; Stein, 1957b on cotton; Canabrava, 1951 on cotton; Leeds, 1957 on cacao; E. Taunay, 1939–1943 on coffee; and Boxer, 1962 on gold).

The current industrial expansion of South Central Brazil, centered in São Paulo, seems to herald a break in this cyclical dependence on a single commodity. For the first time in Brazil's history it has its own source of urban industrial products and capital. The strong regional nature of this industrialization, however, has meant that many less developed sections of Brazil have become dependent upon São Paulo and there are frequent complaints in the north about "Paulista Imperialism." Although there is some justification for these complaints, the fact remains that for the first time Brazil is no longer dependent upon other national entities for most of her manufactured goods.

Location Map 2. South Central Brazil

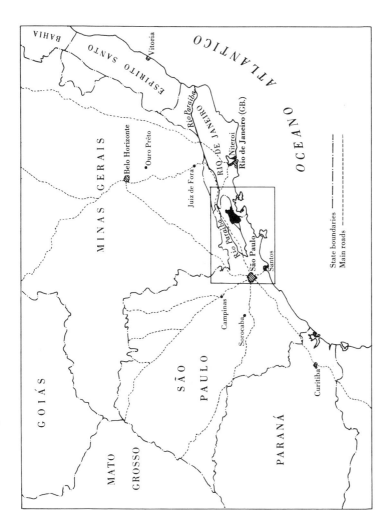

State boundaries ————
Main roads - - - - - - -

GOIÁS

MATO GROSSO

MINAS GERAIS

Belo Horizonte
•Ouro Prêto

Juiz de Fora•

•Campinas
Sorocaba•

SÃO PAULO

São Paulo
Santos

Rio Paraíba

PARANÁ

Curitiba•

ESPIRITO SANTO
Vitoria•

Rio Paraíba

RIO DE JANEIRO
Niteroi
Rio de Janeiro (GB.)

OCEANO ATLANTICO

BAHIA

Cunha has almost never produced commodities for direct export and hence has not been directly involved in the international trading economy. The *município* has instead had an economic history of production of food, supplying regions so involved. Thus Cunha has been in the rather odd position of being productively primary, that is, engaged in the production of subsistence crops, but commercially secondary; her production had only local, not international, value. Such dependence upon subsistence production has had both advantages and disadvantages. Commercially the region could not develop as far as the areas producing for export, but at the same time it was not as deeply involved in commercial production, with all that this implies, concerning exploitation of both the land and the people. This point will be further developed below.

The first Portuguese settlements in Brazil were along the coast, where a series of small port towns were established in the seventeenth century. One of these was Paratí, which was founded on the western end of the Bay of Ilha Grande, one of the largest and best natural ports in Brazil. The very first European inhabitants of the Cunha region were adventurers and pathfinders (Wagner Vieira da Cunha, 1944:641), who entered the mountains from the coastal settlements seeking emeralds and Indians to enslave. A series of small settlements were established in the hinterland as "jumping off" places for further exploration, or as points to rest and obtain supplies.

At the same time other groups with the same interests were pushing out from the newly established town of São Paulo. One of the first routes opened was along the Paraíba Valley, and here too little way stations were established, at intervals of the distance which it took to travel in a day. The regularity of the spacing of the cities in the valley today, strung like beads along the Paraíba River, testifies to their origin. Each of these little settlements became a center for further exploration, and groups of adventurers entered the mountains flanking the valley from both Taubeté and Guaratinguetá. By 1650 the link between Paratí and Guaratinguetá had been made, and the town of Cunha became an important way station on the road from the sea to the Paraíba Valley and the interior. The early townsite for Cunha (described in Chapter XI) developed around the church. The town soon gained a reputation as a haven for criminal fugitives from the coast who had fled the colonial authorities in Paratí.

Cunha first boomed, however, during the Brazilian gold rush between 1695 and 1750, even though it was not itself a mining region. After the first gold strikes were made in Minas Gerais in 1693 and 1695, travel on the road between Paratí and the interior increased many times. Thousands of gold hunters traveled inland from the sea through the town and many gold shipments were carried, on muleback, in the opposite direction. This road through Cunha was known as the "*Caminho Velho*," or "Old Highway," and was one of the most important routes into the interior. From Paratí the road bifurcated at the town, one branch leading directly down to Guaratinguetá and the other going north to Lorena. Of these, the former was shorter and was generally favored. From the valley the road led along the Paraíba River until it turned north to the valley of the Rio Doce and the interior of Minas Gerais. It thus skirted the high ridges of the Serra da Mantiquera (Boxer, 1962).

Cunha supplied food, animals, and other necessary goods to the travelers and greatly profited from the increased movement stemming from the gold rush. It thus became a notable commercial center at an early date. The profits were apparently made in more ways than one, since the colonial Portuguese government in 1700 put heavy guards on the road in order to prevent waylaying and smuggling of gold (Wagner Vieira da Cunha, 1944:642). The actual settling of the land, however, only began after the gold rush had subsided in the eighteenth century.

The early settlement of the land was very much like that

of the rest of the Paraíba region. Petitions were made to the Portuguese crown for the granting of *sesmarias*—huge land grants of a square league in area (about 36 square kilometers). These always fronted on a road and opened onto the wilderness at the back. The *sertão* (backlands) technically still belonged to the state. The early recipients of these grants were often *Paulistas* of mixed Portuguese and Indian extraction, although grants were usually made only to those who were wealthy enough to own a few slaves and could develop the land. Thus, from the earliest periods of Cunha's history, the exploitation and settlement of the land came about with slave labor. In the early years these slaves were Indians, but the local tribes soon disappeared and later more and more Africans were imported.

The men who received these grants were not at first very prosperous. Nevertheless, they were the early local landed elite. Sometimes grants were made to several members of the same family so that small colonies of related persons developed. The house was usually established some distance away from the road so that the owner could oversee his property more easily. This house, in time, became a *fazenda*, a residential nucleus where the landowner lived with his relatives and slaves. In addition it was common for the *fazendeiro*, the large landowner, to allow several poorer free families to live on his land rent free. These dependent families lived scattered over the *sesmaria* area and formed the basis of the *Caipira Paulista* peasantry.

The major commercial activity in Cunha in the seventeenth and eighteenth centuries was taking care of the travelers and commerce along the *caminho velho*. What Charles Boxer said for Minas Gerais held largely true for Cunha: "The individuals who did best for themselves derived their wealth not from mining alone, but from a judicious combination of mining, farming, slave trading, and merchandising" (1963:53). In this way, Cunha, even though not a mining region, was able to prosper, as is shown by the construction of the enormous *matriz* church, as well as some large homes during this era.

It might be pointed out that at this period of time, the town of Cunha as an urban center could rival many of the towns in the Paraíba Valley. Von Spix and Martius, for example, writing in 1818, comment on the surprising poverty of settlements in the Valley. Lorena, for example, now a town of 35,000 people and the seat of a diocese, was described then as "a village consisting of about forty houses and of no importance" (Von Spix and Martius, 1824:302), while Pindamonhangaba is noted as consisting of "some rows of low huts lying scattered upon a hill, [which] does not appear to be in a thriving condition" (*Ibid.*, 308).

The ordinance census of 1803 gives a clear picture of the social organization in Cunha for that year. At the top was the *Capitão-mor*, who was both the largest landowner and the official representative of the Portuguese crown in the region. He owned 39 slaves, the largest number of slaves held by anyone noted in the census. There was a total of fifteen *fazendeiros* who owned more than twenty slaves each. The majority of these, in addition, had a number of dependent families living on their lands. These families were listed under the names of the landowners as free men but living on the land "*a favor*," that is, rent-free. Although they are carefully distinguished from the slaves, they are nevertheless noted as dependents of the landowner, for small freeholding farmers were listed separately.

At this time almost every free *agricultor* owned a few slaves. There were some 40 or 50 families who owned from 10 to 20 slaves each, and an even larger number who only owned one or two slaves. These last might be considered small *sitiante* farmers.* Some of the dependent families living on

* The various Portuguese terms for people who make a living off the land will be used continually throughout this book. They have unfortunately no very precise meaning, but they do make some important distinctions. A *fazendeiro* is the owner of a *fazenda*, a large commercial agricultural enterprise. A *sitiante* is the owner of a *sitio*, a small farm, operated largely through the labor of the owner and his family. The *sitiante* does have free

Table IIA. Occupation List for the Cunha Region, 1803
Taken from the ordinance census of the year 1803. The census was done by three separate Ordinance Companies of the Portuguese Army, each of which had an assigned area. The first Company carried out the census of the *sede.**

Occupation	1st Ca.	Total
Military†	53	159
Magistrates and Civil Employees	13	13
Secular Clergy	5	7
Farmers (*Agricultores*)	51	177
Merchants (*Negociantes*)	20	30
Artisans (*Artistas*)	30	34
Dayworkers (*Jornaleiros*)	7	13
Beggars	4	9
Unemployed	4	4
Slaves: Total	*558*	*1,289‡*
Total Free Population	*615‡*	*1,465‡*
Total Population	*1,173‡*	*2,754‡*

* This material was obtained from the excellent *Arquivo do Estado de São Paulo*, and the author wishes to express his gratitude to this organization and its staff.

† This number may be an idealized figure of three companies of 53 men each.

‡ These figures are approximations; the data are conflicting.

the big estates also owned a few slaves. Table IIA lists occupations for Cunha in 1803. The first column refers to people living in the town itself (*sede*) and nearby areas. Even at this early date it can be seen that the town was fairly well

access to his property however, and thus is to be distinguished from the *lavrador*, a rural farm worker who is either landless or does not own sufficient land on which to live. In Cunha the distinction is made between the *parceiro*, a sharecropper, and the *camarada*, a paid agricultural worker. A ranch worker was generally called *camarada*. There is much variation in usage, however. One professional who also owned a fine *fazenda* listed his occupation as a *lavrador* on official documents. See the glossary for definitions of other Portuguese-Brazilian terms used in this book.

developed and had a total population of over 1,000. The large number of soldiers in the census was presumably to guard the road and may have been somewhat exaggerated.

The total population of the Cunha region (it was not a *município* in 1803) at this time is given as 2,754. Among these there were 1,111 whites, 336 free mulattos, and 18 free Negros. There were, in addition, 1,289 Negro and mulatto slaves. The tremendous importance of slavery in the early history of the population of Cunha is thus shown, as is the very small number of day laborers, either urban or rural, in the region. Clearly such manual work was done by slaves.

The major commercial production at this time (according to the census), was foodstuffs, primarily corn, beans, and rice. The larger *fazendeiros* also raised horses, presumably to sell to travelers. The food produced was sold to supply people on the *Caminho Velho,* and possibly the town of Paratí itself. There is no record at this time that there was any production in Cunha of products, such as sugar, that would be directly marketable abroad.

It is very doubtful if any but the very richest *fazendeiro* merchants at this time lived a very luxurious life. Slaves were relatively costly and the system of simple hoe cultivation used was relatively unproductive. A *fazenda* was usually a largely self-sufficient enterprise which produced food for its own consumption and sold what was left over. Thus, Stanley Stein wrote:

In the midst of forest that encroached on all sides, in touch with the outside world only when travelers stopped for the night, and early *fazendas* were more than the way stations surrounded by clearings typical for the years before 1800. They were nuclei of settlement. From these pinpoints of population there went out each day the free and the slave to clear the forest, to plant and harvest. In exchange for coffee and other products sent to Rio they received iron for implements worn in the siege with the forest, and slaves to wield them, also cotton goods and salt. In common with all pioneer plantations everything was temporary: The essential job was to feed, clothe, and house the people of the settlement (1957a:21–22).

It seems certain that the basis of the *caipira* peasant culture developed out of the way of life of these early settlements. As among the *caipira*, urban contact was minimal, even though some commerce was carried on for essentials which could not be made on the *fazenda*. The form of agriculture was very simple and education and religion in the more distant rural zones would tend to drift more and more into local "folk" patterns.

The existence of the road to Paratí, however, linked the *sede* of Cunha with the sea and hence the great urban centers of Rio and Europe. The town was stimulated, both socially and economically, by this contact and developed an urban quality at a very early date. It was an important government outpost by 1700, since the Portuguese were trying to control traffic to the gold fields. That it remained so into the next century is shown by the number of soldiers listed in the census of 1803. There is evidence of a long history of wealth in the town. The church, built in the first half of the eighteenth century, was decorated with carvings brought from Portugal and with lavish use of gold leaf. Some of the townhouses are impressively large and are said to be nearly 200 years old. Thus, an unusually sharp division between the urban and the rural ways of life seems to have been characteristic of Cunha throughout most of its history.

The rural zones of Cunha, in contrast, always remained economically and socially rather backward. The commercial production of Cunha, as has been noted, has always been dependent upon outside factors. The presence of the road gave some opportunity for commercial production of food, but there were no really large nonsubsistence permanent populations to supply. Even the market on the road dropped off with the

Location Map 3: Paraíba Valley

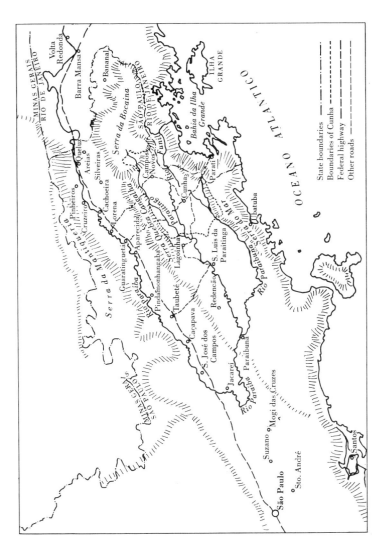

State boundaries
Boundaries of Cunha
Federal highway
Other roads

OCEANO ATLÂNTICO

ILHA GRANDE

Bahia da Ilha Grande

Parati

Ubatuba

S. Luís da Paraitinga

Redenção

S. José dos Campos

Jacareí

Suzano   Mogi das Cruzes

São Paulo

Sto. André

Santos

Rio Paraíba

Serra do Mar

Rio Paraíbuna

Cacapava

Taubaté

Lagoinha

Pindamonhangaba

Cunha

Guaratinguetá

Aparecida

Queluz

Cruzeiro

Areias

Pinheiros

Cachoeira

Lorena

Silveiras

Serra da Bocaina

Serra da Mantiqueira

Bananal

Barra Mansa

Volta Redonda

MINAS GERAIS
RIO DE JANEIRO

SÃO PAULO
RIO DE JANEIRO

MINAS GERAIS
SÃO PAULO

Campos Novos

Tinguá

end of the gold rush in 1750. For years there was no impetus for opening up the huge undeveloped backlands of Cunha for commercial production of any kind, and the region was left uninhabited except for the *caipira* families on the margins of the *sesmarias*. Thus the marginal peasantry of Cunha was allowed to develop in a relatively unhampered way due to the general weakness of the commercial agricultural sector.

Until about 1830 the history of Cunha was about like that of most of the *municípios* of the Paraíba Valley region. The rural zones were inhabited by a large number of slaveholding *fazendeiros* devoted primarily to subsistence production. Some of the towns were stimulated by contact with the mining regions and had developed a premature urban quality (cf. Harris 1956). The backlands remained largely undeveloped and uninhabited. The few Indian tribes had been eliminated by enslavement and intermarriage with the early Paulista settlers. Without a commercial commodity there was nothing to stimulate settlement, and the whole Paraíba region remained largely peripheral to the gold-mining regions of Minas Gerais.

By the end of the eighteenth century, however, production of marketable commodities had started on the rich flatlands of the valley floor. The history of the Paraíba Valley is largely the story of its commercial production and the various cycles of products which followed one another. Lucille Hermann, in a monograph written about the city of Guaratinguetá, has examined each of these cycles respectively and has shown the patterns of economics, social organization, and demography characterizing each. She has distinguished four economic cycles for Guaratinguetá (1948:321-23):

Cycle of the subsistence economy 1630–1775
Cycle of the small sugar plantations 1775–1836
Coffee cycle 1805–1920
Present cycle 1900–1944

The first cycle is characterized by an extremely small population scattered along the roads, little commerce, and extreme poverty among the population in the way of manufactured goods. It had a subsistence economy with little competition for land, a predominance of small-scale agriculture, and a social pyramid which was very broad at the base and with very small elite and middle classes. Politically the region was dominated in this early period by the *Capitão-mor*, but there were no struggles for land or power because most of the great landowners were related and land was plentiful and of relatively little commercial value. The population was largely Indian and Portuguese. A folk culture predominated, with great emphasis upon conformity and very little mobility (Hermann, 1948:13-52). In short, the society in this first period was very much like that of Cunha until most recent times.

The second and third cycles created great changes in all aspects of the society. Both these were cycles of monoculture production, and had the same general characteristics, but the coffee cycle had much more profound effects. The subsistence economy and the peasantry were undermined and finally obliterated during the great years of the coffee boom. The new society which took its place had several characteristics which distinguished it from the original subsistence culture. It changed demographically as large numbers of Negro slaves were brought in as nonsubsistence producers of the commercial crops. The value of the new products created competition for land which led to its legal division and control. The first effect of this was fragmentation under the Brazilian law of partible inheritance, but later, during the coffee cycle, annexation of land, because of its great value, became common and immense *latifúndios* developed. Exterior commerce favored the development of social classes and conspicuous consumption. This tendency increased during the coffee cycle. Small landowners were pushed out and an economically, socially, and politically dominant rural aristocracy developed.

While the socioeconomic pyramid reached its maximum, the middle classes enlarged as well. Politically, the newly emerging rural elite successfully challenged the hegemony of the *Capitães-mores*, but in turn fought over control until a compromise was reached which included members of the middle class. Cunha developed many of the characteristics of the second cycle, but never developed anything to equal the rural aristocracy which dominated the Paraíba Valley during the great days of coffee. Coffee was by far the most profitable and important crop grown in the Paraíba region. It was first produced on a small scale in Rio de Janeiro and entered the valley in the last decade of the eighteenth century through the *município* of Areias. By 1830 it was a common commercial crop throughout most of the region and it proved so profitable that production was rapidly expanded. The extent of its expansion can be seen from the following figures for a few of the *municípios* of the Middle Paraíba Valley:

Production (in arrobas: about 15 kg.)

Município	1836	1854
Taubeté	23,607	354,030
Pindamonhangaba	62,628	350,000
Lorena	33,649	125,000
Guaratinguetá	22,442	100,885

(From Taunay 1945:55)

It is difficult to overestimate the degree to which coffee production dominated the Paraíba Valley, and even the Brazilian national economy, from 1830 to 1930. The term "coffee baron" is used when speaking of the great producers of São Paulo, but the *fazendeiros* of the valley were, literally, barons of the Brazilian Empire. The region held a galaxy of glittering titles testifying to the importance of the coffee producers to the Imperial Government. Each member of this aristocracy owned hundreds of slaves and had usually annexed all the land for miles around. Thus their political and economic superiority can be understood. They were not only linked up with the national economy, in a very real sense they owned the national economy.

All of this production was carried out with Negro slave labor, and after 1800 a great many Africans were brought into the region despite a series of laws by the British and Brazilian governments against importing slaves. Many of these slaves were brought in from Paratí along the *Caminho Velho*. The difficulty of importing slaves, however, meant that the region suffered a chronic labor shortage, and this was one of the major reasons why coffee production declined in the valley after after 1860.* By that year most of the available land in the valley which was suitable for agriculture had been planted with coffee trees. As these aged, therefore, production began to decline. The lack of labor meant that the *fazendeiro* was unable to keep his estates in order by replanting trees or even preventing erosion (Long, 1949:63).

The final blow to the Paraíba coffee boom was the emancipation of the slaves in 1888. According to Escragnolle Taunay, many of the coffee *fazendas* were abandoned in mid-production by the slaves, as news of their freedom swept down the valley. Many of them left to visit the "court" at Rio de Janeiro and stayed in the city. This was so sudden and severe a jolt that coffee production in Brazil for that year, which had been planned at 10.7 million sacks, was reduced to 6.5 million sacks (Taunay, Vol. VII, 1939:468).

The development of coffee production in the Paraíba Valley had many effects on Cunha. As has been noted, most of the

---

* In 1883 the *municípios* of the valley had the following slave populations:

Areias	2,293	Pindamonhangaba	4,177
Bananal	7,168	Cruzeiro	1,000
Guaratinguetá	5,312	Queluz	2,255
Lorena	2,464	Taubeté	5,155

(From Taunay, Vol. V, 1939:451-53)

territory of the *município* is too high to grow coffee as the presence of frost during the winter kills the trees. Only in a few secluded valleys such as that of the Rio Paraitinga did extensive coffee plantations develop. The fact that Cunha could not produce coffee meant that the area remained on the periphery of this boom, as it had been on the periphery of the gold rush, and Cunha thus became an economic and political dependency of Guaratinguetá.

Nevertheless, Cunha did commercially prosper from the boom. The *município* became the food-producing region for the surrounding coffee zone. By 1860 the coffee boom had reached its peak, and what Stanley Stein noted in Vassouras apparently also happened throughout the Middle Paraíba Valley. Coffee *fazendeiros* "reduced foodstuff acreage and concentrated their labor force upon coffee production" (1957a:47). By this time, moreover, the small subsistence planters in the valley had been forced out of production by the slave and land monopolies of the coffee barons. The result was food shortage, and its prices soared. "Between 1852 and 1859 the price of basic foods more than doubled at the wholesale level and quadrupled at the retail level" (Stein, 1957a:48).

Thus Cunha became a major center for commercial food production, supplying corn, beans, rice, and hogs to the slave *fazendas* of the Paraíba Valley at inflated prices. It is worthy of note that most of this commercial production of foodstuffs in Cunha was also done with slave labor. Thus in 1883 Cunha had 1,744 slaves (Taunay, Vol. VII, 1939:451), and most commercial production was in the hands of a small number of great *fazendeiros*. Many of them were descendants of the traditional families who had received the original *sesmaria* grants. The socioeconomic pattern thus was somewhat similar to what Lucille Hermann found in Guaratinguetá, but there were two major differences. First, the fact that Cunha was specialized in food production meant that the area could revert to subsistence production without difficulty. Second,

Cunha never was as deeply involved in commercial production as the valley communities. Much of the land area of the *município* remained unplanted, and the *caipira* peasantry was not driven away, as had been the case in the valley. Two additional factors augmented the economy of Cunha in the middle decades of the nineteenth century. One of these was cotton production, which will be described in some detail below, and the other was the renewed interest in the Paratí road brought about by the coffee boom. Many of the great coffee planters preferred to ship their product to Rio by sea rather than overland. In this way, movement on the road revived. In 1837 and 1838, thirty animals loaded with coffee passed daily through the tollgates of Taboão on the way to Paratí. By 1854–1855, however, this traffic had increased to one hundred-fifty animals a day. Over two and one-half million kilograms a year were shipped through Paratí. Thus Mario Wagner da Cunha wrote, "It was the exploitation of this intense traffic of goods of great economic value that stimulated the population of the area and the cultivation of the land" (1944: 643).

With the possible exception of the present, these decades were the time of Cunha's greatest commercial prosperity. Great new homes were put up in both the town and rural *fazendas*. The local "colonels" lived in affluence and it was a time which many local residents remember as Cunha's "golden age." This opinion, however, is not usually shared by the local colored population, whose ancestors had supported all this wealth with hard labor.

Cunha can grow cotton, and this crop, for a brief time, became of considerable importance in the local economy. It marked the area's first entrance as a primary commercial producer selling on the international market, even though the boom lasted only a few years. The American Civil War produced a severe cotton shortage for the English and other European cloth mills. The price immediately rose to the point where production was feasible in Brazil, despite rather inefficient means of production, ginning, and transportation. The boom started in the Sorocaba area of São Paulo State and quickly spread into the Middle Paraíba Valley, where the cotton was often planted between the coffee trees, which did not help preserve the soils (Canabrava, 1951:101).

Unlike coffee and some other tropical products, cotton can be grown in higher areas and it thrived in the dry climate of the *Alta Paraíba*. The first planting in the region was done in 1865 and was so successful that shortly the highland region, including Cunha, had become the major cotton-producing area of the valley (Canabrava, 1951:82). Cotton thus became an important commercial crop at about the time when coffee production was beginning to decline and it may be safe to say that the prosperity of the Cunha *fazendeiros* at this time was due as much to it as to food production for the valley. The people of Cunha, at any rate, insist that cotton had once been one of the most important crops in the *município*, despite the fact that Cunha never became one of the major cotton-producing *municípios*. Planting was limited to the lower river valleys and the areas which already were being exploited commercially. Most of the area was not involved.

According to Stanley Stein, the establishment of cotton cultivation in São Paulo was largely "the result of the efforts of the Manchester Cotton Supply Association, which sent seed to the provincial authorities" (1957b:45). Cotton was known as the "poor man's crop" as it was as easy to produce on a small scale, using slash-and-burn techniques, as on a large plantation. It had traditionally been grown by peasants as a minor cash crop (Stein, 1957b:47), and the rapid expansion of production after 1860 was probably due to the sudden interest and activity of the *fazendeiros* in planting this newly profitable commodity (Canabrava, 1951:83). The boom continued for about a dozen years. After 1870 cotton from the United States began to reenter the world scene again and the price began to decline. By 1875 U.S. production had largely returned to normal and the price had dropped to the point where the São Paulo cotton planters were driven out of business. Thus, although cotton played a brief but important role in the development of the commercial *fazendas* of Cunha, at the present time there is almost no production of this crop in the *município*.

Cotton in the State of São Paulo

Year	Production in the State (in kilograms)	Price on the Santos Exchange (in milreis)
1861	0	—
1862	1,305	—
1863	5,040	15.5
1864	106,605	18.5
1865	2,898,645	15.7
1866	3,344,898	16.2
1867	8,185,973	10.2
1868	7,176,255	11.9
1869	6,142,288	14.9
1870	5,475,682	11.4
1871	10,204,610	8.6
1872	9,286,250	10.9
1873	9,283,256	9.0
1874	6,127,174	7.7
1875	4,074,968	6.9
1876	2,173,946	—
1877	643,074	—

(Canabrava, 1951: 297-301)

The economic expansion of the *município* of Cunha greatly stimulated its demographic growth. This can be seen from the population figures for the area during the nineteenth century (Wagner Vieira da Cunha, 1944:643):

Year	Population
1799	 2,472
1836	 3,403
1872	 7,873
1886	 10,856

The census of 1890, however, gives the municipal population as 20,457, a figure which could be due to gross overinflation of the data or, more likely, to the possibility that many rural families, previously ignored in the census, were, this time, counted. Whatever the case, the increasing proportion of free labor is apparent. In 1803 it was shown that slaves made up 46 per cent of the total population, whereas in 1883 they made up only about 20 per cent. Since the urban population remained relatively stable, the change probably indicates a growing *caipira* population in the rural zones.

Unlike the *municípios* of the Paraíba Valley, commercial production, as was noted, never extended over the entire area of Cunha. This is why there are existing tracts of virgin forest in the region today. Commercial production depended upon transportation and thus the *fazendas* developed in a belt about 10 to 15 kilometers wide, all fairly near the Paratí Highway and the area which had the best agricultural soils in the region. Marginal to the commercial production lived the scattered *bairros* of the *caipira*.

The decline of coffee production in the Paraíba Valley ruined Cunha's major market, and brought an end to much of the commercial activity in the *município*. The worst single blow to its prosperity was the completion in 1877 of the *Central do Brasil* railroad linking Rio de Janeiro and São Paulo along the Paraíba Valley. This eliminated, at a stroke, all traffic on the *Caminho Velho*. The road fell into ruin, and by the end of the century was impassable for vehicles of any kind and very difficult even for pack animals. While commercial food and cotton production after 1860 was able to sustain the rural economy of the region for another decade or two, the key element in Cunha's continued urban contact and prosperity—the road—was finished.

The economic history of Cunha thus presents a fairly uniform picture. The *município* was divided into three parts. The first of these, the town, was dependent largely upon commerce with travelers, but was also linked socially and economically with the second part, the area of commercial production. This area was devoted largely to food production. The labor supply was at first Negro slaves, but after 1888 the *fazendeiros* let their former slaves and others stay on as sharecroppers, since the main commodity was foodstuffs and it was easy to simply take the surplus. Beyond the commercial *fazendas*, was the third section of the *município*, a marginal zone inhabited by peasant *caipira* families. The economic system thus had considerable flexibility, as the local landowners were not dependent upon the sale of a commodity to buy food for their workers and production could expand or contract depending upon the market conditions. Thus after 1875 the region slipped back more and more into subsistence production but was in fact ready for any new market possibilities that might develop.

One important event seriously disturbed the general somnolence of the Paraíba region, and especially Cunha, during the first decades of the twentieth century. This was the Constitutionalist Revolution of 1932. After Getulio Vargas seized control of the Brazilian government in 1930 the great Paulista elite felt that their national influence was threatened and considerable unrest developed in the state. This erupted into open violence in July, 1932, when the state police, the federal garrison in São Paulo, and several civilian groups, rebelled against the national government. This Paulista force was very well armed and was supported by most of the political groups in the state (Bello 1966:290-1). The war lasted for over two months and the hottest fighting went on in the Paraíba Valley, including Cunha itself.

The national government had control of the sea and hence

was able to land troops at Paratí. Federal forces climbed the escarpment of the Serra do Mar, but found the Paulistas entrenched in the town of Cunha, which had been evacuated of its civilian population. Even though only a few companies of men were involved, the fighting was intense and bloody and went on for several weeks. The Paulistas were slowly forced back and on September 20th abandoned the *município* (Figueiredo, n.d.:257). The war generally went badly for the Paulista forces, despite heroic statewide efforts. The São Paulo leaders had expected aid from other states and abroad, but did not get it. The city surrendered on September 29, 1932. Vargas did not exact severe reprisals, but he did disband the São Paulo military police, exiled his leading opponents in the state, and sent *interventores*, later including Dr. Adhemar de Barros to take over the state government.

Cunha was badly hurt. The town had been bombarded and looted. One local shopkeeper said that his entire stock had been stolen. Battles had taken place in many rural areas from Cunha to Campos Novos de Cunha. Many fields and homes had been destroyed and animals killed. A number of local *fazendeiros* were ruined by the war to such an extent that they were never able to rebuild. The war and the subsequent Paulista defeat also had important local political consequences which will be described in Chapter V.

Chapter III

The Rural Society: a Tradition

Caipira is a word used in São Paulo to refer to the peasant farmers of that state. The word, according to one Brazilian dictionary (Souza, 1939:68), means a "man or woman who does not live in a settlement, who has no education or social graces, and who does not know how to dress or present himself in public." This definition in itself reveals the extent of the social gap between urban writers and the peasant, for in fact the *caipira* have a distinctive and elaborate culture, rich in its own values, organization, and lore.

The concepts of "peasant" and "peasant community" have been the subjects of considerable debate and research among anthropologists and others since the publication in 1930 of Robert Redfield's *Tepoztlán: A Mexican Village*. The debate on who is or is not a "peasant" is extensive and there is no space to review it here (see Wolf, 1966). For most purposes the definition of Raymond Firth will serve (1964:17):

Peasant refers to a socio-economic category. It describes a socio-economic system of small-scale producers with relatively simple, non-industrial technology. The system is a rural one, though . . . it depends on a rural-urban antinomy and interrelationship, particularly upon the existence of a market. Definition of a system as "peasant" implies that it has its own particular local character, partly because of intricate community interrelationships and partly because, in economic and social affairs, it both contributes to and draws upon a town in trade, cultural exchange and general ideology.

There is some argument that Brazil, with its huge slave *fazendas*, monoculture, commercial elite, and numerous mining towns, did not develop a genuine subsistence peasantry in the sense that one existed in Mexico or Europe. The *caipira*, however, very decidedly fit most definitions of a peasantry, with stable populations, deeply rooted to the land, growing a variety of crops and yet with some commercial links to the town (Monbeig, 1957:192). A major difference is that the concentrated "village" type of settlement did not exist in this part of Brazil, the *caipira* community typically being dispersed, as will be described below. It seems clear that an extensive peasant culture existed throughout much of south-central Brazil until fairly recent times. In Cunha, however, the culture is so severely in decline that this chapter is drawn largely from secondary sources.*

The Caipira Culture

The origins of the *caipira* and their society are to be found in the very first settlements by the Portuguese in the region. Indeed, the description by Stanley Stein, quoted in the previous chapter, of the way of life of the first settlers in the Paraíba Valley during the sixteenth century would almost exactly fit the way of life found in some of the remote regions of Cunha today. It is important to point out that commercialization and extensive monocrop agriculture are antithetical to the *caipira* way of life, which depends upon subsistence agriculture. They can justly be described as "marginal" peasants (Oberg, 1965:1426).

The production of subsistence crops with the machete and hoe was from the very beginning relegated to Negro slaves and Indians on the large land holdings. Once established, this pattern was continued by escaped slaves, poor whites, and mixed bloods who, for

* Because of this historical interest and the very richness of its folklore, the *caipira* Paulista culture has been the subject of intense interest and numerous studies by Brazilian social scientists. The most notable of these works are the studies by Emilio Willems (1947); Alceu Maynard Araújo (1957 and 1964); Carlos Borges Schmidt (1946 and 1951); Antonio Candido (1964); J. V. Freitas Marcondes (1952); and Donald Pierson (1948).

one reason or another, were forced off the plantations to take up their abode in the hinterland. Over the centuries this stratum of marginal peasants increased and spread, and the pattern hardened. . . .

Although this "*roça*" form of production is known in Portugal, the basic cultivated plants (maize, cassava, and beans) are Brazilian Indian and it was probably adopted from them (Gourou, 1959:118).

The peasantry of Southern Brazil, unlike their counterparts in Spanish America, were never wholly subjugated by Church and Crown and hence were not concentrated into villages. Indeed the agricultural hamlet or village, taken to mean a concentrated settlement of subsistence cultivators, hardly exists at all in Brazil (Deffontaines, 1938:379). Towns are very common, but these have specialized urban functions and the majority of the rural population does not live in them (see Chapter VIII). Traditionally in Brazil each nuclear family preferred to establish a homestead on the land to be worked by members of that family, even if the land was owned by someone else. There were very decided obligations between families, however, and a series of linked homesteads formed a definite social group, known in Portuguese as a *bairro*, or "neighborhood." Several writers* have called particular attention to the importance of these units. Their greatest chronicler, Antonio Candido, describes them this way:

This (the bairro) is the fundamental structure of caipira social life, consisting in the grouping of a few or many families more or less bound by feelings of locality, by convenience, by practices of mutual aid, and by folk religious activities. The residences can be close to each other, suggesting at times a rather sparse village form, or they can be separated in such a way that the observer often cannot make out, from the isolated houses spaced at fixed intervals, the unity which binds them (1964:44).

* Most notably T. Lynn Smith (1963) ; Charles Wagley (1963:159 et seq.) ; and Antonio Candido (1964).

The lands of Cunha consist largely of a labyrinth of little steep-sided valleys. Settlement generally took place along the valley floor since that was where water and the best alluvial land were available. It seems likely, therefore, that the nature of the terrain as well as the form of settlement contributed to the dispersion of the population. In Cunha, however, I found that the word *bairro* was used less as a term of social identity than as a word used to describe a named geographical region with known boundaries. In this paper, therefore, the word "neighborhood" will be used to describe the social group and the term *bairro* will be used according to local usage.

A neighborhood would consist of one or more named *bairros*, each one usually a little valley, linked to a center, typically consisting of a chapel and *venda*, that is a little general store. The center could be a part of a *fazenda* and owned by a great landowner, or it might be independent, belonging to one of the *caipira* families. The center had important communal functions, which will be described below.

A total of 375 *bairro* names were gathered in Cunha, and as there are many duplications of names the actual total would be somewhat higher. The largest and most important *bairros* are several square miles in area and have up to fifty families living in them. These large *bairros* almost always had their own centers. At the other extreme, a few were but an *alqueire* (2.42 hectares) in extent, and contained just a handful of people. Thus the *bairro* itself was not necessarily the functioning social unit of the *caipira* culture, for such a unit had to include a center. The number of centers might be judged from the fact that there were in Cunha at the time of the study seventy-five rural *vendas* and fifty-six Catholic chapels in addition to eight Protestant chapels and churches in the rural zones.

The economic base of the *caipira* culture was the subsistence production of a few food crops. These typically included corn (*Zea mays*), beans (sometimes of two types, which gave two harvests), manioc, and sweet potato (Maynard Araújo, 1957:

30-39). Since these formed the foundation of the rural diet, the neighborhood was thus essentially able to feed itself. Beans, potatoes, peanuts, onions, garlic, tobacco, squash, and sugar cane were grown as commercial crops, but only on a small scale (Schmidt, 1951:176). In addition, hogs and chickens were raised on the corn, but these, too, were generally sold or given to the religious *festas*.

Caipira agriculture was traditionally of the simplest swidden type. The only implements used were the hoe, the axe, and the *podão*, or billhook. The plow, in a hilly region such as Cunha, was almost never used. This type of hoe agriculture demanded considerable concentrations of labor at times, as well as extensive unused lands. Thus developed the most important and characteristic social feature of the *caipira* culture: mutual aid (Ianni, 1963:140). This aid took two forms:

. . . when a man is unable to handle his work alone, he will resort to the "exchange of days." He requests assistance from a neighbor and repays the service with a day's labor. In this way he succeeds in getting together at the time of his greatest needs a half dozen or more companions. When he himself is asked to help, he repays the debt religiously.

The *mutirão* in connection with agricultural activities is more rare than the "exchange of days," and the two should not be confused. The *mutirão* is used, generally, in the final stage of the construction of a house since the technique employed requires that the work all be done at one time. It ends in great festivities. . . . With this alone, those who come to help in the work feel well paid (Schmidt, 1951:177).

Houses are typically made of wattle-and-daub, with thatch roofs. Such a house could be constructed in a short time with the aid of a *mutirão*. Building materials, which consisted of sticks and mud for the walls, various types of vines to hold the frame and walls together, and *sapé* grass for the roof, were freely available in many rural areas. Traditionally, neither bricks nor tiles were used in *caipira* construction unless supplied by a nearby *fazendeiro*. Traditional furniture consisted of woven mats and homely wooden artifacts made by the peasant himself. Even pottery was once produced in Cunha. In this way, the *caipira* culture was to a high degree independent of urban industrial production. The only things that could not be produced locally were metal objects—most importantly tools—and cloth. This final fact meant that, for most *caipira*, clothing was a valuable commodity and not likely to be thrown away. Emilio Willems wrote in 1945:

Even those who have the resources to buy more varied and better quality clothing are usually satisfied with a patched shirt and a pair of trousers . . . even in winter men and women go about barefoot, the former without a jacket, and the latter in only a simple calico dress. The sharecroppers sometimes wear shirts and trousers that have been patched so often that they resemble the plumage of some strange bird (1947:99).

The relative independence of the *caipira* culture enabled it to develop and flourish at a time when the urban element of the community was stagnant. The *caipira* society was necessarily an expanding one. Antonio Candido has pointed out that the basic characteristics of this culture were: "(1) isolation, (2) possession of lands, (3) domestic labor, (4) neighborhood aid, (5) availability of lands, (6) margin of leisure" (1964: 61). Until recently Cunha had effectively limitless lands with almost no external control over them. Under such conditions the culture could and did grow at a rapid rate. Every man, when he married, established his own household on his own piece of land. Thus the *caipira* was continually leaving his home *bairro* and establishing another in the next valley. The result was not a "hollow frontier," however, but a continually expanding folk population cutting its way into the forest.

Bairros were frequently linked by kinship ties. A small *bairro* might be wholly occupied by and named after a single extended family which occupied it. It was not uncommon to have the houses of several members of one family strung out at regular intervals along a narrow dirt road. When a *bairro* developed as an offshoot of another the two would often continue to remember their former kinship relations and be more readily willing to offer mutual economic aid. In this way neighborhoods developed.

The *caipira* of these mountain regions are demographically very stable and will live in the same *bairro* for generations if at all possible. In this way they differ from much of the rest of Brazil where, according to some authorities (T. Lynn Smith, 1963:144), the lower classes are highly nomadic and without attachment to the soil. The author was told in Cunha that people coming from different *bairros* in Cunha could actually be distinguished by their different accents and use of special local expressions, a linguistic fact which alone indicates a great stability and isolation of the population in the rural zones. Certain large extended families were known to have lived in the same neighborhoods for generations. The phrase, "His people come from *bairro* so-and-so," was heard frequently in interviews in the town.

Intermarriage between members of adjoining *bairros* was frequent, although neither the *bairro* nor the neighborhood was necessarily exogamous. Girls traditionally married very young, and a difference of ten years of age between a man and his wife was not unusual—a fact which may explain the large number of widows in Cunha at the present time. Commonly several members of one *bairro* or extended family would marry members of another such group nearby. In this way several *bairros* would come to be tied together through marriage and the neighborhood would tend to become one complex web of kin. Since the neighborhood was not strictly endogamous, the people living in it would have some ties with members of other *bairros* and neighborhoods and the whole region, including the urban zone, was thus loosely bound together. In practice, however, in the rural zones, locality was more important than kinship in the important activities, such as mutual aid. Thus kinship ties that, due to isolation, were not continually reinforced, would be eventually ignored, if not wholly forgotten. The *caipira* were bound together by kinship, mutual economic interest, and religion. They were also bound, however loosely, to the urban society, from which they obtained a few necessary commodities. The integrative focus, linking the various *bairros* and families both with each other and with the larger urban community, was the neighborhood center. This consisted of both a chapel and *venda*, and no rural neighborhood would be complete without both elements. The two were frequently, although not necessarily, located near each other. Traditionally a school did not form part of this center. Both chapel and venda had different functions and were social centers for different activities.

Alceu Maynard Araújo has given an account of how a new center would be formed (Vol. III, 1964:10). A wayside cross, often marking a grave, would be transformed into a "holy place." This in time would become the site for a new chapel. As the population and social activity developed, someone would open a store and a new neighborhood would be established. Its size would thus be an area with a population large enough to support both a *venda* and a chapel. This seemed to be between 30 and 50 families. In some areas of sparse population the nearest center might be up to fifteen kilometers away, but it was usually within walking distance. The chapel was the center for local religious and social activity, both on a weekly and annual basis.

Once a year at the anniversary of the installation of the chapel, the priest comes to say mass. This Sunday is a great festival day. The preceding week there is a septenario or novena, and the prayers are directed at nightfall by the neighborhood chaplain, whose social influence is marked.

The chapel becomes a reunion point. The dance of the *moçam-*

bique is practiced Sunday mornings on the ground alongside the chapel. Sunday afternoons there is a prayer session directed by the chaplain . . . (Maynard Araújo, Vol. III, 1964:12).

Religious activities were very important in the *caipira* culture. Cunha was famed throughout much of the state of São Paulo for the richness of its folk ceremonies, and even at the present time people still come for hundreds of miles to witness certain *festas*. An examination of the religious cycles of Cunha will not be attempted here as several important works have already been written on the subject.* It is interesting to see that despite considerable influx of Negro slaves into Cunha, the base of the folk religion and folk belief, unlike that of Bahia, remained largely Portuguese and Catholic. Catholic holidays were celebrated with processions, feasts, and dances. Mock battles between "Christians" and "Moors," called the *congada*, reenacting the "Song of Roland," were performed at various times (Maynard Araújo, Vol. I, 1964:216-296). It seems likely, therefore, that the *caipira* religious practices originated among the early Portuguese settlers of São Paulo, and that the pattern had stabilized by the time slavery on a large scale entered the region. Thus the slaves themselves adopted and elaborated upon the relatively unsophisticated beliefs of their masters. This seems more likely when it is noted that slaves in a relatively poor region such as Cunha lived on a much closer day-to-day relationship with their Portuguese masters than occurred on the great plantations of the North.

Alceu Maynard Araújo (1957) has demonstrated how in Cunha the most important religious festivals were timed so that they would not interfere with agricultural activities. Thus the great *festas* took place during the "vacant times" of the yearly cycle, that is, at times when there was no important agricul-

* The most systematic treatment of caipira religion is to be found in Alceu Maynard Araújo's monograph (1957), which was augmented in specific details in his later publications (1964). Another important study is that of Emilio Willems (1947, 1949a, and 1955).

tural work. In addition, it seems likely that the enormous elaboration of the folk religion in Cunha is a relatively recent phenomenon. The decline in commercial activity of the region at the end of the nineteenth century and the first few decades of the twentieth century meant that the *caipira* was free to devote more and more of his surplus production to his religion, rather than share it with a landlord.

Religious activities served as an integrative force for the neighborhood, focused upon the chapel. In addition, to a degree religion served to integrate the *muncipio* as a whole, as there were a few major *festas* which were held in town and reunited a large portion of the municipal population. The *festa* of the *Divino Espírito Santo* was the most important of these and required months of preparation throughout the Catholic sections of the *município*. The point should not be overstressed, however, since for many *caipira* the town was too far away for them to attend these major festivals and the celebration of the neighborhood saint's day remained the most important annual religious event. There are, to this day, people in the rural zones who have never seen the town. Nor should it be assumed that all this religious activity served as an important link between the folk culture and the formal Catholic Church. It was, in fact, a truly local expression. According to Emilio Willems, "The chaplains who are entrusted with the convocation of the faithful and the direction of the ceremonies frequently interpret the Catholic doctrine in their own way, twisting its meaning or putting it to the service of ends which would only with great difficulty find the approval of the priest" (1947:104). Many priests actively opposed many of the expressions of folk religion (Maynard Araújo, Vol. I, 1964:226-27), and in recent years one vicar banned all such activity from the streets of Cunha.

One aspect of the festival cycle in Cunha which is worth noting is its economic side. In Cunha many of the religious *festas* are immensely popular and will draw visitors from many surrounding *bairros* and from nearby towns and cities as well. Important festivals are advertised in the cities of the Paraíba Valley with printed leaflets detailing the order of attractions. As in most of Latin America, especially devout individuals will volunteer to arrange and organize each festival for a given year. The *festeiro* must collect the food and drink for the feast which forms the main event of the day, and in return is permitted to carry the banner of the saint of the *festa* and indeed keep and display it for the rest of the year. The *festeiro* thus gains great prestige, but rather surprisingly is not expected to take any financial loss. I was able to inspect the reports on one major *festa* which had been held in Cunha in 1966 and found that two of the three men involved had received more in contributions than they had given away. To take a loss, however, was considered an honorable thing to do, and there was some bitter complaint when during one major festival the priest sold sixty head of cattle to help pay for a new chapel, whereas many felt they should have been killed and the beef distributed to the poor, as was customary.

No festival would be complete, moreover, without the *mascate*, the traveling peddler. Even the very smallest, least consequential local *festas* would bring one or two of these from the town selling candy and trinkets. More important *festas* would have several dozen open air stands selling a large assortment of items. A number of local people augmented their incomes by making and selling pastries and sweets (*doces*). Fruit stands were common and there would invariably be one or two small hand presses where raw sugar cane was crushed and the juice (*caldo-de-cana*) sold to passersby. The more prosperous and professional *mascates*, many arriving by jeep, would sell religious articles or items of clothing: scarves, shirts, trousers, and hats. It is probably safe to assume that many of the *caipira* bought most of their clothing this way, as few of the *vendas* carried such items. In fact the number of *mascates* at these holidays well reflects the increasing material prosperity of the region. During Holy Week, and other important holidays celebrated in the town itself for a period of several days, everyone who could would go into commerce. An endless array of holiday foods would be sold, meats as well as pastries and *doces,* also fruit juices, soft drinks, hard drinks, and the *quentão,* a mixture of hot rum and ginger. For these occasions professional *mascates* from the cities of the Paraíba and even São Paulo itself would come up to Cunha with their trucks laden with merchandise, mainly shoes and clothing. The main plaza in front of the *matriz* became so crowded with commerce in 1965 that the priest lost his temper, called the police, and banned every salesman from the center of town.

Integration with the Larger Community

The *caipira,* isolated as he may have been, was nonetheless a true peasant and thus by definition did have links with the larger municipal and national societies. These links were social and political as well as economic, and despite their complexity are essential to an understanding of the dynamic forces which have changed the region.

One of the most important institutions in the rural regions which served to both integrate the neighborhoods and link them with the larger municipal community was the *venda,* or little general store. Here the *caipira* bought most of the tools and foods which he could not produce himself. The major exception was clothing. Cloth was usually sold only in the town, though sometimes items of clothing were sold by traveling peddlers who frequented the rural festivals. Importantly, the *venda* owner served as a commercial middleman and bought many of the cash crops of the small farmers of the region. The *venda* also served as a social center for more secular activities than the chapel afforded.

On Saturdays the men go to the small general store. Only on rare occasions will a woman be seen at the store on these days. The purpose of the trip is to purchase supplies for the coming week, but there are few who do not take a few drinks of rum while at the store. Then they become loquacious and there is much joking and horseplay. . . . The *caipiras* are found of *pinga* (a sugarcane rum) and frequently they fail to buy kerosene for the lamps in order to use the money to purchase a supply of *pinga* for the week (Marcondes, 1952:49–50).

To understand the nature of the *caipira* society and the interrelations between the urban and peasant sectors, it is necessary to examine briefly the commercial development of the region and the nature of the classes which developed out of it from the colonial period. It was shown in the last chapter how Cunha was populated as a result of commercial expansion by the Portuguese. The *caipira* peasant culture developed out of the commercial *fazendas* and established itself as well on the fringes of the commercial zones. The *fazendas* themselves were worked by African slaves, but since these slaves in Cunha were primarily employed in the same activity as the marginal peasant groups, they soon adopted the same cultural patterns as the latter. This was especially true since frequently the slave-owner himself had a largely *caipira* standard of living. In fact, the very early class structure of the community might be described as made up primarily of mixed Indian-Portuguese landowners and their slaves, both African and Indian. Here the *Capitão-mor* would represent the Portuguese crown and be leader of the community, but this position derived from the fact that he was the largest local landowner. He had no other special grants or qualifications.

In the earlier period, most of the landowners were themselves semi-peasants in their way of life because of the general poverty of the region. With time, however, the situation became more complex. The commercial success of some of the larger land-owners and their continued contact with the Portuguese urban centers through the mining roads allowed some of them to educate their children and raise their own standard of living to a point where they could afford to build large rural mansions and town houses and develop interests beyond the locality. Their success strengthened their hold on the commerce of the region and their political importance and they thus became the local landed elite (see Chapter V). Other settlers, more isolated or less ambitious than their neighbors, remained largely cut off from the commercial activity of the region and maintained their basically peasant way of life, even when they were distantly related to the elite and legally entitled to land.

Thus the basic social structure of the rural zones for most of Cunha's history was made up of three elements: the great landowners with links to the cities together with their families; the slaves; and the marginal *caipira*. With the abolition of slavery in 1888, the commercial *fazendeiros* found it to their interest to allow the former slaves to continue to live on their lands in return for a share of their production as rent. In this way, two classes of *caipira* evolved (Candido, 1964:6): the *sitiantes* who lived without major obligations to a landlord, and the *parceiros*, the sharecroppers. This was largely the social situation in Cunha at the end of the last century.

The great *fazendeiros* formed the true elite of the region. These men were in contact with the state and national governments and were involved in the money economy. They were educated, had urban interests, and kept contacts with others of their class both in Cunha and elsewhere. They also had effective political and economic control of the *município*. The belt of great *fazendas* extended across the center of the *município*, largely in the areas where the original *sesmaria* grants had been made on both sides of the road. Some other very large ones, however, existed in more isolated areas. (This is shown in the map.) Each of these big *fazendas* had a number of sharecropping families living on it. Beyond the areas of effective control of the *fazendeiros*, usually in the less desirable mountainous regions or isolated areas far from the roads, lived many scattered *bairros* of *caipira sitiantes*. Some of these in fact had control over very considerable tracts of land but due to the nature of their culture and economy they engaged in little commerce. Extensive production on their part would only invite the politically powerful *fazendeiros* to expect a share.

After 1888, however, with the general paralysis of the economy of the Paraíba Valley, the *fazendeiro* group found its wealth declining. In the first part of this century, in fact, many *fazendeiros* left the region, or their children left to go to school in the cities and did not wish to return. Today in Cunha one can find the ruins of several great manor houses which were abandoned when the last owner died. Frequently the land was sold to others from outside the region, but at times it was simply abandoned and local sharecroppers took over as *sitiantes*. One case was mentioned in Cunha of a *fazendeiro* who, when he died, left all of his land to his slaves. As the dominant urban society lessened its political-economic grip on the peasantry, more and more of the sharecroppers began living *a favor* without paying rent. Land was bought, traded, and sold among the peasants without any kind of authoritative sanction from the urban society and the *fazendeiros* did not interfere as long as the land was almost valueless due to the absence of markets.

Thus Cunha, in the first part of the century, had an extensive folk culture with minimal urban contacts. While a number of commercial *fazendas* existed in many parts of the *município*, in general the picture was one of stagnation of the urban sector and florescence of the folk culture, because the *caipira* were free to utilize their surplus production on themselves and their religious activities. Emilio Willems wrote the following in 1945:

. . . the reciprocal relations between city and country (are not) well balanced. It is true that the rural residents must reach the center to obtain rapid transportation or communication, to seek administrative and religious services, to pay taxes, to vote or obtain information about the course of local politics. . . . But the functions of the town as a center of ecological dominance suffer in comparison with nearby cities (1947:21).

Chapter IV

Economic Changes

By the first part of this century, at a time when much of the South of Brazil was beginning to experience the economic changes which were to lead to the present industrialization of São Paulo, Cunha remained isolated and rural, a little pocket of eighteenth-century Brazil. This was due, as has been described, largely to local economic stagnation and isolation of the whole Paraíba valley region. The interesting fact is that the *caipira* peasant culture of Cunha, far from experiencing a gradual decline under the impact of continued urban expansion and small industry, actually reached its zenith at this time, as the urban commercial influence of the town diminished. Only about thirty years ago did the first waves of the effects of industrial urbanism hit the *município,* and these waves have continued with increasing vigor and effect. This chapter will first briefly examine the industrial development of the state of São Paulo and then describe the economic effects this has had in Cunha. Rural social changes in the peasant culture will be shown in Chapter VII.

The Development of Industrial Society in São Paulo

Industry has a long history in São Paulo. According to Stanley Stein, "The protective tariff of 1844 began the first period of textile growth, 1844–1885, and . . . fostered small mills . . . in the south-central area (Rio de Janeiro and São Paulo). In addition to the stimulus of the tariff, the prior accumulation of investment capital in former years of agricultural prosperity was a decisive factor in both cases" (1955: 431). In addition, "The State of São Paulo was the heart of world coffee production and the capital city was the center of the coffee trade; the prewar crisis for 1913 had brought many rural workers to the capital in search of employment. The wartime combination of investment capital, cheap labor, and consumer demand stimulated industries there in general" (Stein, 1955:440).

This pattern has continued to the present day. "Brazilian government policy has long been to favor new industries both by protection against foreign competition and by direct aid through loans, tax exemptions, compulsory purchasing arrangements, and a variety of other measures" (Wythe, 1955: 62). The great boom in Brazilian industry came after World War II with an all-out drive on the part of the Brazilian government to industrialize, and the considerable investment of foreign and domestic capital into Brazilian industry. "During the Kubitschek administration a substantial amount of progress was made towards fulfilling many of the targets, especially in industry and some of the planned infrastructure. The agricultural sector, however, lagged behind" (Baer, 1965:67). "While the real product increased by 128 per cent from 1947 to 1961, the real agricultural product increased by only 87 per cent" (Baer, 1961:69). "The evidence available . . . suggests that part of the inflationary process acted as a mechanism to finance industrialization by redistributing income from the consuming classes (mainly the wage-earning classes) to the investing classes, both private industry and government . . . it is fairly certain that this lag extended to the agricultural wage-earning sector, too" (Baer, 1961:194). Baer also believes that most of the relative increase in agricultural prices was absorbed by the agricultural distribution sector rather than the farmers themselves.

Important to the discussion here are the demographic changes due to this industrialization. In 1960 the state of São Paulo had 828,182 people engaged in industrial activities, about half of whom were in the capital city. The number is augmented by the tendency of Brazilian industry to use "labor intensive techniques either at the core or at the periphery of the industrial unit" (Baer, 1961:148). Such labor, moreover, though poorly paid, can have a lower level of skill than capital intensive industry requires, and rural people thus can find work.

Lured by the increased opportunities offered, the population of São Paulo State increased from 1,400,000 in 1890 to 7,200,000 in 1940, and 13,000,000 in 1960. The city of São Paulo itself grew from 64,934 in 1890, to 1,326,261 in 1940, and 3,825,321 in 1960 (data from the Brazilian censuses, I.B.G.E.). While the major part of this growth is probably due to population movement within Brazil itself, it is important to bear in mind that there was considerable international immigration to Brazil throughout its history, nearly five million between 1874 and 1957, about half going to São Paulo (Smith, 1963:121). The fact that the state government made a deliberate effort to attract Italian immigrants as a labor force at the end of the nineteenth century accounts for their importance in the state. Structurally important from the standpoint of commerce are the Syrians and Lebanese even though they make up a total of only about 0.8% of the number of immigrants.

There can be little doubt, however, that by the 1960s São Paulo represented an industrialized urban society with a large scale industrial labor force. The importance of this fact is hard to underestimate. It may be the most significant event in the history of Brazil. This industrialization produced a profound structural change in the midst of what had been a huge, but essentially static, dependent agrarian society. For the first time in Brazilian history millions of people were directly involved in the urban monetary economy and hence increasingly aware of and involved in urban problems, urban ideologies, urban needs, and urban politics. This change is the real Brazilian Revolution, or perhaps, as Celso Furtado has said, the Brazilian prerevolution (1962).

The development of São Paulo had centrifugal effects upon

the valley of the Paraíba, which began to seriously develop industrially in the past two decades. By 1958 the cities of Taubeté, São José dos Campos, and Mogi das Cruzes had all become "medium-sized" centers of industrial production, and Cruzeiro and Guaratinguetá were both listed as "small-sized" centers (Grupo da Geografia das Indústrias, 1963, map opposite p. 184). While the population of the predominantly agricultural zone of the Alta Paraíba between 1950 and 1960 actually fell slightly, from 79,237 to 79,162, the population of the valley itself increased from 370,495 to 500,657 (I.B.G.E. Census Reports, 1950 and 1960).

Development within the Paraíba Valley tended to follow lines of transportation. Those cities which have developed most are those linked to São Paulo and Rio de Janeiro through the railroad and highway. Because these swing north to Volta Redonda, other cities to the south, such as Areias and Bananal, have remained largely rural and poor. The point is made because later emigration from Cunha tended to be to the more developed valley cities.

As Gunnar Myrdal points out, "The localities and regions where economic activity is expanding will attract net immigration from other parts of the country. As migration is always selective, at least with respect to the migrant's age, this movement by itself tends to favor the rapidly growing communities and disfavor the others" (1963:27). Rural exodus from Cunha will be discussed in detail in Chapter VII. What is important here is to examine the economic basis for such mobility. That an important part of the demographic expansion of São Paulo is due to this migration has been shown by Brazilian government studies (quoted in Baer, 1965:173). Such migration is largely due to regional income inequalities. The per capita income in São Paulo is consistently nearly four times that of the northeastern states (Baer, 1965:170). In addition, rural zones tend to have a degree of "disguised unemployment," workers who are not fully employed but through family support are able to live. Many of these young people have formed part of the exodus. Rural exodus in fact has become one of the main themes of Brazilian society (Camargo, 1960).

The Effects within the Município: The Market System

The rapid economic and demographic expansion of São Paulo, including the Paraíba Valley, had profound effects upon Cunha. A whole new set of economic opportunities appeared, and where the people of Cunha themselves did not take advantage of them, others came who did. Of these changes by far the most important were the development of an extensive market for meat and dairy products and the new labor opportunities offered by the industries and services of the cities. Any market system, however, must involve production, distribution, and demand. Brazilian agricultural production has generally lagged behind demand owing largely to archaic production methods and poor distribution structures. São Paulo to an extent is an industrial society existing on a preindustrial agricultural base.

The huge nonagricultural population of the cities of São Paulo offered a vast potential market for almost all kinds of food products. Cunha was stimulated again, as she had been in the 1850s, to produce food for a large nonsubsistence population. This time, however, the demand was much greater, and there were major differences in the kinds of products needed. The old Paulista coffee planter fed his slaves mainly cornmeal, manioc, and beans, now and again supplemented with a bit of pork or bacon, and sugar (Stein, 1957:174). In other words, the marketable commodities were simply an extension of the subsistence products that the *caipira* produced anyway. As Werner Baer has pointed out, however:

It is generally known that the expenditure pattern on food of the urban population is different from that of the rural population. This is especially true as the income of the average urban dweller rises. The rate of increase of demand for animal proteins—especially meats and dairy products—is larger than the rate of increase of demand for such traditional items of consumption as rice and beans . . . the rise in production of livestock in the fifties was substantially smaller than the increase of the urban population. The relative shortage of the type of food products increasingly consumed by the urban sector is also revealed by the relative rise of various types of food prices (1965:152–53).

Within the *município* of Cunha itself, the prices of meat and milk have held consistently higher than any other product (see Chart IVA). This has had important economic repercussions in an area such as Cunha where the topography makes mechanization of agriculture difficult. Beef and milk production require high initial investment in land and cattle, but later labor and other costs are low. Thus cattle raising and dairy farming tend to be highly profitable to those with extensive land holdings.

The initial reactions to the new markets by the commercially oriented landowners in Cunha tended to be a great increase in production of the traditional products of the *município*, drawing upon the enormous reserves of *caipira* labor available. The favored and most profitable product was beans, due to the ease of handling this product and the relatively high prices (shown in Chart IVA). Even now the more traditionally minded *fazendeiros* with large labor pools available still produce these products.

Meanwhile a considerable number of immigrants from Minas Gerais, forced out of their home state by land pressures, came to Cunha with their cattle herds and a little cash to buy land. These people, though often scorned by the traditional residents, were in large part responsible for the development of meat and dairy production in Cunha. Eventually most of the traditional *fazendeiros* and *sitiantes* as well have found it to their profit to shift production to animal products.

Today in Cunha the Mineiros and the Methodists make up a sizable proportion of the commercially active *fazendeiros* and *sitiantes* in Cunha. Both groups have reputations for being hard-working, tight-fisted, and commercially able. The Mineiros, unlike the Methodists, have not attempted to establish

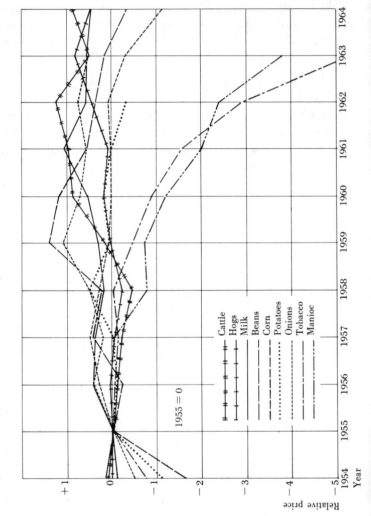

Chart IVA. Constant Commodity Prices in Cunha, 1954–1964

1955 = 0

Cattle
Hogs
Milk
Beans
Corn
Potatoes
Onions
Tobacco
Manioc

Relative price

Year

a separate subcommunity in the *município,* but have worked within the framework of the society as they found it. Like the Methodists they are politically active. They have largely achieved social acceptance, although the phrase *"Êle é um Mineiro"* ("He is a Mineiro") is still used to describe someone who is very careful with his money. Demographically, it should be said that the commercialization of the *município* has been due at least as much to the activities of these two groups as to modification in the way of life of the *caipira* peasantry or the traditional elite toward greater commercial activity.

The development of the meat and dairy industries is shown by the statistics.* Both cattle and dairy production have increased considerably in Cunha. An almost universal comment made by the people was, "Today the only things of importance in Cunha are meat and milk; nothing else matters anymore here." At the same time the traditional crops have declined in importance. The author, who came to know a town surrounded by miles of rolling pastureland, found it at first hard to believe the statements of informants that only a few years ago most of the area was planted with corn. Few fields remain today near the town. Urban market potentialities have, therefore, had a considerable effect upon municipal production.

A key element in this change, however, is the development of a large-scale distribution system to take advantage of the Paulista market potential. Only in this way has Cunha avoided some of the problems of regional inequality and been able to share at least peripherally in the economic expansion due to industrial development. The change is reflected in the focusing

---

* In 1886 the census for that year states that there were between 500 and 600 cattle in Cunha. The agricultural census of 1940 counted 12,140 and that of 1950, 27,183, the first time there had been more cows than people in the *município.* The Department of Statistics of the state estimated the herds in Cunha between 1954 and 1960 to be about 40,000, falling within recent years to about 33,000; possibly as farmers sold off their animals to take advantage of high prices. Milk production, as will be seen, has increased accordingly.

of commercial and social attention upon the capital city of São Paulo and the complex of industrial towns around it. In 1945 Emilio Willems wrote, "There exists a system of exchange which unites Cunha with some *municípios* of the Paraíba Valley, principally with Guaratinguetá, Cruzeiro, Lorena and Valparaiba. As a more distant market, the capital of the state has little attraction" (1947:21). At this time, in fact, Rio de Janeiro was a more important market than São Paulo. This situation has now reversed and the city of São Paulo itself is now undoubtedly Cunha's major customer.*

An essential element in the development of Cunha has been the change in the marketing distribution system, most notably in animal products, from small local traders to large-scale government licensed market organizations. Emilio Willems wrote in 1945 (1947:21), "The very Cunha merchants, those called local 'profiteers' (*atravessadores*) suffer from the competition of tradesmen who come up from the valley of the Paraíba to purchase directly corn and beans, chicks, eggs and hogs." Moreover, unlike many Brazilian towns, Cunha has never had a municipal market, as an attempt to found one in 1944 failed, ostensibly because it was built on "land of the Saint," where an earlier chapel had stood (Willems, 1947: 106). In fact, it probably failed because the *caipira* economic structure largely functions within the neighborhoods rather than through the town.

Even in 1945, however, the expansion of distribution systems was being felt. Emilio Willems noted that "Even this form of intermediate commerce (by the merchants of the Paraíba Valley) is being supplanted by traders who come di-

* One indication of the fact that Cunha is now undoubtedly in the Paulista sphere of influence may be seen in the area of personal transportation. The most popular means of individual transportation is by bus, and the bus line from Cunha ends in Guaratinguetá. From that city, however, there is only one bus line with four daily buses going into Rio de Janeiro whereas there are three lines with more than twenty buses daily into São Paulo. The entire trip takes about five to six hours in good weather, in either direction.

rectly from Rio de Janeiro to acquire foodstuffs and fowls from the producers themselves" (1947:21).

Extensive marketing arrangements which link Cunha with the city of São Paulo do exist at the present time. These are, however, only for animal products. Beef cattle are sent live into the Paraíba Valley, where they are slaughtered and the meat refrigerated and shipped to the city. The largest *frigorífico* (slaughtering and cold storage plant) was located in the town of Cruzeiro, although in 1965 it was in serious financial difficulties, a fact which might cause enormous loss to some of the *fazendeiros* of Cunha. Cattle are sent from Cunha to the valley, either by individual *fazendeiros* or by one of the local or regional middlemen who buy cattle in the *município* and sell them in the valley. There are five such middlemen in Cunha and each of them has certain regular customers, often relatives. Most of the middlemen have *fazendas* of their own as well. The statistics on beef production are less reliable than those on milk production, but it was estimated in Cunha that at least 7,000 head of cattle are exported yearly from the *município*. In addition the town of Cunha itself consumes some 400 head of cattle a year. One informant complained, "They only sell the scrawniest beasts here—those that they'd have trouble selling in the cities."

Hog production is very important in the region, as it is a highly profitable enterprise and does not require extensive land areas. Hence initial investment is low, and many small *sitiantes* or *agregados* can invest in one or a few pigs or breeding sows and raise and sell them when convenient. Many large *fazendeiros* also are currently raising hogs because of their relatively high prices. A large percentage of the corn grown in the *município* is fed to pigs. Statistics of the state show an astonishing increase in the number of these animals from only a few hundred in 1951 to some 22,000 in 1963. These figures, however, probably reflect their increasing commercial importance rather than an actual increase in numbers to this extent. It does, however, show the rapid response of the farming population to favorable market conditions. It is worthwhile noting that many thousands of suckling pigs are marketed every year as the traditional Christmas and holiday food. Marketing arrangements are diffused. Many animals are sold or exchanged within the *município*. The larger *fazendeiros* usually have their own arrangements in the valley, and there are several middlemen within and without the *município* who have transportation and buy and sell a variety of products throughout Cunha and the Paraíba Valley in a manner similar to the traditional exchange system described by Emilio Willems above.*

Dairy products have become the economic mainstay of the *município*, especially for the smaller landowners. Cunha has long been noted for the quality and quantity of its cheese production. Even in 1939 it was said to be the second largest producer of this product in the area (Ferraz, 1939:14). This extensive early production was due to the fact that cheese was the only form in which the region's extensive milk production could be preserved and marketed, in view of the exceedingly poor transportation available in the *município*. In the more isolated northern district of Campos Novos it is not surprising that cheese is still the main commercial dairy product. Production for this region alone is said to be some 75,000 kilos yearly. Some fifteen or twenty dairymen produce small amounts of cheese individually on their own *fazendas*, but sell it through a single locally based distributor in the Paraíba Valley.†

_____

* The economic role of chickens and other fowl might be mentioned here. Cunha has never developed an extensive marketing system for either chickens or eggs and so the number has tended to decline since 1951, since large commercial farmers are not interested in development in this industry and small producers are leaving the region. The social importance of the chicken is important to note, for it offers one of the major sources of cash income to the small peasant family, which consumes its agricultural crops and cannot afford to keep pigs or cattle.

† In the southern district there are three smaller full-time cheese manufacturers who market the dairy production of those producers outside the distribution network of the cooperative. These three together are said to produce some fifteen or twenty tons yearly.

Most of the dairy production in the region, however, is now sold in the form of fresh milk. Fresh milk production had already started in Cunha when Emilio Willems was there. He notes (1947:87-88) that in 1942 a plastic manufacturer from Guaratinguetá, seeking casein for making galalith, managed to obtain a production of 1,000 liters per day from the local farmers. This production fell off when the use of milk for industrial production was made illegal. While there existed in 1945 a company to distribute fresh milk to Guaratinguetá, it could only accept deliveries before 10 o'clock in the morning, and "this new condition made the daily volume fall to 750 liters, since many producers were not able to adjust to a rigid schedule" (Willems, 1947:89). At that time there were 33 suppliers to the depot.

In 1944 the *Cooperativa de Laticínios de Guaratinguetá* was founded specifically to take advantage of the growing São Paulo market for fresh milk. It became a unit in the federation of the large *Cooperativa Central de São Paulo*, the largest milk company in Latin America, which currently sells hundreds of thousands of liters daily to the capital, while the local units sell to the cities of the Paraíba Valley. In 1965 the Guaratinguetá cooperative was receiving an average of 58,000 liters daily, marketing 8,000 directly, and selling the rest to the central organization. In 1957 the Guaratinguetá cooperative bought out the older *Cooperativa de Laticínios Cunhense*, thus gaining effective control over milk production in the *município*. Since the cooperative is socially and economically the most important commercial institution in Cunha, it seems worthwhile to discuss its functioning in some detail.*

Large-scale distribution of fresh milk requires considerable capital investment and only an organization such as the Guara-

* For information about the cooperative I wish to thank its directorate, Sr. Guilherme de Castro Barbosa. Director Presidente, Sr. Antonio Coelho Guimarães, Director Gerente, and Sr. Gilberto Leonel Fortes Azevedo, Director Secretario. My special thanks go to Sr. Dirceu Torres, Técnico em Contabilidade, for statistics about production in Cunha.

tinguetá cooperative, with current resources of over a billion and one half *cruzeiros* ($750,000) could succeed. As a distribution system the cooperative is a reasonably modern, highly mechanized, and efficiently run organization. There are three collecting and refrigeration plants—one in Cunha, one on the border of the *município* half way along the main road to Guaratinguetá, and the third in that city itself. The milk is brought to the station in the cans of each individual producer, where it is measured and tested for acid and fat content. What the cooperative will pay depends on this. It is then rapidly refrigerated by machine and shipped in 100 liter cans to Guaratinguetá. There the milk is pasteurized and shipped in large tank trucks to São Paulo for bottling.

The Guaratinguetá cooperative is a legally instituted cooperative under Brazilian law. As such every member has the right to vote for the directorate and the independent fiscal council. That this right is exercised is seen from the fact that in the last elections held in 1966 the directorate was very nearly defeated. The producers from Guaratinguetá dominate the cooperative. This might be expected, since of 1,122 members in 1965, only about one-fifth came from Cunha. Nonetheless, this fact tends to take important economic decision-making out of the hands of the *município*.

The most important decisions, however, are made by the federal government. Under Brazilian law the prices of meat and milk are fixed by the Superintendency of Supplies (SUNAB), a fact that frequently produces sharp conflict between the government and the producers. For most of 1965, the price of milk was set at Cr. $105 per liter for milk containing 3.2% butterfat content. Higher fat content brought a higher price and lower content a lower price. This effectively discouraged diluting the milk with water.

Rapid Transportation is the key to fresh milk distribution and the cooperative has a relatively complex distribution system within the *município*. There are six trucks, each of which leaves the town early in the morning and follows a set route for about 15-20 kilometers, picking up the cans of the various producers along the way. These return at various times in the morning and unload the milk for processing. By 11:00 A.M. the trucks have left for Guaratinguetá, and the morning activity is over. The line trucks are privately owned. Some are owned by *fazendeiros*, others by individual entrepreneurs who make a living from transportation. The fact that petroleum and machinery prices have risen at a much greater rate than the price of milk and other agricultural prices has put truckers and farmers in a bind, which has caused considerable conflict. Many producers prefer to deliver the milk themselves to the station, whether by their own jeep or truck, or by horse and mule.*

There is a distinct, though subtle, division between regions in the *município* served by the line routes and those which are not. Regions within the distribution network tend definitely to be the more prosperous and commercially active areas. The line trucks carry messages and packages as well as passengers for a small fee, so that the milk zone is in daily contact with the town. Beyond the region served by these trucks are the broad pasturelands belonging to many important cattle ranchers. Past these holdings may be found a number of isolated *caipira* settlements on the fringes of the commercial establishments and the *sertão*, the great stretches of virgin rain forest which cover the mountains of the escarpment of the Serra do Mar leading down to the sea.

The station of the cooperative in Cunha employs a manager

* The importance of transportation to the production of fresh milk is dramatized when heavy rains make the Cunha roads impassable for motor vehicles. This occurred several times in the summers of 1965–1966, once for a period of ten days. At such times cavalcades of horses and mules carrying cans of milk enter the town from all directions, for the cooperative will pay the same price for fresh milk whether they can deliver it further or not. The cooperative in turn stores the milk in the only possible way by producing cheese. They may in bad weather produce a ton of cheese a day.

and eight workers. The work requires some skill and is highly prized, since these employees are among the few in Cunha who earn the regional minimum wage. There were in December of 1965, 232 members of the cooperative in Cunha. Cunha has many peripheral producers who refuse to sell milk if the price does not seem worth the trouble. In 1964, there were less than 200, and the number rises and falls with the relative price of milk, according to officials of the cooperative.* At an average, the cooperative ships 8,000 liters daily from the Cunha *usina*. In addition, officials in the cooperative estimate that another 8,000 liters from the *município* are delivered to the *usina* at Rocinha. Another milk company buys 1,000 liters daily, and a large powdered-milk firm 1,500 to 2,000 liters per day from producers in Cunha. Both these organizations are located near Guaratinguetá and do not have their own distribution network within the *município* as does the cooperative. The *usina* of Cunha alone shipped 3,162,103 liters in 1965, and total production is probably closer to seven million liters. This is equal to the estimate made by the State Department of Agriculture. The expansion of production over that of 1945 is impressive.

The cooperative has certain social functions in addition to that of simply a distribution network. They sell a variety of products related to cattle raising, from insecticides to gasoline,

---

* The size of individual production varies considerably as can be seen in the table below.

Data for June 1964 Daily Production	Number of Members
1 — 50 liters	153
51 — 100 liters	40
101 — 200 liters	12
201 — 300 liters	1

It should be noted, in contrast, that in the other two *usinas* (stations) of the cooperative, there are fifty members who produce more than 201 liters daily and a few who produce over 1,000. Some of the largest producers in the *município* have *fazendas* along the main road to Guaratinguetá and hence are listed as belonging to the *usina* of Rocinha on Cunha's boundary.

at a reduced price to their members. For this service alone some *fazendeiros* stay in the cooperative even though their milk production is only nominal. Members also have free medical, dental, and veterinary service, although the fact that these are located in Guaratinguetá limits their usefulness for the members in Cunha.

Still the cooperative is the major voice for the diffusion of modern ideas of dairy farming in the *município*. Few members in Cunha at the present time, however, seem willing or able to make the necessary investments to improve production. The most serious problem, for example, that dairymen have in Cunha is the *sêca*, the dry season during the winter when the pastures become dry and the animals must be fed indoors. The most common winter feed is sugar cane, and an estimated 13,000 tons are grown each year in Cunha only for this. The inferior quality of this feed causes the milk production in Cunha to fall 30 per cent in the winter months, and the co-operative has been making an effort to get the farmers to supplement this in a more scientific manner to prevent this decline. They have met with small success. In this region the sign of a truly modern ranch is a silo for storing winter feed, but there are few of these in Cunha.

There is one final function that the cooperative has which is perhaps its most significant social one. It functions as a power bloc to attempt to influence key governmental decision-making. The vital importance of this to the farmers can be seen when one remembers that not only is the price of milk fixed by law, but the price of gasoline as well. It is the state and national governments, in addition, which maintain the roads upon which the distribution system depends. It is essential, therefore, that the dairy producers have some influence in high governmental circles and in important influence groups. As individuals they are unable to exert such an influence, but the cooperative can. Through the cooperative, dairymen were trying to persuade the government to raise milk prices, a step which would politically be very unpopular in the cities. The dilemma was a serious one, since a major price increase would put milk out of the market for many urban poor, yet low prices were causing many *fazendeiros* to stop milk production in favor of more profitable operations.

The cooperative apparently has been able to operate as a pressure group without becoming too deeply involved in party politics. At least it is not embroiled in the endless political battles which seem to occur in Cunha over almost every issue. This may be due to the fact that its economic importance over-rides political feelings. It is, moreover, illegal for a coopera-tive to engage in party politics. Nevertheless, the cooperative wields considerable political influence. Its president, Dr. João Rodrigues de Alckmin, is one of the leading spokesmen for the cooperative movement in Brazil and comes from an old and very important Mineiro family. The chairman of its fiscal coun-cil in Guaratinguetá in 1966 was the State Secretary of Agri-culture, a federal deputy, and an important supporter of the then governor of São Paulo State, Dr. Adhemar de Barros. The cooperative, in short, does have links to the highest state and federal levels.*

There are other cooperatives in Cunha although they have in no way the importance of the *Cooperativa de Laticínios.*

There is a local *Cooperativa Agrícola Mista de Cunha* which was founded in 1943 and was noted by Emilio Willems (1947: 73-74). It was established with the hope of doing for agricul-tural products what the other cooperative does for dairy prod-ucts, which is to sell the agricultural production of its members directly to the urban centers without paying middlemen. Wil-lems writes, "The major difficulty against which the directors of the cooperative struggled in 1945 was the lack of capi-

---

* In 1968 the cooperatives were in serious general trouble in Brazil due, in part at least, to the fact that their highly formal organization made it very difficult for them to evade the multitude of Brazilian taxes and they were losing ground to other private firms.

tal. . . ." This is still the basic problem today. This capital, since 1945, has not even kept up with the inflation, and it requires tremendous effort on the part of its management simply to keep financially solvent. The cooperative is currently little more than a cooperative general store, which sells a variety of products to its members at a reduced price. The original plan of making it a distribution organization was forgotten some years ago. It has thus not fulfilled its promise, and this failure prompted some wealthy Methodist *fazendeiros* to found their own cooperative near the Methodist Church of Jericó, in 1965. This, too, has run into problems caused by inflation, and only time will tell how well it succeeds.

The large-scale commercial development of cattle raising in Cunha has been generally detrimental to agricultural production, even the most traditional ones in the *município*: corn and beans. Chart IVB presents data on production as furnished by the state department of statistics for São Paulo. It should be noted that these statistics tend to reflect commercial rather than subsistence production. They show a general decline in production with the exception of certain high-profit truck crops, such as onions, which need little land. While the statistics are not entirely reliable for Cunha, the overall trend is probably accurate. It is interesting to note that statistics from the São Paulo Department of Agriculture, which attempt to show total production, reveal a decline in agriculture even more severe than that shown in the chart. They also show an increasing milk production until the past few years, in accordance with information supplied by the cooperative.

The decline in agriculture can be seen everywhere. The production of wine and European fruits, for which Cunha was celebrated in the nineteenth century (Redondo, 1895), has all but ceased. The *município* as late as 1957 was the third largest bean-producing region in the state, whereas nine years later the author was told the beans were being imported from Guaratinguetá to feed the town. The fall in agricultural pro-

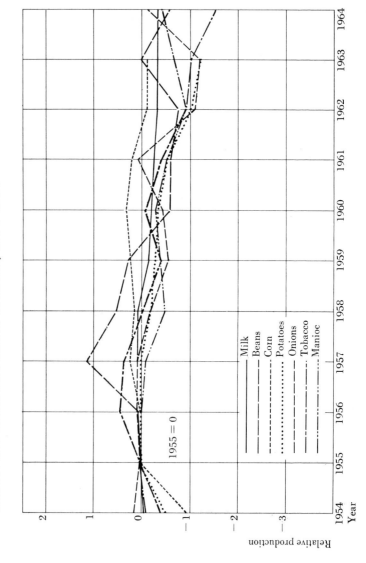

Chart IVB. Production Patterns in Cunha, 1954–1964

duction has been so severe that food prices in Cunha have risen faster than the general cost of living. At the present time, many foods actually cost more in Cunha than in the city of São Paulo and the Paraíba Valley. This is true even of products such as beef, which are in plentiful supply locally. Residents explained that this is due to the fact that there are few agricultural producers remaining who are willing to sell in the town on a retail basis. There are one or two shopkeepers in Cunha who sell food, mainly fruits, vegetables, and processed foods, to rural as well as urban families. The corn-meal (*farinha*) factory in town sells much of its production locally, thus saving the housewives, rural and urban, the trouble of grinding and baking it themselves. (There was widespread complaint, however, that the mass-produced meal was not as good as the homemade article.) The point can justifiably be made, therefore, that Cunha no longer has a true subsistence economy. It no longer feeds itself, but is becoming a specialized ranching and dairy district for São Paulo.*

The point should not be exaggerated. Probably 70 per cent or more of the people still produce their own food and very few of the rural population are wholly specialized in dairy and meat production. One new factor, however, is the increasing popularity of processed and hence externally produced foods. One old *fazendeiro* informed the author, a little wistfully, that in the old days all he needed to buy for his family was coffee, salt, and a little sugar. The main food was corn meal, roasted in a backyard oven, red beans, and manioc flour, all from his own fields, and an occasional chicken or pig to supply meat for special occasions and Sundays. Now he said, they have to buy bread from the town, rice from the valley,

* During a brief return visit which was made during the summer of 1968, I found that Cunha had actually lost its official status as a rural *município*, which had important political and social consequences. The youth of Cunha, for example, are no longer exempt from military service.

and spaghetti from São Paulo—all to suit the modern tastes
of his family.

Thus it can be said that an economic revolution has hit
Cunha. The factors which have brought this about are commercial and demographic. The type of traditional agriculture
practiced in Cunha is extremely labor intensive, utilizing few
tools more elaborate than a hoe. The rugged terrain does not
permit extensive use of mechanization. With the price of
agricultural products declining in relation to animal products,
the landowner, to make equivalent profits, leaves his workers
distressingly little income. The workers, however, have an
alternative in the industries of the nearby cities.

Emilio Willems says that even in 1935, jobs in the Paraíba
Valley, for equivalent work, paid twice as much as they did in
Cunha (1947:86). In 1965 the usual pay for a field hand
(*camarada*) was from Cr. $1,000 to Cr. $1,200 per day, and
less for the very young or the elderly. Even this work was
seldom available on a dependable day-to-day basis. Contrast
this with the fact that the minimum wage in the factories of
São Paulo in 1966 was Cr. $86,000 per month, and the lure
of the city becomes quite explicable. One of the major reasons
for the decline of traditional agriculture in Cunha was scarcity
of labor due to the exodus of many of the farm workers. Many
fazendeiros, when asked why they no longer planted extensive
agricultural crops, replied, *"Falta dos braços":* lack of field
hands. This is but one part of the story, however. Another
part involves the vital economic element, land tenure, which
will be dealt with in Chapter VII.

Chapter V

Authority and Power: a Changing Social Structure

Cities may be defined in many ways. It is common, for example, especially in demographic surveys (Anderson, 1964), to base a definition strictly on population size. By such a definition Cunha, with a past population of only 1,000 or so, would not rate as urban, and in fact it is smaller than many rural villages in other parts of the world. It is the contention here, however, that such definitions are misleading. The *sede* of Cunha is, and has always been, basically an urban center, a fact which the Brazilians recognize by classifying it officially as a *cidade*, a city.

Marvin Harris has pointed out that interior Brazilian towns often are surprisingly urban in their structure and outlook, despite their relatively small size.

In the central and northern portions of the Eastern Brazilian Highlands, there are many communities of less than two thousand people, strikingly isolated from the nation's metropolitan centers, with a retarded level of technological development and a world view which is essentially nonscientific, but which nonetheless present a large number of conspicuously urban features. Whatever the opinion of social scientists may be, the inhabitants of these towns feel themselves to be profoundly different from their country neighbors who live nearby in villages and on farms (1956:4).

This urban ethos is characteristic of Cunha as well. The Cunhenses fiercely resent any implication that they might be a part of the *caipira* culture. The very word *"caipira"* is not one to be bandied about in the town, even in jest. On the other hand it is fully accepted in the rural regions, often with a comment to the effect that "we are all *caipira* here." Cunha's urbanism, however, as will be shown, is as much a matter of structure as of ethos.

Anyone who studies "peasant" societies, especially in Latin America, must consider Robert Redfield's well-known concept of the folk-urban "continuum" (1941). While Redfield was interested in showing a dichotomy which he felt existed between ideal types of "folk" and "urban" society, in recent years attention has focused upon the specific relationships which exist between the peasants and their adjunct urban society. This work has clarified a point which Redfield, as well as many others, did not see, namely that the city, in the preindustrial world, was a part of the peasant's world, not necessarily because the peasants wanted it so, but because the city could not exist without the peasant's labor. To speak only of peasants when one refers to a "folk" society is misleading. Any such society contains both rural and urban elements, both peasants and townsmen.

Moreover, as Gideon Sjoberg pointed out in his book, *The Pre-industrial City*, the characteristics of this "folk-urban" society are very different from the urban culture characterized by Redfield. The preindustrial city, according to Sjoberg, is wholly dominated by a small highly privileged upper class. This upper class not only controls the society politically and economically, but sets the norms of behavior for all its members, those of the lower classes as well. In fact, however, only the upper class can fully participate in the expected religious and educational norms, and only it can maintain the full extended family system and ideal norms of marriage and family behavior.

Any study of a "folk" society, therefore, necessarily implies a study of the urban as well as rural components and thus must become in part a study of social stratification. In this I tend to agree with those "conflict" theorists such as Ralf Dahrendorf, who hold that the basis of stratification, and indeed the "glue" which holds a complex society together, is authority. This is by no means the place to review the immense literature on this problem but I do believe that only through an examination of the total distribution of authority in all of its manifold forms that one can come to understand the social system in a dynamic sense. Changes in social structure are changes in patterns of authority and power, and only in this light can we see weaknesses and tensions which will enable us to predict and perhaps encourage future changes. In this regard, Max Weber's definitions of both authority and power may be usefully accepted.

"Authority," says Weber, is the "probability that a command with a given specific content will be obeyed by a given group of persons," whereas power is the "probability that one actor within a social relationship will be in a position to carry out his own will despite resistance, regardless of the basis on which this probability rests" (Dahrendorf, 1959:166). Authority can thus be of many kinds and may be said to have power content insofar as there are sanctions involved for disobedience.

In this view, authority is the primary social mechanism and power is derived from it. Authority must work through a system of rewards and punishments to get people to obey. Coercive authority, thus, is backed up by the threat of negative sanctions for disobedience, whereas collaborative authority is based upon the promise of reward of some kind for obedience. The "pecking order" form of authority backed up by sheer physical force, while common in many animal groups, is usually replaced by some development of collaboration in most human societies. It is commonplace in anthropology that among people with simple political patterns, such as a hunting band, the headman must frequently impoverish himself to maintain his position. He must, in other words, buy authority from his followers.

The situation, however, becomes vastly more complex if the individual or group in authority have a mechanism for enforcing their demands. Law, whether in a simple or complex society, may be defined as authority backed up by force: negative sanctions. The legal system, therefore, is the organization set up to enforce such authority. Thus a legal system gives an enforced authority pattern backed up by the ability to overcome potential opposition on the part of some of the population. It gives, in other words, a pattern of power. The basic social structure, the basis for social stratification, is derived from the legal system, which distributes power.

It must be made clear that the existence of such a structure does not eliminate collaborative authority within a politically complex society. This is a point that some dedicated conflict theorists miss. It is in the nature of a complex society that many kinds of authority exist at different levels. Simple collaborative authority in a powerful organization, such as the military, may give the holder life-or-death power over those outside the organization. Authority, moreover, can well be maintained without the constant threat of violence. Politics is built upon this kind of collaboration. It is a system of promises of mutual rewards for obedience to the politician's authority. As a general rule, politics works within the framework of the pattern of power set out by the legal system, usually where negative sanctions for disobedience are ineffective or too cumbersome. Influence and charisma can thus be seen as political mechanisms, the former operating on a diadic basis, the latter on a one-many basis.

In a very simple society where there is no established enforcement mechanism, the authority of a chief or headman is almost entirely "political" (i.e., based upon collaboration). His coercive power is small except in certain carefully defined situations, such as a communal hunt or war where the welfare of the group is clearly at stake. The development of class differentiation comes about with the development of a legal system, a law enforcement agency, as well as the development of spatially fixed production techniques such as agriculture. This means that the leader may be able to gain control over strategic resources, such as land, and can thus gain power over the majority of the population. He no longer, therefore, needs to collaborate with all of the people but only with those necessary to maintain his position.

There is no space here to elaborate on the complexities of social evolution or the different models and forms of distribution of authority and power. It is sufficient to say here that Brazil's political system never really fit the standard "feudal" model of society, as many writers, including Sjoberg, saw it. The "feudal state" according to Mosca (1939:53–58) was a political system wherein a warrior elite was able to gain control over a pacific population by controlling access to land. This elite thereby could make and enforce its own laws with minimal concern for the controlled population. The number of people in this system who would benefit from and have a voice in the collaborative political system would thus be quite restricted.

Brazil, however, as was pointed out in Chapter II, developed out of European commercial expansion and opened up as economic conditions in Europe warranted. Brazilian society has always been linked with world economic markets (Simonsen, 1962), and the Luzo-Brazilian elite were always traders as well as warriors, willing to fight when necessary, but constantly with an eye on the profits involved. They even bought their own laboring class from Africa. The Africans in the New World did not constitute a conquered peasantry, as the Indians did in Spanish America, but were brought over individually as slaves to take part in a commercial enterprise, the *fazenda* or plantation. The African had no community of his own in the Americas except the *fazenda* and he was to a degree dependent upon his Portuguese master for many of the

necessities of life.* The *fazendeiro* was the only link between
the slave and the commercial world and he alone could supply
his workers with the products of that society: clothing, rum,
weapons, and basic foodstuffs, such as the *bacalhau* (dried
codfish).

The authority and power of the *fazendeiro* in Brazil was
thus based no more upon his military ability than his position
as trader and distributor of goods of the European society.
The fact that he kept the lion's share of the goods for himself
could not affect the basic structure. The farm laborer, African
or European, could not become a *fazendeiro* by simple re-
bellion, as the upper class was supported by the entire international trading organization. The authority of the sword was
never as sharp in Brazil as in Spanish America and it was not
uncommon, in fact, for a plantation owner to be so confident
of his position of commercial authority that he would arm his
own slaves and retainers, something unthinkable in, say, the
southern United States or Peru.

The *fazenda* was thus not only the basic economic institution
in rural Brazil, but the basic political institution as well. The
economic independence and isolation of the *fazenda* set the
stage for the fundamental fragmentation of political authority
during the colonial and imperial periods as well as the early
years of the Brazilian Republic. The Portuguese colonial government, interested mainly in fiscal return on trade, was per-
fectly willing to leave local political matters in the hands of
the great landholding families and would in fact choose the
most powerful *fazendeiros* in each region to represent the
crown as *Capitão-mor*. The authority of the *fazendeiro*, there-

* There were, of course, attempts by escaped slaves to establish African
style communities in the Brazilian interior, but when these developed to
the point of really becoming focal points for runaways, even the Portuguese
could be moved to military action. Such as the fate of the famous "republic"
of Palmares which in fact successfully resisted attack by the Europeans
until the government called in mixed-blood troops from São Paulo (Carneiro,
1966).

fore, was supreme on his own land and although the fragmentation of authority resembled a "feudal" pattern, it was highly integrated with commerce and hence to a large degree non-militaristic. The Brazilian *Coronel*, despite the fact that he might have purchased a military rank in the local militia, was not a warlord of the *caudillo* type, although he might maintain a few armed enforcers to back up his authority.* Even the abolition of slavery in Brazil in 1888 did not destroy the hegemony of the *fazendeiro* since his economic and social authority over his dependents remained. In fact, Vitor Nunes Leal, in his great study of Brazilian *coronelismo* notes the following (1948:11): "Completely, or nearly, illiterate, without medical assistance, unable to read newspapers or magazines . . . the rural laborer, and not only in exceptional cases, counts his "boss" (*patrão*) as a benefactor. It is from him, in fact, that he receives the only favors that he knows in his forgotten existence."

This, then, was the basic social pattern of rural Brazil until quite recently. There was no law in these areas except that which was made by the members of the landed commercial elite and there was no law enforcement except that provided by their armed enforcers. Boxer writes (1962:44–45) that in 1700 "the powerful Paulista leaders and the richer ranchers with their scores of hired bravoes, armed slaves and hangers-on, behaved like independent princelings, 'insulting persons of the highest rank, without any regard to human or divine laws.' " The towns in this kind of a social system functioned basically as organizational and commercial centers for the rural patriarchate. The culture which developed in these centers was "urban" in that the people did not work on the land but through the institutions of the town, the educational, religious, and governmental systems, the elite perpetuated itself

---

* *The Violent Land* (Terras do Sem Fim) by the Brazilian novelist Jorge Amado (1965) presents an excellent and striking portrait of the way power is maintained in the Brazilian interior.

and ensured its control over the agricultural population. More-over, due to the isolation of these towns they remained pockets of preindustrial urbanism long after the coastal cities were becoming sophisticated metropolitan centers.

It is to the metropolis, then, that one must turn for the second act in the story of rural social change, and to the other main type of urbanism, industrial urbanism. We have already pointed out the powerful economic effects that growing cities had upon agricultural production. The cities have had equally powerful effects upon local authority, and Cunha again dem-onstrates the change. Much of the political history of Brazil, especially in recent years, can be seen as an effort on the part of the landed elite class to maintain its tremendous local au-thority in the face of efforts on the part of the Brazilian gov-ernment to impose a more universalistic system, favorable to the metropolitan middle classes, upon the country as a whole (Greenfield, 1968).

As a defense against the growing power of these classes and the increasing power of the national government, oligarch-ical political networks developed throughout the interior of the country during the latter days of Dom Pedro II. Thus the political system known as *coronelismo* developed wherein the landed oligarchy exchanged the votes of their clients and de-pendents in return for favors from a local *chefe politico* (polit-ical chief), who in turn would use these votes as bargaining counters with the state and even federal politicians. The *chefe* might himself be a *fazendeiro*, but it was not uncommon for him to be a *doutor*, an educated man, a lawyer, physician, pharmacist, or perhaps a priest, whose refinement and prestige could well represent the municipality in the larger cities. It was not uncommon for the political *chefe*, once well established, to arrange his election to state or federal office, leaving his municipal base in the hands of subordinates. He in turn would use his new position to see that his home region received its fair share of state funds (Leal, 1948). Out of these Byzantine

webs of clientele politics developed what Helio Jaguaribe
(1958) calls the "Cartorial State," the main job of which was
to maintain the status quo, namely the local independence of
the authority of the *fazendeiros*.

The base upon which the whole structure rested was the
município, the lowest level (urban) administrative unit. These
in the past were highly independent units, as T. Lynn Smith
notes:

. . . for Brazilians, and especially for the overwhelming majority
of them who live in the interior . . . the fundamental government
unit is the *município* . . . in the Brazil of the past, and it remains
true today even after several decades in which centralization has
made tremendous strides, the *municípios* appear to have been the
primary units of which the state was merely a loose confedera-
tion. . . . In the past about the only contacts between the state and
federal governments, on the one hand, and the resident of the rural
areas, on the other, were the assessment and collection of taxes and
even these were done through the *município* (Smith, 1963:570).

The municipal political chief had a very high degree of independent authority and power. He would by necessity control
the key offices of the *município*, namely that of *prefeito* and
head of the city council and he could usually exchange the
votes under his control in return for local autonomy and the
right to name state and even federal officials (such as the
judge, police chief, and tax collector) in his district (Leal,
1948:30–1). The local leader and his allies, therefore, were
usually in a position to ignore legal limitations upon his
authority.

Once in control of the *prefeitura* (city hall), moreover,
with control over the social and economic resources of the
municipal government, there was a great deal that a political
chief could do to maintain his position. Two of the main
mechanisms he could use were *filhotismo* and *mandonismo*.
Filhotismo (from the Portuguese *filho*: son) was simple political favoritism. This could involve the whole range of mu-

nicipal services, and could involve anything from tax evasion
to public employment. Thus, says Leal (1948:27), "It is
known that public services in the interior are extremely defi-
cient, since the municipalities do not use their resources for
their needs. . . ." A large part, he maintains, is spent with a
view to elections. This fact, in turn, throws the burden of
municipal development onto the state government which in
turn would reward its own political friends. Thus collaborative
authority in this system is not maintained through appeals to
general development, but through specific gifts to individuals.

The other aspect of maintaining local authority is *mandonismo*, (from *mando*: power) the persecution of one's
political enemies. Or, as the Brazilians pithily put it:

> para os amigos pão
> para os inamigos pau.
> (for our friends, bread
>   for our enemies, clubs.)

(Leal, 1948:23–24)

Hence law enforcement too, under this system of politics, tends
to become personalized, with punishment meted out to enemies
of the individuals in power. It was not uncommon in the past
for the great political clans of the interior to violently feud
with each other, with the *coroneis* hiring their own private
"enforcers." But in São Paulo open violence has been declining
in favor of political maneuvering and minor harassment.*

Cunha, until 1932, followed this "cartorial" pattern with
exceptional clarity. Since that date, however, many changes
have occurred which are slowly bringing the local autonomy
of the *município* to an end. These could have major relevance
for Brazil as a whole.

---

* In Cunha, for example, some years ago, one *prefeito* who paved the main
street of the town, as a promised municipal project, "ran out of funds" just
before he was able to finish paving the street in front of his main political
rival.

The traditional elite of Cunha was made up largely of families of the great slaveholding *fazendas* which produced food for the coffee plantations of the Paraíba Valley. Throughout the *município,* especially in the regions near the main road, can be found the remains of the traditional great houses (*casas grandes*). Some of these still exist and are inhabited by old Cunhense families, with the slave quarters boarded up or turned into sheds for equipment or animals. But most of the old mansions are gone, destroyed by fire or sheer neglect. The modern *fazendeiros* prefer smaller, modern brick houses to the huge traditional ones of *taipa* and wood.

Although the landed elite of Cunha was not comparable in wealth and power to the coffee barons of the valley, the size of some of these houses in both the town and rural zone show that the most powerful local families, at least during the time of the coffee boom, had a very comfortable life. It is the members of this elite whose names remain on the streets and plazas of the town: *Colonel* João Olympio, *Major* Sant'Ana, *Colonel* Macedo, *Comandador* João Vaz, and the like. These men were literally and figuratively the "*coroneis*" of Cunha's past, landed gentry who kept their big houses in the country and were the supreme overlords of their *fazendas* and the people living on them. The most powerful of them also kept houses in the town, where they could keep an eye on local politics.

A century ago there was a serious power vacuum in the rural regions of Cunha, as in much of Brazil at the time. The "clan politics" apparently prevailed here as well, but without any group powerful enough to impose order on the region. The colonial Portuguese and later imperial governments made some effort to reduce banditry on the roads, but were not entirely successful. There is some evidence that before the hegemony of the group led by Dr. Salvador there was considerable internecine warfare and bloodshed between these great families in Cunha. Such fighting took place over land,

and, as in Guaratinguetá, became more intense as the coffee boom in the valley increased its value. Local residents speak of a "time of troubles" in the nineteenth century, and of the "one hundred crosses" marking graves of those assassinated on the road between Campos Novos and the town of Cunha. The bloody era of clan politics, however, is no longer well remembered in the town, as it ended over 80 years ago, except in a few isolated regions in the mountains.

One person who brought an end to the "troubles" and is remembered, usually with great affection and respect, is Dr. Thales de Salvador. According to Emilio Willems (1947: 57–59) and accounts of those who remember him in Cunha, this man, a mulatto trained as a physician in Bahia, arrived in Cunha in 1877 seeking the dry climate to cure a lung condition. As the only doctor in the region he set up a free clinic and soon became widely popular among all classes of the population. He turned to politics, allied himself with several of the leading elite families, and rapidly built a large and loyal electorial base in the *município*. He had political supporters and friends throughout the region, but his principal allies were three local families who were members of the landed elite. The head of one of these families held the job of mayor of Cunha continuously for twenty-two years. The second family controlled tax collection, and the third dominated the city council (Willems, 1947: 59). According to Emilio Willems the *prefeito*, with time, came to consider himself the "owner" of his position, as well as its privileges. He once drove one farmer out of the *município* for presenting the mayor with a bill for a basket of fruit which the latter had ordered (1947: 59). The political machine which these families established with the doctor controlled the *município* for half a century. It was oligarchic but peaceful.

The story of Dr. Thales de Salvador is a nearly perfect example of the *doutor* as politician. Civilized, urbane, and paternalistic, he was the ideal man to link together the rough

caipira of the mountains with the great coffee elite of São
Paulo. With his powerful local support he was elected city
councilman and mayor several times. He allied himself with the
immensely powerful political group of Rodrigues Alves in
Guaratinguetá and in 1892 with their support he was elected
a federal deputy and in 1913 a senator. Much of his effectiveness, therefore, in dominating the wilful *fazendeiros* of Cunha
came from his position as political broker between them and
the valley. At this time, the state government was gradually
building its own legal system in the *município*, Cunha was
made a *comarca* (legal district) in 1893, and the doctor was
quite influential enough to see to it that this system, including
the police and judiciary, remained under his authority. He
thus became final arbiter between state and local interests,
and was in fact in an unshakable position as long as the coffee
elite ruled in the capital. Another factor in his long domination
of the region was the general economic decline of the whole
Paraíba Valley region. The peacefulness of his era may have
been due less, perhaps, to Dr. Salvador's own forceful personality than to the fact that the land was economically no longer
worth fighting about. (In fact, the only derogatory remark
about Dr. Salvador which was ever reported to me in Cunha,
was that he tended to discourage economic change.)

The year 1932 brought an end to this quiet, if slightly
decadent, era. In the Constitutionalist Revolution of that year,
as mentioned in Chapter II, the forces of São Paulo lost to
the armies of Getulio Vargas, and the power of the old Paulista
elite was broken. Vargas imposed, with backing by the national
army, federal intervention in the state's politics. Cunha was
evacuated and sacked, with a local *interventor* later installed
as well. The power of Dr. Salvador, nationally, was destroyed.
He had risen with the coffee elite and he fell with it. Although
he still remained very influential in the eyes of the local people
his authority as a political broker was gone and he died four
years later. The politically powerful families of the traditional

elite, who had remained in Cunha despite the collapse of the coffee economy in the Paraíba Valley, saw their authority eliminated by intervention, and most of them left the *município*. Few members of the traditional families still remain in Cunha. Those who have remained, with one or two exceptions, have relatively little political power. The son of Dr. Salvador, a lawyer, now lives in São Paulo, although he maintains a house in the town of Cunha. The stage was set for a new arrangement of political forces in the town.

A fundamental aspect of this rearrangement was a change in the nature of the leading oligarchy from domination by rural *fazendeiro* clans to domination by a more sophisticated urban-official group. This is a general pattern in southern Brazil where the "clan" oligarchy is gradually being replaced by a "functional" oligarchy, related less by kinship than by the members' professional ability to compliment each other's work in an increasingly complex social environment. These dominating oligarchic groups are frequently called *panelinhas* (the term is used in Cunha with this very meaning), defined by Anthony Leeds as "a relatively closed, completely informal primary group, held together in common interest by personal ties and including a roster of all key socio-politico-economic positions" (1964: 1330). These groups attempt to coordinate informally the various power and economic elements in any given area so that they can support and protect each other. They are self-perpetuating and recruit new membership as necessary to insure their own continuity. They are linked vertically with other higher level *panelinhas*, leading ultimately to the national capital. The *panelinhas* thus crosscut and interlink the various systems of the social structure: industries, banks, politics, bureaucracies, etc. A stable political situation in a region means that one *panelinha* so dominates the political and economic structure that no challenge is possible. At a local level, unlike what Leeds found at the higher levels of Brazilian society (1964: 1338), there is intense political competition for control. A change in the political climate often brings about a restructuring of the dominant *panelinha,* and often personal elements are involved.

While the full nature of the dominant oligarchy in Cunha at the time of Dr. Salvador is difficult to reconstruct, it seems to have been made up almost exclusively of a few families of the landed elite, with positions in the militia, who gave their political support to the doctor in return for representation and protection by him at the state and federal levels. There seems little doubt at this time that the state and federal officials of the *município* were largely under the thumb of the landed aristocracy.

After the failure of the revolution in 1932 and the death of Dr. Salvador in 1936, a new *panelinha* formed which was very different in form and membership from the old one. A number of new elements of authority and power entered the scene. Cunha no longer had the powerful voice in the state and federal governments that it had formerly and hence the local politicians and leaders had to compromise more and more with officials of the state and federal government, who could, and sometimes did, implement political intervention. The new *panelinha* thus was no longer made up of the great landed *coroneis* and their families but had to include certain major state officials who were no longer simply agents of the local elite. The details of this political reorganization will be presented in the next chapter.

Law and the Legal Order

Perhaps the most important element in the political transition and restructuring of power in Cunha has been the growth and development of a São Paulo State legal system within the *município*. By this is meant the whole apparatus through which a government enforces its authority, including police as well as the judiciary. Ultimate political power lies in force or the threat of force, and in Cunha the past two or three generations have seen such power pass out of local hands and into those of statewide bureaucratic systems. Even though on the national scene the Brazilian federal government successfully asserted its power over that of state in 1932, this has seldom been reflected at the municipal level, where the state government of São Paulo has nearly always dominated. The development of such an organization in a region is of fundamental importance both in theory and in fact. It marks the difference between a society where real power lies with local leaders—personal law—and a society where power lies with an enforcement agency—metropolitan law.

Under the older system of "clan" politics, effective law was made by the *fazendeiros* and their "bravoes, armed slaves, and hangers-on." Neither the central government nor the state were in a position to enforce universally its own rules except in regions where it had a garrison, and, as has been noted, for the most part these larger polities were not concerned with local conditions as long as taxes and duties were paid properly. It might be said that in many parts of the interior of Brazil this type of system still exists, but in São Paulo the state for many years has gradually been expanding its real power into its rural regions. Throughout most of its long history Cunha was judicially merely a subdistrict of the *comarca* of Guaratinguetá and its only judiciary was a *Juiz de Paz*, justice of the peace, a locally appointed official who had little actual state authority besides the right to perform marriages. The position required little formal training and in fact the job was probably little more than a sinecure for one of the local elite.

Cunha, as mentioned earlier, was made a separate *comarca* in 1893. Although at the time this meant little actual change in the restructuring of power in the *município*, due to the tremendous political influence of Dr. Salvador, the change did have some long-range effects. It meant, for one thing, that the town was to have, instead of a mere *Juiz de Paz*, its own

Juiz de Direito, a judge of law. This is an important position in Brazilian jurisprudence, candidates must be fully trained lawyers and they are selected by examination by the Supreme Court of the State of São Paulo. Thus the judge is almost invariably brought in from outside the *município* and is educated in the cities. In addition a number of other state officials were brought into the town, such as a *delegado* (police commissioner) and *promotor público* (district attorney). Most important of all was the introduction of a state police force into the *município,* the famous *Fôrça Pública* of São Paulo, a group which gradually over the years has eliminated private armies and bandits from all regions of the state (Smith, 1963: 584). While the potential independence of these state officials was doubtless checked by the enormous state and federal authority of the doctor, after his fall in 1932, the local elite no longer had this authority over the legal system.

An examination of trial records in Cunha since 1893 shows clearly an increasing effectiveness and organization in the judiciary. There has been a constant increase in judicial activity of all kinds. Most notable, the number of trials for crimes of violence has gradually increased during these years, even though most informants felt there is less violent crime now than in the past, an indication of the increasing effectiveness of the legal order. It was universally attested that hidden crimes of violence had been nearly eliminated in Cunha. The roads were free from bandits and had been for years. The last major political shooting incident occurred over ten years ago and even then caused a major scandal.

Crimes of violence still do occur in Cunha, but seldom without subsequent investigation by the state. There are an average of about 25 police investigations a year in Cunha. Local residents still remember an incident which occurred a few years ago when a man considered to be a dangerous criminal escaped into the mountains. A large detachment of state troopers was sent up from the Paraíba Valley to search the *município* and after considerable time and effort the man was recaptured.

When the value of land began to rise again after the 1930s, the state legal apparatus was firmly in control. Disputes over land were thus more and more conducted through the courts. This, as will be shown, worked to the detriment of the illiterate *caipira* peasant, but to the advantage of the small-scale commercial farmer who found in the courts a potential defense from the local elite.

At the present time, the legal system has a virtual monopoly over force in the *município*, and it is important to examine its structure. There are three elements involved: the *Fôrça Pública*, or state police; the *delegado*, the police commissioner and his assistants; and the judiciary, headed by the *juiz de direito*, the judge, and *promotor público*, the district attorney, and their assistants. Each of these is a separate organization with separate lines of authority to the city of São Paulo.

The *Fôrça Pública* of São Paulo is a well-trained and equipped paramilitary force. It has its own chain of command which leads eventually to the governor of the state. Locally in Cunha the *Fôrça* is represented by a corporal and a varying number of soldiers. The normal compliment is 22, but there are seldom that many in the town. In addition there are four rural policemen. Most of the soldiers are career men. In Cunha the majority are young and unmarried since those with greater seniority and married soldiers usually choose to live in a town larger than Cunha. Two or three of the group have married local girls and have elected to settle down, establishing homes of their own in the town. The rest live in the police station, an area set aside for them in the local jail building.

The new Cunha jail was completed a couple of years after the old jail and city hall burned down in 1961. Because of its modern design it is currently used as a maximum security institution for the whole Paraíba Valley. There is room for 32 prisoners, but there are seldom that many at any given time.

Very few of the prisoners come from Cunha itself. Prisoners are allowed to have tools, books, and whatever else they need to amuse themselves or to make small objects to sell. At the time of the study, the jail held 17 prisoners and only three of them came from Cunha.

The presence of the police is generally accepted. In a small, highly conservative and mainly rural region such as Cunha there is relatively little crime and little opposition to authority. Most police activity has to do with crimes of sudden violence, often caused by alcohol. There was a small group of "no-goods" in the town and one policeman said that "every now and again we have to bring them to the station and teach them to behave." In general it seems police-community relations were good because the class most likely to rebel, the urban laborers, frequently have the same background as the police, and there is a definite bond of understanding between them. Further-more, the state police is one of the main avenues of social advancement for this class and many hope to keep this option open. The story was told by one laborer in Cunha how one day, in debt, with his family actually going hungry, he was in the public garden contemplating a robbery when one of the local policemen came by, found out about his problem, and loaned him enough money to pay his debts. On the other hand, the Brazilian police can be very tough on those who oppose them and Cunha is not an exception. The combination of kindness and toughness breaks up any kind of organized class of opposition to the established order, and creates an almost overwhelming system of social control. Those most likely to rebel against the system are brought in to enforce it. Cunha is an area where the poor are resigned rather than hostile.

The *delegado* is an appointed civilian official whose author-ity also derives from the governor of the state but in separate lines from that of the police. He is responsible for investigating crimes in his area and for this the *Fôrça Pública* is at his command. In actual practice in Cunha the job is something of a sinecure, since the police do most of the investigative work and his job is mainly to prepare an accused criminal for trial. At the time of the study the *delegado* appointed for Cunha did not live in the town but commuted one day a week from the Paraíba Valley. Most routine work was done by his local assistant.

The judiciary has been the key institution that has led to the enforcement of state and national laws in Cunha at the expense of local control. The judiciary of the *município* consists of two officials with extensive legal training, the *Juiz de Direito* (judge of law) and *Promotor Público* (district attorney—literally, public prosecutor), several judicial assistants, and clerks. There are in addition four judicial assistants who work full-time in the rural zones serving notice of trials.

The *Juiz de Direito* is the head of the entire legal system in Cunha and probably the most powerful individual in the *município*. He must be, as has been mentioned, a professional lawyer and is selected by examination by the state supreme court. Thus in a small town such as Cunha the *Juiz* is and nearly always has been an "outsider" not related to the old families of the region. The state judiciary, moreover, is a constitutionally independent branch of the government and traditionally jealous of its prerogatives. This means that the selection of a judge, at least during the past three decades, is largely independent of local interests, and he is effectively immune to local political pressure (Scheman, 1962). This does not mean that a judge cannot be influenced by local people, but there is no one in Cunha who has any effective power over him. This puts the *juiz* in an immensely strong position. He is an outside official of the state of São Paulo, highly educated, with a direct and independent line of influence, through the judiciary, to the very top echelons of the state government. He has effective authority over the whole legal organization, including the *Fôrça Pública*. He, in reality, is the ultimate local authority.

Few would flout this authority since he is one of the major decision makers in Cunha. He can order the arrest and trial of anyone, and, except for major crimes, tries them himself. While the trial is subject to review, this very review is done by the state legal system and moves the decision still further into the realm of city law and away from local influence. Most important in a rural region is the fact that the judge makes all decisions over land tenure. Thus, through the judiciary, the state has gained ultimate control over the very base of the economy—access to land.

The state-appointed judge, therefore, rather than the locally elected mayor, is the *de facto* chief official in Cunha. The event noted by Emilio Willems above, where one of the early mayors drove one of the local farmers out of the *município* for daring to send a bill for fruit, could not possibly happen now without at least the tacit consent of the state authorities. It is not surprising, therefore, to find from Alceu Maynard Araújo's notes on Cunha (1945) that the dominant politico-economic *panelinha* of Cunha in 1945 included both the *Juiz* and *Promotor*. A sign of the judge's position is the tremendous deference paid to him by even the most important local citizens.

This point is very important. It is the legalization as well as the commercialization of land which has led to the present changes in Cunha society. If land were not protected in some way by an independent authority, a landed elite could soon take over again. But the judiciary does offer some protection to the moderate-to-small farmer who knows how to take advantage of the law. This has important consequences which will be presented later. It is enough to say now that there has been a tremendous increase in legal registration of land in Cunha, since only through registration can a landowner obtain the protection of the law. In 1920 there were only 828 titles registered in Cunha. In 1966 there were over 2,000.

There are five orders of judicial districts, *comarcas*, in São Paulo, and Cunha, being a *comarca* of the fourth order, is one of the smaller ones. A *Juiz* receives an appointment for two years and then has the option to stay where he is, or compete for a more important position. While the majority of judges who come are ambitious and prefer to move on as soon as possible, a few like the smalltown life and the feeling of local importance and elect to stay on. A large part of the stability of the municipal government in Cunha in the two decades following the death of Dr. Salvador was due to the fact that one judge entered the *município* at that time and stayed for a number of years. He was a good friend of the *prefeito* and decidedly a member of the local *panelinha*, as was the *promotor* (Maynard Araújo, 1945).

Most informants in Cunha, of all social classes, seemed to feel that the majority of judges who had been appointed to Cunha had been honest and hardworking, though inevitably there were some reports of corruption. One judge who resided briefly in the town was said to have accepted money for almost any small decision. Such reports were, however, in the minority. One or two judges took advantage of their control over land tenure and established their own *fazendas* in the *município* by condemning unregistered land. While they were within their legal rights to do this, the local peasants frequently were not amused at being ousted from their fields.

There was general agreement that the more recent judges in Cunha had been among the best. One of them was largely responsible for the opening of the local *ginasio* (secondary school) and he taught in it for a number of years. The judiciary in Cunha at the time of the study was most impressive. Both the *Juiz* and *Promotor Público* were young, intelligent, and hardworking. Importantly, both were legal technicians in that they saw their responsibilities as scrupulous application of the written laws of the state and nation. Both stayed rigorously free from local involvement in politics and economics. The *Promotor* actually lived in the Paraíba Valley and came into town only during the week. While in Cunha he stayed in one of the local hotels. He once told the author that he would not even enter one of the local bars for fear that he might compromise his reputation. The *Juiz*, while he did live in the town, was not willing to join any of the local *panelinhas* and he refused to even try to make friends with the local politicians. This is quite a change from the earlier situation where the judge and local politicians formed a cohesive power group.

The important point to be made here is that these men are professionals (bureaucrats in Max Weber's sense, 1958: 196) and while highly ambitious they are interested in making their way within their professional organizations rather than any specific locality.*

Thus judicial decision-making in Cunha has become more and more legalized and almost wholly independent of the local leadership. The ones who were most upset by this change were members of the local elite who had lost their influence with the judiciary. Most of the townspeople, especially the humbler citizens, seemed to be satisfied with the course of events. Whether the recent separation of the political and judicial parts of the government is a temporary idiosyncratic matter, or whether it reflects a real change in the social structure remains to be seen. The author, however, feels that this course of events will continue and even accentuate as Cunha is brought more and more into the ambit of São Paulo and the twentieth century.

---

* In the terminology used by Fred Riggs, the system, at least locally, has become more "refractive" and less "fused" (1964).

Chapter VI

The Elaboration of Politics

Em matéria de política não há desonestidade.
(In political matters, there is no dishonesty.)

There are a variety of reasons why Brazilians vote for specific candidates, but seldom do they have anything to do with the issues involved. The Brazilian rural voter is generally conservative and basically pessimistic, usually with good reason. He doesn't expect that the government is really going to do anything to help him out anyway, and thus if he can get something tangible for his vote at election time, he is more than happy to do so. This sets the basis for the system of clientele politics which is one of the most interesting and important aspects of Brazilian political life.

It is not entirely correct to say that the political form known as *coronelismo*, as described in the previous chapter, is the only political style in Brazil, although in the rural regions it is certainly the most important. Alberto Guerreiro Ramos has, in fact, proposed five different successive models of Brazilian political styles (quoted in Graham, 1968:95). These are:

(1) clan-style politics characteristic of colonial Brazil and focusing around patriarchal families; (2) oligarchical-style politics, most appropriate for the period between 1822 and 1930 and centering on regional political bosses; (3) populist-style politics, best exemplified by the Brazilian Labor Party (PTB) and representing a larger concentration of political support than the first two political styles; (4) pressure-group politics, appearing only within more recent years and concentrated around specific economic in-

terests, and (5) ideological politics, which reaches its maximum development during the Quadros and Goulart government.

None of these "styles," it must be emphasized, fully supersedes the others but can only develop within a framework established by former styles.

The succession is important since each "style" effectively set up a pattern of authority and power, a political culture, and a series of vested interests which had to be accommodated or changed before any new form of politics could develop. Thus the existence of all-powerful local landowners in the interior led naturally to hierarchical networks of clientele politics as soon as votes became important on the national and state levels as a means of obtaining authority over the governmental bureaucracies. Naturally the rural elite would be happy to sell the votes of their dependents, who would never dare vote against their *patrão*, to the highest bidder. As the national and state governments became more and more important, both from the point of view of legal control and from the tax revenues and patronage possibilities involved, the interplay between the rural landowners and the governmental organization involved became more and more intense. Brazil has been called, with some justice, the most highly politicized nation in the world. Politics is always uppermost in the Brazilian's mind and the political struggles, even at local levels, become fierce and bitter (Harris, 1956:197). The reason for this is not hard to discover: Politics is immediately, directly, and personally important in Brazil.

The last chapter partly explained why this is so. Under a system where almost total power is granted by the central government to local politicians in exchange for their votes, the losing candidate can lose more than an election, he can lose his property and a number of his civil rights as well. This is why the "clan" politics in the Northeast often becomes such deadly business; land and even life may be at stake. In

Southern Brazil things are not so extreme. It is well to remember, however, that even here the country was, and to an
extent still is, a preindustrial agrarian society, so that the
industrial economic system, until very recently, has not been
a key to social mobility as it was in the United States and
Europe. Economics was always very closely tied in with
politics in Brazil. Social mobility lay mainly in the political
arena and this was true for people at all social and income
levels. Thus to the Brazilian townsman, politics is important
as the way up.

To properly understand the clientele system of politics, one
should attempt to view it from the standpoint of the local
political *chefe*. He is himself a client of some more powerful
state politician who is interested in but one thing, the maximum
number of votes at minimum cost. On the other hand, no
Brazilian politician has the resources to even begin to supply
the basic needs of his region in any universal way. It is no
accident that physicians and pharmacists are frequently prominent in Brazilian politics as they are in a position to gain
favor with the voters by donating medical aid. In order to
stay in office, therefore, the local leader must utilize the resources under his control and his authority to its ultimate
extent to obtain the maximum number of votes possible. For
this reason the municipal bureaucracies are politicized and their
members chosen for political reasons rather than personal
skills. This is why local bureaucracies in Brazil are frequently
so ineffective: The employee is kept on for politics rather than
performance. In addition the local *chefe político* usually does
have some ready cash at election time, supplied by himself,
his patron, or local merchants who want to remain in his
favor. With this he can buy a few votes outright, stage a few
churrascos (outdoor barbecues, which are vital to any political
campaign), and perhaps entertain a visiting state dignitary to
prove the importance of his connections. Invariably he has
some relatives, affinal or consanguineal, in the region who are

also politically oriented (he probably has helped them become so) and can be counted on for a few hundred votes. If he has been in office for some time, he will already have given most of the better local jobs, such as clerkships, teaching positions, etc., to sons and daughters of important local merchants and *fazendeiros*, or to his own relatives to keep them from nagging him to death. Sometimes these positions and their salaries can be divided up so as to give half jobs to two young people instead of a full-time job to one. This way he can also avoid paying the legal minimum wage for full-time work. It should be noted that in rural Brazil there are many families who have considerable land holdings but relatively little cash so that even a teacher's salary in these cases can be very helpful, earning him the gratitude and votes not only of the landowner, but of his family and dependents as well. In addition there are in the town, a number of menial lesser jobs such as janitors, street-sweepers, etc., which the local elite wouldn't touch, but which can be turned over to poor but respectable citizens with numerous relatives in the back country.

One interesting aspect of the political culture surrounding the clientele style is the degree of personal loyalty frequently to be found between patrons and clients at various levels of the structure. This loyalty may persist in behavior patterns even if it does not always involve ideological support. In Cunha, for example, one town laborer, poor but intelligent and politically astute, once bitterly condemned a local politician whom he always supported at election time. When asked how he could vote for such a shark, he replied, "because he gave my father a job." This aspect of the political culture also existed between upper and lower echelon *políticos*. Major politicians of southern Brazil such as Adhemar de Barros and Borges de Medeiros, despite somewhat shady general reputations, were noted for scrupulously paying off their political debts. It should also be noted that a breach in the loyalty between patron and client, especially on the part of the client, was considered a cardinal sin and would not be taken lightly by either party. Here too, nimble political footwork was required, when to change sides profitably, without retribution.

This brings to light another aspect of the clientele system, the nature of promises and rewards. All of Brazilian politics is carried on at a very personal level between the leader and his subordinates. Promises made in Brazilian politics are not grand schemes and generalizations made by the politician for mass consumption, but very specific exchanges between individuals; thus one vote may be exchanged for a pair of shoes, ten for a minor job, one thousand votes for a new bridge, etc. Unlike the usual "politician's promise" these specific items can be planned and bargained for in advance, and they are usually delivered, if the promiser wins; though not otherwise.

In this way these networks are built and in Brazil this can become a fine art. Since this was in the past one of the main roads to advancement, especially in the interior, many of the nimblest minds in the nation went into politics at some level or another.* The system, in its own way, has a strong ethic of its own and personal loyalty to family, friends, patrons, and clients are put ahead of loyalty to any abstraction such as "state" or "progress." It is personal rather than universal. This type of political pattern, moreover, often comes into being when the demands upon a political system are far greater than the services it has to offer. In these cases, it is not uncommon for political entrepreneurs to selectively use what resources they have simply to maintain themselves in power. This was as true in the time of Boss Tweed's New York (Callow, 1966:47) as it is in the interior of Brazil today. Critics of Brazilian "nepotism" and "corruption" would do well to bear this in mind. On the negative side, the system tends to build up patterns of behavior and a series of vested interests which paralyze real economic and political change.

* See, for example, the story "The Return of the Prodigal Husband," by João Guimarães Rosa, in his *Sagarana* (1966:57-98).

The last chapter, indeed, showed that at the beginning of this century Cunha was an unusually clear-cut and stable example of the clientele style of politics under the leadership of Dr. Thales de Salvador. Besides the handful of powerful *fazendeiros* in the *sede*, the rural zones of the *município* were organized by "district inspectors." In the commercially active zones of the *município* these were usually important *fazendeiros* and the position was one of considerable power. In the independent *bairros* of the *caipira* peasantry they were apparently usually themselves peasants who held the job because they were widely respected and had many kinship and *compadre* ties in the locality. In both cases the nominal job of the inspector was to keep the peace. In fact they were frequently very influential politically as well, in the standard pattern, earning their authority by delivering votes at election time. The position no longer has the importance that it once had since the state now has full time police and judicial officials in the rural zones. It is an honorary title given to influential *fazendeiros* or *sitiantes*.

The controlling municipal *panelinha* in Cunha which reformulated after the devastation of war in 1932 and the death of Dr. Salvador in 1936, reflected the increasing importance of local townsmen and metropolitan bureaucrats at the cost of the local landed elite. The rural *fazendeiros* were still important, but different groups of them came into prominence, most notably commercially successful cattlemen such as the Methodist groups in the southern part of the *município*. The important local businessmen were also included, especially the Lebanese families who became very active in politics and contributed a great deal to campaigns. Finally the group included *ex-officio* the key state officials, the judge, and *delegado*.

The *chefe político* of a rural region such as Cunha does not necessarily have to be rich or even widely popular, but he must at least be able to coordinate the disparate fragments of political and economic power in the community through his political authority. Such authority is gained partly by personality but most importantly through connections with the state and national governments. A local political chief in São Paulo today, as was pointed out in the last chapter, no longer has the kind of direct power which the powerful clan leaders had in the past. His appeal is collaborative and political and he must be able to persuade those who count that somehow they benefit from keeping him in office. This is done by showing the local elite that he is able to obtain favors from the state or national governments.

Dr. Salvador, with powerful connections in São Paulo, was able to do this for generations. After 1936 the man who first reorganized the political structure of the *município* was a wealthy French businessman living in Cunha. He lost everything he owned, however, in a disastrous fire and lost his position to Sr. Euclydes Carvalho, a man from Taubeté who had lived for some years in the Methodist regions of the *município* and had strong friendships there as well as important family connections in the Paraíba Valley and São Paulo. This man devoted himself to politics for the next twenty years and between 1938 and 1958 was in effective control of the *município*, being elected *prefeito* (mayor) three times.

His coalition controlled politics in Cunha for about two decades. It had, in the late 1940s and early 1950s, about 1,200 votes, whereas the organized opposition had between four and five hundred. These can be seen from electoral returns for these years. Blocks of votes of these sizes appear again and again for certain candidates, the same candidates, incidentally, who were selected by the political chiefs of Guaratinguetá.

The coalition broke up, however, and Sr. Carvalho fell from power in 1959 due partly to external political pressures and partly to purely local matters. Sr. Carvalho is a politician of the old school. He is considered to have notable administrative ability but he is trained in the political traditions of the Paulista coffee elite, and he always kept close ties with this group.

His style is thus courtly and formal and he has little charisma. Over the years various politically ambitious men had broken with him and created a small but intense opposition group, headed by a pharmacist of Italian descent. For many years Sr. Carvalho's skill as a politician was made manifest by the inability of the opposition to make any headway despite the fact that they at times had the active support of the state governor. In time, however, for a number of individual factors, many families came to oppose the mayor personally even though they might continue to support him at election time.

Under Brazilian law it is impossible for a *prefeito* to succeed himself in office, so it is customary for the local *chefe* to introduce a friend to serve for the alternate term. It is expected that the friend will only serve in a nominal capacity while the real power remains with the *chefe político*. He usually has himself elected chairman of the city council until he can run again as *prefeito* in the next election. Sr. Carvalho had already performed this maneuver twice before, and in 1959 he presented as the alternate candidate his close friend and political protégé, Nilo Simón, the son of a highly respected Lebanese merchant and a wealthy *fazendeiro* in his own right. Nilo, like his mentor, is a born politician, but he is decidedly one of the new-style Brazilian politicians with a friendly directness and considerable charismatic appeal, as reflected in the fact that he is everywhere referred to by his first name whereas this is never the case with Sr. Carvalho. Even before the election Nilo was gathering up all the loose strings of power which he could find, and these were plentiful, especially in the rural zones. Nilo was so popular he was even able to win the nomination of the opposition party and he won unanimously.

But the old *chefe* had miscalculated and Nilo carried out a *coup*. With the authority and powers of the office of *prefeito* behind him, he proceeded to organize all of Sr. Carvalho's fragmented opposition and created his own party. Immediately he turned on the older man and sued him for malfeasance of

office. The suit was eventually dropped but the point was made
clear. The old coalition was split right down the middle, and
even many families were sharply divided on the issue. One
important Methodist family quit talking politics entirely because of the intensity of feelings generated. Many of the older
members of the community and the more traditional town
families, especially those who owed jobs and favors to the old
mayor, supported him, and an attempt by the new *prefeito* to
purge the city hall met with enough opposition that he backed
down. On the other hand, most of the young people and much
of the important rural commercial class supported Nilo. Feelings were very strong, as might be expected from the nature of
the *coup*. Even at the time of the study the former mayor would
not mention the name of his former friend but would use
instead a series of colorful Portuguese euphemisms. He and
his supporters felt that he had been betrayed by his closest
friend whereas supporters of Nilo Simón felt that the old
político finally got what he deserved and hinted darkly about
numerous unproved misconducts on the part of the ex-mayor.

A part of Euclydes Carvalho's defeat may be laid to the
changing class structure and political style in Cunha. While
it certainly cannot be said that clientele politics is extinct in
the region, it is on the wane and the electoral base is broaden-
ing. The revolution in rural production from peasant-style corn
and beans horticulture to dairy and meat production has meant
that even the wealthiest *fazendeiros* no longer have dozens of
client families dependent upon their goodwill. To win elections
it is no longer enough to appeal to a few big landowners with
promises of favors or jobs for their children. Moreover, the
new ranching elite is basically capitalist in orientation rather
than patriarchal. The political chief of Cunha more and more
had to contend with a growing group of self-willed, independent ranchers, with land holdings of intermediate size and few
client families, who wanted real services from their municipal
government: roads repaired and schools well staffed. Sr. Carvalho is far too intelligent a politician not to have seen the

change, but his roots were in the past, his style personal and hierarchical rather than charismatic and equalitarian, and his connections and allegiances were the dying coffee elite of the Paraíba Valley rather than with the dynamic populist politicians of the metropolis.

Nilo Simón, however, is very much a politician of the populist style, although he is very capable as well of weaving his own webs in the clientele system. Unlike the former *prefeito* who, despite pressures to the contrary, remained loyal to the remnants of the coffee planters in the valley, Nilo for a time deliberately courted the support of the old master of populist politics in São Paulo, Dr. Adhemar de Barros, even though he never committed himself fully to Adhemar or any other patron. Nilo's administration was flamboyant and spectacular, and Cunha changed greatly during the four years he was *prefeito*. The most dramatic event was the burning of the city hall in 1961. Although no one was hurt, the massive 200 year old structure was completely gutted, taking most of the municipal archives in the flames. The end result, however, was that the state government soon had to build a new jail on the site since the old one had been a part of the demolished *prefeitura*. More important, however, was the fact that this was the time of the town's greatest growth, and many new buildings were put up, private as well as public. State and municipal money was spent freely on large and small projects. In his final report on his administration the new *prefeito* listed forty-eight projects which he had undertaken or brought to completion. This was without much doubt the most productive period in Cunha's history. In the meantime, however, the charge of corruption had been leveled at his administration from many sides. It was said that the municipal treasury was open to anyone who asked, and many asked. Several charges of corruption and malfeasance were brought against him by his political enemies and the stigma remains in the minds of many of the local people, even though none of the charges was ever proven.

Whatever the cause, at the end of Nilo's term the credit of

the *município* was seriously imperiled. This was in part due to the fact that money for many promised state projects was not released either because of administrative tangles or because the Brazilian inflation had made their budgets inadequate. To counteract the charges of corruption and financial irresponsibility, Nilo made a politically astute move by presenting as his candidate for mayor in 1963 the town auditor, Antonio Antunes, known as Tunicão, a man of considerable financial ability and unquestioned honesty. Tunicão ran against the fragmented remains of the old coalition headed by Sr. Euclydes Carvalho and won. His administration, however, was paralyzed for two years while the *município* paid off the debts accumulated in the previous four years. This in turn, has produced many complaints in Cunha about a "do nothing" administration and has led to a split between Tunicão and Nilo, leaving politics in Cunha divided three ways.

The Role of the State in the Politics of Cunha

The account given above confirms the general rule that politics in rural Brazil is based on local issues and personalities. A voter in Cunha can be characterized as a *"Carvalhista"* or *"Niloista,"* rather than a Socialist or Christian Democrat, or even Conservative or Liberal. It is impossible, however, to understand the nature of the changes which have occurred in Cunha's politics without an understanding of the role of the state government of São Paulo in both politics and economics. It should be noted at the outset that, as in the case of law enforcement, the Brazilian federal government has little direct importance in Cunha. It is general policy of the federal government to let the wealthy state of São Paulo support its own local services within the state boundaries so that the national government can concentrate its economic efforts in other parts of Brazil where they are most needed. In Cunha the federal government collects taxes and runs the mail service, but does little else.

In the traditional system of clientele politics it is an expected part of the pattern for bureaucracies to be staffed for reasons of politics rather than reasons of skill. Local governments can get little done because what little money they have is spent on elections rather than on public services. What few public services are obtained, therefore, must come from the state governments and these are awarded as favors by successful state politicians to the local *chefe políticos* who have supported them. A local Brazilian politician proves his ability not by how honest an administration he runs at home, but by how much money and how many projects he can wrangle out of the state government in return for the votes he controls (Leal 1948). Under this system, of course, if the municipal and state governments are in opposition, nothing is done locally at all.

This system, however, is changing rather drastically in São Paulo State and Cunha reflects the change. Despite the long domination of Dr. Salvador in local politics and despite his great prominence in state politics, the number of specific state projects which he obtained for the *município* was relatively few. The most important being the construction of a school building some fifty years ago. The tight control which the local landed elite had on politics, however, as well as the general economic stagnation of the region and the disinterest of the *caipira* peasantry, meant that little pressure was put on the doctor to do more for the *município* as a region. Those who had the power were satisfied with the *status quo*.

Cunha has long had close political ties with the city of Guaratinguetá, one of the greatest centers of the coffee boom in the Paraíba Valley. This city, moreover, was the home of one of the greatest figures in Brazilian history, Francisco de Paula Rodrigues Alves, minister of finance and *Conselheiro* (counselor) of the Empire, governor of the state of São Paulo, and twice elected president of Brazil.* It was the support of

* He dominated the politics of the Paraíba Valley effortlessly even when, as President of Brazil, he at times opposed the interests of the coffee planters (Bello, 1966:193). Even after his death in 1919 his family continued to be important in Paulista politics.

this group which insured the long political careers of former Cunha politicians. The Alves political fortunes declined, however, after 1932 under the attacks of Dr. Adhemar de Barros, who had been a federal *interventor* of Getulio Vargas in São Paulo State, where he built an immensely effective political machine and was elected governor three times. Despite considerable efforts of supporters of Adhemar de Barros to take over in Cunha, his P.S.P. party (*Partido Social Progressista*) never made much headway against the old *prefeito*. A serious incident in 1953, the last time that political violence occurred in the town, where an innocent bystander was killed by a stray bullet, was blamed on the opposition and the P.S.P. was so discredited that not until 1964, when Sr. Carvalho's support had been fragmented, did Adhemar win even a plurality of votes in Cunha.

In the state elections of 1954, elements of the Alves group, and with it the leaders of Cunha, opposed the political maverick, Dr. Janio Quadros, and saw to his defeat locally, although with his great charismatic appeal to the metropolitan voters, he was elected governor of the state. Under the rules of Brazilian clientele politics this opposition to the new governor would mean no new projects could be expected from the state government for the next four years and this is what the political leaders of Cunha expected. Quadros, however, as Guerreiro Ramos pointed out, was not an oligarchical style politician and was more interested in over-all state development than immediate political maneuvering. One of the aims of his administration was to develop certain backward rural zones, and Cunha was included. To the astonishment of the Cunhenses, politicians and nonpoliticians alike, Quadros continued and even increased state aid to the *município*. Within two years of his election, according to local informants, he began a series of projects within the town and rural zones. This aid continued under the administration of Dr. Carvalho Pinto, Quadros' successor from 1959 to 1963, and, though with diminished impetus, Dr. Adhemar de Barros.

The local administration of Nilo Simon greatly benefited from this state support. The question arises as to what extent the mayor was responsible for the various projects. His supporters give him credit for everything. He did work hard, spending considerable time in the state capital and with the state legislative leaders. His detractors say, on the other hand, that everything had already been planned by the previous mayor, Euclydes Carvalho, and would have come anyway. The main point is that by this time the key decisions on expenditures for municipal development were in the hands of the state governor and legislator. The mayor might plan any number of projects for his *município*, but all needed approval in the capital city of São Paulo. No projects passed without gubernatorial support. It seems probable that in fact both local mayors merely gave focus and direction to a conscious policy of development by the state government.

In general it may be said that the services which have made possible the economic and social development of the town and to some degree even of the *município* as a whole have been due in large part to investment by the state government. The state operates in Cunha the following:

The education system, in large part

A health service

A pediatric center

An agricultural station

The judicial system

The police force

The *caixa econômica* (a state bank)

A statistics agency (in Pindamonhangaba since the fire of 1961)

Records agencies

A meteorological station (shared with the federal government)

In addition it has given to the *município*, in whole or in part, the following:

The school building

The courthouse
The new jail and police headquarters
The hydroelectric plant
The water-filtration plant
The municipal slaughterhouse
The sewage network
Two road graders

At the time of the study the state had several major projects underway although some of them were going forward rather fitfully. The most important undoubtedly was the construction of a new paved road from Guaratinguetá to the sea, passing near the town. This road, barely begun when this study commenced in 1965 was completed two years later. In addition new buildings are under construction for a new *ginásio* (secondary school) and the agricultural station.

Thus most of the new services which have drawn the rural middle class into the *cidade* of Cunha, stimulating its commerce and industry, came from the state as well as most of the investment which produced the large expansion of the civil service since 1945 (as will be detailed in Chapters VIII and IX). It is probably safe to say that without this investment the town of Cunha would be little larger today than it was twenty years ago, despite the increased commercial wealth of the rural regions.

The municipal government, moreover, is losing the politicization that is characteristic of the "cartorial" system, with new pressures from the state and electorate. It is becoming very important functionally, especially in the rural zones.

It is responsible for road maintenance vital to the *município's* economy, keeps the city clean, maintains the electric and water system, and its own administrative apparatus. In short, the day-to-day operation of government in Cunha is largely in the hands of the officials in the city hall. On the other hand, major capital investment is very difficult for the municipal government, which generally lacks a broad tax base, especially in an agricultural region where even existing taxes are difficult to collect. There are some exceptions—both the *ginásio* and the new *escola normal* began as municipal projects —but these were intended more as stimuli to further state investment rather than as independent projects.

It must be noted that little of this investment has gone into the rural zones. The major contribution of the state to these areas has been through gifts of equipment and small grants to the municipal government for road work and to enlarge the rural educational system, but a massive program of rural aid, agronomy, agricultural education, rural electrification, etc. has not been attempted. An agricultural station exists, but it barely functions since it lacks a trained agronomist, is understaffed, and is mistrusted by many traditional farmers. The health service does yeoman's work with meager resources, but cannot do more than a fraction of what needs to be done in the rural zones.

It can be demonstrated, therefore, that the traditional clientele politics so characteristic of rural Brazil in general, and important in Cunha's past, is beginning to disintegrate and new styles are appearing. The new political leader, though skilled in the older political ways, has definite populist appeal as well. The new class of commercial ranchers beginning to dominate the *município* are less interested in local politics than they are in improved services and protecting their commercial interests at the state and federal level. In a sense the cooperative serves as a kind of pressure group for them. As for the style of what Guerreiro Ramos has called "ideological politics," there has always been a very small group in the town who vote for ideological reasons, and staunchly refuse to change. There were in the past, for example, a couple of people in the town who always insisted in voting communist and when the P.C. disappeared from the ballot they then voted blank. They made no secret of this and no one worried about it, though they were considered a little strange, and it was felt perhaps they read a little too much for their own good. As for ideological or party politics on a mass basis, there is little sign of that as of yet in Cunha.

There is decidedly some evidence of an increasing political sophistication among the people of Cunha. This has gone along with a greater awareness of the outside world generally. Improved means of communication and a greatly increased literacy rate mean that the population is more and more in contact with the urban culture and the problems which concern the cities. There are fifty-four television sets in Cunha, and the majority of urban houses (some 396) and even many of the rural houses have radios. It must be said that these are largely used for entertainment rather than for information, but a certain amount of the latter may get through. There are still only about 40 people who have newspaper subscriptions in town so that newspaper reading is largely still restricted to a minority of the urban elite. Nevertheless, papers pass from hand to hand in Cunha with great rapidity and the number of people who do read them is considerably more than forty. Some of the young people, who cannot actually afford a subscription, regularly read the papers of others.

The reading of the majority of the literate population, however, is restricted to the required school text books, which are practically memorized. The schools do inform children about their nation and the world in general and attempt to instill a sense of national unity. This effort has been only partly successful, however, as the majority of Cunhenses insist that they are Paulistas first and Brazilians second. Also popular among the young people are the *fotonovellas*, the Brazilian equivalent of comic books. These, however, are hardly designed to increase the political awareness of the reader. It was the creation of the local *ginásio*, the secondary school, which was apparently largely responsible for the increase in awareness of national and international problems. Through that school, the well-educated town elite, mostly trained outside the *município*, shared its knowledge with the local young people. As a general rule, only those people in Cunha with more than a primary education had any interest in discussing national and world affairs. Although the author found that this curiosity was greatest among the professionals, a number of the young people were also very interested in world problems and some of them were surprisingly well informed.*

It is to be doubted, however, if even now more than a handful of the people in Cunha vote on the basis of international or even Brazilian national issues. There is, however, some evidence for a growing allegiance, especially among the educated urbanized group, toward state and national political figures over and above the allegiance toward local *chefes*. All of these figures tend to be important in São Paulo State politics. Thus Janio Quadros still had a strong following in Cunha, as did Carvalho Pinto and Adhemar de Barros. How many of the people of Cunha would vote for these candidates over the opposition of their local chiefs is uncertain, though some would undoubteldly do so. Thus, while the great majority of the 4,000 voters in Cunha still vote as directed, political independence is growing with improved education, communication, and economic independence of the voters.

The probable explanation for this is not hard to find. Increasingly the better informed people in Cunha see that the most important decisions that affect their lives are not being made at the local level, but in São Paulo and even Brasilia. Moreover, increasingly, as the state becomes more important in the region, decisions made in these capitals do affect their lives as the *município* and local government are bypassed. Thus, a major change is taking place in the political structure of Cunha parallel to the change in the economic structure; that

---

* The topics of greatest interest in Cunha were, in order: economic conditions in the United States, racism in the United States, Caryl (Carlos) Chessman, and the death penalty, the war in Vietnam, the Dominican intervention, and the ecumenical movement.

is increasing involvement by the people directly with great metropolitan institutions. There is a growing change from municipal isolationism to extensive involvement in the political apparatus of the industrial state.

Chapter VII

A Changing Society: the Rural Zones

Cunha is now a complex and highly stratified society, and is daily growing more complex. The way of life of a wealthy townsman with his automobile and television set has very little in common with that of the *caipira* peasant, with his hoe, his hut of *pau-a-pique*, and his numerous religious festivals. The gap, moreover, is growing wider. It is difficult, however, to say that there are X number of social divisions in Cunha, since the patterns of stratification vary depending upon which variables are taken into account. Social stratification is like every other kind of classification, the "classes" which are obtained depend upon the objectives of the study and the methods used. Most sociologists since the time of Lloyd Warner (1960) have tended to analyze social strata on the basis of prestige factors, though a number of others have attempted to determine social classes through the study of distribution of property, especially if these are important in production. There will be no attempt in this study to review the immense literature on social stratification,* though the problem as it is specifically related to Cunha will be taken up in Chapter IX. This chapter is basically concerned with the nature and forces involved in social change, especially in the rural zones, and modifications in the distribution of land and wealth. Some discussion of changes in stratification patterns, therefore, is necessary here.

The role of prestige and influence in the social organization of Cunha will be examined in later chapters. These are impor-

---

* For good discussions of this literature, see Dahrendorf (1959); Ossowski (1963); and Bendix and Lipset (1966).

tant problems in their own right, but of limited usefulness in the study of social change since, as was pointed out above, change in complex societies is largely due to shifts in authority and power patterns. Although prestige is derived from power differences in a community, as Lenski has pointed out (1966:45), there are too many other factors involved for it to be equated with power. Furthermore, prestige is "conservative" in that it tends to lag behind social change and may give a semblance of power where it does not really exist.

The case is different with regard to property, since there can be no doubt that wealth brings power, especially if it involves authority over scarce resources or the means of production. Thus Ossowski points out (1963:42) that what he calls "simple gradation" (single factor) analysis as a way of determining social stratification, is almost always based upon wealth. A scheme of social stratification based upon property holdings is appealing, in addition, because it offers the possibility for ready quantification, but, like the study of prestige, it can be misleading in the study of social dynamics. Andreski says (1968:25):

The possession of wealth gives power. But as soon as we enquire into the meaning of the word "possession" we see that the economic power is derivative. The terms: possession, property, ownership, designate the right to control, to use and dispose of objects, the access to which is prohibited to all except the owner.

The "ownership" of property, therefore, is not an intrinsic element of property itself (although some conservatives seem to think so) but is in reality based, once again, upon patterns of authority, the acceptance by the society that an individual should have exclusive rights over certain assets. The nature of this "acceptance" is largely determined in complex societies by the legal and political institutions of the community. Thus those individuals who have the means of enforcing their claims of "ownership" are more likely to maintain their property than those who do not.

In the last analysis, therefore, economic authority and power should be seen as derived from political and legal authority and power. The real situation is, of course, vastly more complex than this, but the priority is important in order to fully understand the economic and social changes which are going on in Cunha. Power derived from force is primary to power derived from wealth, and the pattern of political and legal authority and power thus largely determine the pattern of property distribution and privilege. In "personalized" political systems, therefore, where the governmental institutions serve only the interests of a single individual or a small oligarchy, property and privilege will tend to concentrate in the hands of those few. In extreme cases, those who run the state also own the state (Lenski, 1966:212-219).

In an agrarian society, one of the key economic variables is land, the basis of production. Land tenure, the control of access to the land, is thus one of the most important sources of power in such societies. Historically in Brazil, as was pointed out in Chapter V, the fragmentation of political power meant essentially that every landowner was himself responsible for defending his claims to the land. Furthermore, as was also pointed out, the landlord's degree of authority in the local political situation, and hence his ability to defend ownership claims, was to a large degree determined by his position in the larger national economy.* Thus land tended to concentrate in the hands of the *fazendeiros*, the commercial producers, as only they could effectively maintain land "ownership." In addition, it follows that the more deeply involved a region was in commercial production, the more valuable land would become, and the more difficult it would be for the moderate to small landholder to maintain his rights to his property or his production.

Thus power can be derived from authority over property, "wealth," as well as from authority in governmental and other

---

* Once again, Jorge Amado's book, *The Violent Land*, graphically describes such a situation.

institutions. This power can be expressed in a negative sense, by depriving people of property which they had formerly enjoyed, or even their means of livelihood itself, or it can be expressed in the positive sense by offering rewards for obedience. The distribution of economic power, however, depends upon the political organization of the society. Kenneth Boulding points out (1968:44) that as the importance of the "threat" pattern of power declines, that derived from the commercial and economic system increases. The development of a "capitalistic" economic organization (as opposed to "feudal" in Sjoberg's sense, 1952) means, ideally at any rate, that the state defends ownership of private property on a universal rather than oligarchic basis. This is implied in the development and spread of a money economy since money is a universal measure of wealth (i.e., authority over property) which has the additional advantages of being divisible and quantifiable.

The preceding chapters have pointed out the important changes which have taken place in Cunha during the past years with regard to the kinds of authority and power dominant in the *município*. The fact is that in Cunha the individual property owner is, for the most part, no longer directly responsible for defending his claims to ownership by himself. State institutions have taken over this job and most property ownership, especially that of land tenure, now must be confirmed by the state judiciary. The judiciary, as was noted, is increasingly independent of the local elite, which means that it is becoming increasingly possible in Cunha to advance economically without becoming deeply involved in local political institutions. In short, Cunha is becoming more and more involved in the institutions of a monetized, commercial, capitalist state.

Land Tenure in Cunha

In an agricultural community such as Cunha, the most important kind of property is land, the means of production itself. Land means many different things to different groups of people in Cunha. To the *caipira* peasant, it is something to be worked, day by day. It is the very basis of his existence, furnishing him with food and housing and the small surplus necessary to exchange for a few commercial items, such as rum and clothing, at the local *venda*. To the plantation owner and wealthy *fazendeiro*, however, land was not something which one worked directly. Instead one's legal rights to land access and tenure were something which gave him authority over his clients and sharecroppers, which in turn could bring him prestige, labor to enhance the value of his property and his life style, and votes to maintain his political position. For both landlord and peasant the monetary value of the land was of secondary importance. Land was not as a general rule purchased. It was instead claimed, from the Portuguese crown, the local Indians, one's weaker neighbors, or frequently from no one in particular.

By the beginning of the twentieth century, as was shown in the fourth chapter, Cunha was so isolated that it had few commercial markets of any kind. Most of the population lived on a subsistence level with very little contact with the monetary economy and paying little or no rent to the great landholding families of the region. The handful of landed aristocratic *coroneis* who once dominated the region since the time of the coffee boom, had, with few exceptions, moved out of the *município*. (In 1966 only one of the *fazenda* "big houses," *casa grande*, was still occupied.) The picture of the dichotomous social system—the powerful and the powerless, the masters and the slaves—characteristic of much of Brazil, and accurate in its general lines for most agrarian societies, was softened in many areas of Southern Brazil, The *caipira*, living in the areas on the margins of commercial production were, and still are, a fairly independent group, fighting a continual, though losing, battle against exploitation by the urbanized *fazendeiros* of the towns.

Some idea of this independence can be seen in the more

remote regions of Cunha today, despite the widespread dis-
integration of the *caipira* culture. The author once interviewed
a very wealthy *fazendeiro*, a man who owned thousands of
acres of virgin rain forest in the mountains adjoining his
ranch, and had some 14 families of sharecroppers working for
him directly. During the course of the conversation he mentioned that there were some thirty or more additional families,
descendants of Indians and runaway slaves, who had been living on his land since as far back as anyone could remember,
and who never paid any rent at all. When asked if he had ever
tried to force them off, he replied, "Oh, no, I've always had
as much land as I needed, and besides some of them are
armed."

The new commercial activity caused by the rapid expansion
of São Paulo city markets also created a sudden rise in the
value of land. It became increasingly a commercial commodity
and a scarce resource, bought, traded, and fought over, especially since the newly prosperous commercial ranchers had little else to do with their money than reinvest it in animals and
land. The continued Brazilian inflation makes saving money
seem rather foolish. Emilio Willems notes the following: "In
1919, a *fazenda* of 800 *alqueires* (about 2,000 ha.) located
near the town, and on the main road, when at auction, could
not find a buyer for twelve *contos de reis* (about 12,000 *cruzeiros*). In 1945, one alqueire of the same land was worth more
than one thousand *cruzeiros* and the whole *fazenda* thus represented a value of approximately Cr. $800,000" (1947:90). In
1966 land in Cunha was selling at a price of from Cr. $500,000
to Cr. $1,000,000 per alqueire, which probably represents an
increase in *real* value of from seven to ten times the 1945 price.

The fact that land has increased so greatly in *monetary*
value since 1919 is in itself significant, since money is the
language and symbol of ownership in the complex state, and
is not commonly found in peasant societies (Lenski, 1966:
207). As the value and commercial activity of the land soared,

legal ownership of the land became more and more important. As has been shown, the state legal system for several decades has gradually been taking upon itself the role of determining ownership of land. This worked to the advantage of the commercial rancher and farmer, skilled in manipulating both money and the law, but it was disastrous to the *caipira* peasantry. As Antonio Candido pointed out, the *caipira* culture depends for its existence upon control of effectively limitless lands. The increase in population which occurred in the first part of the century reduced the *sertão*, the frontier, to marginal distant areas so that further *caipira* expansion became increasingly difficult. Thus by the 1920s the great majority of the peasant population was living on land which was potentially of great commercial value.

In the 1930s and 1940s came the extensive dispossession movements. Here the urban judicial system backed by written urban law, interpreted by local judicial officials, and with the whole force of the state police behind it, attacked the *caipira* society at its very basis of existence, the land. According to some of the poorer people of Cunha, during this era, many people lost land which they had always assumed was theirs. Due to illiteracy or general alienation from the urban culture, and sometimes just to avoid taxes, they had never bothered to legally register their lands, and others with greater knowledge of the ways of the town and its laws, simply deprived them of it. More than one prosperous rancher living in Cunha today has earned a reputation of *Tubarão de terra* (land shark). Many of the new owners were interested solely in cattle ranching as the most profitable land-intensive form of commercial production and so the residents were not allowed to stay on even as sharecroppers. The dispossession was not always a gentle business. Stories were told about how on occasion peasants, including old people and children, were hauled bodily out of their homes, their furniture put out in the street, and the building then set on fire. It is said that one judge con-

fronted several *caipira* families simultaneously with demands
that their back taxes for several years be paid in cash by the
next day. They were, of course, unable to pay, and their land
was forfeited. There are records of one whole *bairro* being
evicted in such a way, and there may well have been other
cases as well. It is interesting to note that for the most part the
initiators of these dispossession movements were not members
of old Cunhense families trying to get squatters off their land,
but newcomers from Minas Gerais and elsewhere, coming in
with some money and considerable political savvy.

Many local people realized what was happening and took
steps to legally defend themselves against dispossession. The
great increase in the number of registered land holdings between 1920 and 1940 (from 797 to 1,531) is not so much due
to an increase in the actual number of land holders, but to a
growing awareness on the part of the rural population that they
had to abide by urban rather than the *caipira* rules of land
ownership, since the ultimate decisions on land tenure and the
ability to enforce these decisions lay in the town.

Today in almost every part of the *município* there is widespread knowledge with regard to what land is registered and
by whom. A common gambit to avoid paying excessive taxes
is for an owner to register only a part of his land. Thus if
anyone investigates he can always claim that it was that part
under investigation which was registered. This is easier for a
large landowner to do than for a small one, and it is not uncommon for a *fazendeiro* to have two to three times as much
land in use than he has registered. This leads to many conflicts
between neighbors, and the judge of Cunha said that disputes
over land ranks next to disputes over women as a source of
violence in the *comarca*. Most of the court trials that I personally saw in Cunha were related to land ownership.

One case will illustrate some of these problems: *fazendeiro*
Eduardo Campos, an ambitious but by no means wealthy man,
owned one fairly large *fazenda* of a few hundred *alqueires*,

which he had registered, and several other pieces of land which he had never bothered to register. He had four or five field hands who worked for him on his *fazenda* on a full time basis. It was his habit to plant each of his unregistered sections of land early in the season, and this gave him and his workers a yearly claim at least to the crops planted on the land, if not the land itself. This year (in 1966), he arrived with some of his hands to begin farming as usual, only to find that a neighbor, with the aid of a few *lavradores*, had already started planting on a section that Sr. Campos considered "his." The *fazendeiro* then proceeded to pull out a gun and fired six shots into the ground. This effectively discouraged the neighbor and his crew, who fled in all directions, and Sr. Campos thus kept control over his land.

This case reveals several interesting points about land tenure in Cunha. It shows that personal violence as a defense of land ownership still exists in the region but it is by no means the deadly business it was a century ago—and still is in some parts of Brazil. Perhaps more important is the fact that Sr. Campos was brought to trial for assault, thus, confirming the general rule that land disputes in Cunha are now fought in the courts rather than in the forest. Indeed, there are records of a suit, filed some ten years ago by one of Cunha's most influential landowners, to dispossess one of his own sharecroppers who, he claimed, had not paid adequate rent in years. Such legal nicety would be unheard of in the interior of Brazil today or probably in the Cunha of fifty years ago, where a peasant reluctant with his shares would simply be tossed out, if not worse.

The distribution of land holdings in Cunha is best shown in graph form and Chart VIIA reveals the changes in land tenure over a period of forty years. There can be seen a definite trend toward an increase in the number of middle-size holdings, while the number of large holdings are relatively declining. This is due mainly to the Brazilian system of partible inherit-

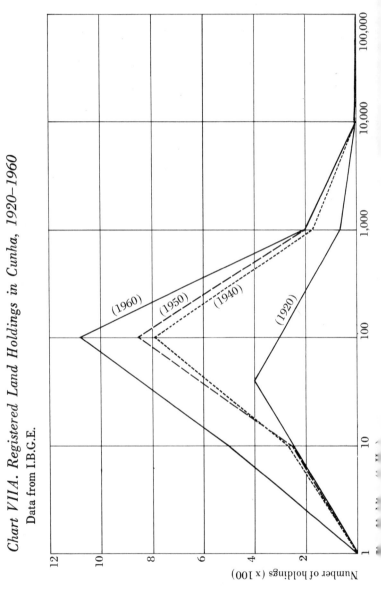

Chart VIIA. *Registered Land Holdings in Cunha, 1920–1960*
Data from I.B.G.E.

ance (Wolf, 1966) wherein property is divided equally among the children of a deceased individual. This system of inheritance, although derived from Roman law, is so ancient that it has become a part of the folk tradition and, together with the increased commercialization of the soil, has fundamentally changed the nature of rural Cunha society.

Transportation in the Município of Cunha

It would be wrong to say that the commercial transformation is complete in Cunha. A key to commercial development is accessibility to markets, and here the vital factor is transportation. One of the main reasons why the *caipira* culture flourished in Cunha at the turn of the century was the fact that much of the region was almost inaccessible. Even today the physical isolation means that many areas of the *município* are still not threatened with high land prices and commercialization. These areas are becoming fewer and fewer, however, as new roads are cut into the *sertão*, often following development of the lumber industry. The development of transportation networks, therefore, is a key link in understanding the social and economic dynamics of rural Cunha.

The roads of Cunha are legendarily bad. One visitor said that they were worse than those of Spain during the Civil War. Even in 1965, one journalist wrote that to travel on the main Cunha highway from Guaratinguetá to Paratí in times of rain was "not courage, but madness" (*O Estado de São Paulo*, Jan. 15, 1965:15). In January 1961, when the town's city hall caught fire, fire trucks were summoned from the city of São Paulo, but arrived, after great communal effort, 48 hours late. They were just in time to be able to pull down the century-old walls of the building. On this occasion the Paulista fire chief became something of a local celebrity when he arrived on a mule ahead of his bogged trucks.

While the roads are difficult and even dangerous in times of rain, they are nevertheless reasonably good in dry weather.

The state government, in addition, currently keeps heavy machinery on the main road to tow trapped vehicles out of the mud. The more important roads are usually kept open except for a few weeks in January and February.

The state of São Paulo maintains one road in the *município*: that between Guaratinguetá and the mountains overlooking Paratí. The state is currently paving this road, a fact of major importance which will be examined later. There are, in addition, some 700 kilometers of rural roads which are maintained by the municipal government. The *Prefeito* once said that maintaining the roads was the main responsibility of the local government. In a region such as Cunha where fresh milk is the main product one can see why this is necessary. Every day the line trucks cannot run, the farmers lose considerably. Thus the more important roads, the main highway to Guaratinguetá, and the milk routes, are fairly well maintained. Many of the more distant roads are not well taken care of, and a few of them have been impassable for years due to a fallen bridge or washed-out section. Interestingly, as an indication of the isolation between the two districts, the road between the *sede* and the village of Campos Novos is in very poor shape and difficult for a vehicle, even in dry weather. The people of Campos Novos prefer to maintain their direct links with the city of Lorena in the Paraíba Valley rather than those with their own center.

Traditionally, roads were maintained by the local residents of each *bairro*. Under the municipal code of 1893, each individual was obligated to attend *muterões*, called by local highway inspectors, to repair the roads. *Fazendeiros* were required to send a quarter of their field hands (Willems, 1947:38). In 1927 a municipal "travel tax" was imposed and a group of full-time workers was hired solely to maintain the roads. Emilio Willems writes that in 1945 the *muterão* for the upkeep of the roads was a very rare thing. This is true today, although such communal effort still exists. In times of special emergency such as a fallen bridge or stalled truck, a local policeman or inspector may call on everyone in the neighborhood to help in the repairs, but this is not in the sense of a true *muterão*.

The municipal government currently hires eleven full-time workers to maintain the streets. Others are hired on a daily basis when needed, from the local farms. These are low-paid day laborers who work on the roads with hoes and shovels much as it was done twenty years ago. The town now owns two mechanical road graders, and while one is old and rather small, the other is a large, modern apparatus given to the *município* by the state government. These machines can open up a road for vehicular traffic in a few hours when it would have taken days by hand labor. Their size and weight limit their work to more level regions, however, and they never get to the high northern parts of the *município*.

According to local officials, there were about 800 kilometers of roads in the *município* in 1965, yet not all of these were passable to motor traffic. Emilio Willems states that in 1945 there existed only 280 km. of municipal roads; less than half the present total (1947:20). The road to Paratí was at that time impassable for motor travel. Now trucks, buses, and private cars pass daily to this seaside town which is rapidly becoming a major resort center. Thus, it can be said that the system of roads in Cunha has improved considerably in the past generation.

The improvements of roads and increased financial prosperity of Cunha has greatly stimulated the ownership and utilization of motor vehicles in the area, and vice versa. The first car appeared in Cunha in the 1920s and old-time residents still remember its arrival, although there is some debate over the exact date. The enormous problems of distances, mountains, and abominable roads have made the acceptance of the automobile very slow. Their cost, both to buy and maintain, made them prohibitive for all but a very few of the citizens. In 1945 Emilio Willems wrote: "Motor vehicles are rare and their passage raised curiosity from the local residents. Seven people, all belonging to the upper class, own automobiles. There are also five trucks in the *município* of Cunha. . . ." (1947:13).

By comparison with the 12 vehicles which were in Cunha in 1945, the following were registered in Cunha in 1964:

152 jeeps
 10 passenger automobiles
  6 buses
 20 pickup trucks
 28 trucks of over 5-ton capacity (metric)
  1 motorcycle
  4 motor scooters
 28 other vehicles not specified

The development of the jeep (*jipe*) brought about a great change in the utilization of motor vehicles in Cunha. The four-wheel drive and low-gear ratio of this type of vehicle meant that it could travel even the roads of Cunha. At the present time the statement "It's too wet even for a jeep to pass," means that the town is effectively isolated. Standard passenger automobiles are only useful at dry times of the year, and on few roads in the *município*. They are owned mostly by urban dwellers whose travel is limited to Guaratinguetá and other cities. To a great extent these serve as status symbols for the owners.

The jeep is a rural status symbol but is functionally important, as it has opened up large areas of the countryside to rapid transportation. While there are still a few diehards who prefer the horse and refuse to own the things, many of the *fazendeiros* now have jeeps as do a few of the more prosperous *sitiantes*. The commercially oriented farmer who deals in milk production prefers to own a jeep. The very largest *fazendeiros*, especially if they produce beef cattle, prefer to own a truck or, if possible, both.

This development of rapid motor transportation has had

enormous commercial importance. Many *sitiantes* who raise truck crops could not prosper without it. Its importance in the dairy industry had already been illustrated. Rapid movement has had a great social impact on the rural people. In good weather even the remotest inhabited *bairros* are only a few hours away by car. Health and educational inspectors, judicial officials, and the police travel throughout the *município,* and all but a few living in the *sertão* have had some contact with them. Any major social activity or *festa* will bring sightseers by truck, bus, or car from the town and sometimes as far as from the Paraíba Valley. Even a simple country dance will bring one or two jeeps full of young people from the town looking for a good time, and the genuine and distinctive *caipira* folk music is being interspersed and replaced with popular themes from São Paulo City. In addition it is not uncommon for the rural people to ride into town on a bus, truck, or passing jeep to visit relatives or to shop.

It has become increasingly possible for rural workers to work in the country while living in the town, and this is true at every social level. There are in Cunha now dozens of *lavradores ambulantes* (rural farm hands) who work at various times for a variety of landowners. In this way improved transportation in the *município* has been very important in the increased contact between the rural population and urban individuals and organizations.

In the town of Cunha the proliferation of motor vehicles has created a small subindustry to take care of them. Two gasoline stations and three garages now exist in town. This means that to own an automobile is much less difficult and expensive now than it was in the past.

A bus line has existed in Cunha for several years. The company currently owns six vehicles and another is on order. These are specially built, front engine, rural buses. The newer buses are larger in anticipation of increased business when the new road is completed. Two buses leave Cunha daily for

Guaratinguetá and two return. There is also a daily bus to and
from Paratí. The cost of the whole trip into the valley is
about $.35, though a part of the trip is prorated. The bus
will stop to pick up or let off anyone along the road. The
morning bus out of Guaratinguetá usually carries several
school teachers who get off at several points along the way,
sometimes making connections with one of the milk trucks.
School children generally are allowed to ride free. Many rural
people use the bus to go to and from their homes and the town.
It is not uncommon, especially on Fridays and Mondays, for
the bus to be overflowing with 20 or 30 standees, including
several small children, and the front full of luggage and
produce. The bus company is wholly owned by one of the
wealthy Lebanese merchant families of Cunha, whose shops
are located in the town. The local family bought the company
seven years ago from a businessman in Guaratinguetá and
moved its equipment into Cunha. It is a fully licensed company
and quite efficiently run.

The Decline of the Caipira Culture

New markets, commercialization of land, improved transportation, and partible inheritance are all acting to bring
about a change in the traditional folk society. Many *caipira*,
as has been shown, lost their land as a result of increasing
land values. Other rural people have effectively come to an
equilibrium relation with the commercial forces by accepting
land registration without losing the essential quality of subsistence peasants. As a general rule, however, these people
are not culturally *caipira*, since the very fact that they have
been able successfully to defend their land titles in the courts
implies a degree or urban sophistication.

The great majority of *caipira* who have kept their peasant
culture have done so through the protection of a *patrão* (boss),
rather than through the protection of the courts. This *patrão*
has legal ownership of their land but in return for certain

services allows the peasant to work it. There are several patterns which this can take. The most common form is simple sharecropping. Any landholder with even moderate holdings in Cunha commonly has one or more families living on his land who are allowed to grow a certain amount of corn, rice, and beans in return for a share of the crop. The sharecropper family will usually be allowed to raise pigs, chickens, and often even a cow or two without obligation. A skilled worker, one who can easily go elsewhere, will be allowed to farm as an *agregado* for a 20 per cent share of the crop. In more traditional situations, and with less fortunate workers, the sharecropper works as a *meeiro* and pays 50 per cent of the crop. The *agregado* is perhaps more common in Cunha, but the *meeiro* is also well known.

Another common pattern is for a *bairro* or part of a *bairro* to have been left untouched by large landowners. In such cases the peasants are able to raise most of their food on their own soil, but are available to work on the *fazendas* for a share of the crop or for wages. In this way such independent *bairros* serve as potential labor pools for the *fazendeiros* and their own holdings are therefore not threatened. In such cases the peasant's land is almost always registered, and this explains the large number of tiny holdings in Cunha. These land-holding peasants as well as the *parceiros* on the *fazendas* generally hold on to the culture patterns of the *caipira*, including neighborhood aid.

Two factors here work against the peasant. The first is the economic change in the *município* from agricultural production which needs intensive labor, to animal production, which does not. Thus his *patrão* may find it more profitable to raise cattle than beans and corn, and he may try to take over the land for pasture. Another factor is demography. The *caipira* society needs unlimited space to expand. Once the land is commercialized and its limits fixed through registration, expansion is impossible. Cunha is a relatively healthy region, and rural families are large; the average rural family has about five children. The *caipira* is thus caught in a terrible land squeeze. Even if he owns his own land and it is adequate for him to live comfortably, it is doubtful if it can support all of his descendants. The majority of these children, therefore, must leave their family land and find some employment either within the *município* or beyond. It is always possible for an individual to establish a squatter's claim in the *sertão*, in the traditional pattern, but this usually involves a sharp cut in his standard of living and few choose this option unless they are deathly afraid of the cities. The majority prefer to leave the region unless they can obtain some land through marriage.

The Brazilian law of partible inheritance specifies that when a man dies, his property is divided so that one-half goes to his wife, and the other half is divided *equally* among his children. In turn, when the wife dies, the remainder is also equally divided among the children. This pattern of inheritance is so deeply ingrained among the Brazilian population, commercial farmers and *caipira* alike, that any other pattern, such as primogeniture, is unthinkable. The importance of this law is hard to overstress, since it has strongly contributed to the breakdown of the great *fazendas* as well as the *caipira* neighborhoods.

Since under this law all children inherit the property of their parents equally, those who leave have the same rights to the land as those who stay. Not uncommonly an individual who leaves the *bairro* will simply allow his brothers to farm his land without compensation. Frequently a *sitiante*, when asked if he owns his land, will reply something to the effect that, "it really belongs to me and my brother, but he lives in the city and hasn't been back for years." This pattern allows the departing brother a haven to return to if he should find life in the city too rigorous. On the other hand, if he sells the land it will give him a "nest egg" which will assist him in his search for work in the city, and many choose this option. The latter pattern, however, is highly disruptive, not only to the family but to the whole *caipira* structure, for it breaks up the neighborhoods and puts the land more and more in the hands of the commercial farmers who can afford to pay cash for land, and takes it away from the peasant who cannot.

The following descriptions of two small *bairros* well illustrate the forces which are slowly undermining the *caipira* society. Both *bairros* are part of the same neighborhood which is still largely intact despite the fact that it is near the town and has several important roads cutting through it. This neighborhood comprises six named *bairros*. About forty households live in this area, most of whom belong to one of three traditional extended families which have lived in the neighborhood for generations. The neighborhood center lies in one valley, with the other *bairro* valleys radiating out from it. The whole neighborhood is about twenty square kilometers in area.

The center consists of two *vendas* a few hundred feet away from each other. The first is run by the son of one of the largest resident landholders; the other by a *mineiro* (an individual born in Minas Gerais). The recently rebuilt chapel, though some distance away from the *vendas*, is one of the largest, and perhaps the most important, in the *município*, the site of one of the major festivals in Cunha. A school formerly existed in the center, but has been abandoned.

Three large *fazendas* isolate the neighborhood to the west and south. All of these have absentee owners and resident managers. One of them is the property of the church; the others are owned by one of the former judges of Cunha, Dr. Bruno, and Sr. Jacob, a merchant who lives in the town.

Sítio: A Bairro in Fragmentation. Sítio is a very small *bairro*, totaling only 8 *alquires* or 20 hectares in area. It lies at the bottom of a small, round valley with steep hills surrounding it on three sides. A small stream runs through the valley, the land is good, the main road runs nearby, and the entire floor of the *bairro* is intensively cultivated in corn, rice, and beans. Yet Sítio is about the poorest *bairro* that the author saw in Cunha, an observation confirmed by many of the people of Cunha. While the residents of Sítio all own land, the *bairro* is surrounded by cattle ranches so that there is no room to expand and there are now simply too many people living in the valley.

From above, the *bairro* looks like a small rural hamlet, with several houses of *pau-a-pique* and thatched roofs. Upon approaching, however, the visitor sees that some of the houses are closed and falling into ruin. Of eight houses, only three have full-time residents, although two others have part-time residents. The *bairro* had once been a single *sítio*, a one-family farm. Upon the death of the original owner the land was divided among his children. Final transferal among his four heirs, however, had not been made at the time of the study, nor were the people of the *bairro* in any hurry to have this done. The legal transactions cost money. All of the residents, except one, are related. The exception is an unmarried stranger who moved into one of the abandoned houses one day without warning. He plants a little corn, helps with the work when asked, and is otherwise generally left alone. The oldest brother of the landowning family lives outside the valley, though still in the neighborhood, on land belonging to his wife. He owns one of the *vendas* of the neighborhood center and has six grown children, all of whom live in the *município*, most of them nearby. The three remaining children of the original owner of Sítio all continue to live in the *bairro*.

Sr. Carlos is the most prosperous, or rather the least poor, of the residents. His house is brightly painted and has a tile roof. He owns, in addition, three horses and a few pigs. He is also the most insistent about the lack of land for planting in the region. The family's relative prosperity is due to the fact that of nine living children he has three grown sons who help him in the fields. Three older sons have married and left the *bairro*, two for the Paraíba Valley, and one for another part of the *município*. Two daughters have married and also live elsewhere in the *município*, while one little girl, the youngest child, lives at home. The family farms their share of land in the *bairro*, but it is not enough for the four of them and so they sharecrop extensively as *agregados* on the *fazenda* of Dr. Bruno to the west.

Sr. Roberto comes from another part of the *município*, but he married a sister of Sr. Carlos and settled on her land. Their house is of wattle-and-daub and *sapé*, but it is only three months old and is cared for very well. The interior has little furniture, only beds, benches, and woven mats, although in the corner of the living room was a newly decorated altar covered with fresh flowers, a common fixture in the *caipira* home. The interior was freshly whitewashed and the floor carefully swept. The reason for the fine condition of the house is that Sr. Roberto also has nine children, and of these there are three adult unmarried daughters who live and work in the house. Two sons also live at home, but only one is old enough to help with the field work. Two other sons and two daughters have married and left the *bairro*, although they all continue to live in the neighborhood. Roberto and his son plant corn and rice on their land in Sítio, and also on property belonging to one of his daughters-in-law, who lives nearby.

Sr. Jorge was born in the neighborhood, although not in Sítio. He married the youngest sister of Sr. Carlos, and now has four children, all of whom are unmarried and live at home. His house, effectively hidden in the midst of his corn fields— another common *caipira* trait—is of mud and thatch like that of Sr. Roberto, but is in relatively poor shape. This is probably the poorest of the traditional households in the *bairro*, despite the fact that two of Jorge's sons, aged 19 and 14 years, help their father plant on his own land and that of the *fazenda* of Dr. Bruno.

Finally, one cousin on the mother's side of the family still keeps a house in the *bairro*. At times she and her husband come and stay in Sítio when he is seeking work on one of the nearby *fazendas,* and he usually does some planting on the *bairro* lands as well.

The people of Sítio are almost all engaged in subsistence production and have very little commerce. It can be said that the most important product exported from this *bairro* has been people. The original *sitiante* probably could live comfortably on the land of the *bairro.* His living descendants now total, however, four children, with two sons-in-law and two daughters-in-law, twenty-eight grandchildren, and untold great-grandchildren, all of whom have some potential rights to this farm of only fifty acres.

At the present time, twenty people live in the *bairro*: ten adult men, six women, and four children. Economically the *bairro* could not exist or even feed itself without its members working on other lands. Since its residents sell little, its main commercial activity is as a labor reservoir for the *fazenda* of Dr. Bruno. The people of Sítio, however, still cling to the traditions of the *caipira* culture and keep a tightly knit family structure, where the members help each other in time of need. The traditional quality of the area is shown by the fact that, despite intense land presures, a total stranger was allowed to move in and live *a favor* on the *bairro* lands. The strength of the traditional family ties is shown here also. Although all the married children have left the *bairro,* almost all of them have tried to stay in the neighborhood. Of the thirty-two adult descendants of the original *sitiante,* only two sons of Sr. Carlos have left the *município.*

Varzia de Vitória: A Bairro in Transition. Varzia de Vitória is a large *bairro.* This valley is about two kilometers long and about 100 meters wide. The valley floor is flat and fertile—good agricultural land. It is an unusually interesting *bairro* because among its eight households and ten landowners may be found examples of several of the different kinds of land and agricultural patterns characteristic of Cunha.

The *bairro* was once owned by one family, and still bears its name, but over the years most of the land has been sold. Of the Vitória family, only one member still lives in the *bairro*. She is a 70-year-old lady, the widow of the first owner's grandson. She still lives in the original big brick house of the Vitórias' and owns thirty-five hectares of land, half of which she rents to her brother, who lives within the *bairro*. The other half is sharecropped on an *agregado* basis by her nephew, who lives in the house with her, and his wife and six children. She has no children of her own, but has raised three adopted children, *filhos de criação*. Only one of these, a boy of 14, still lives with her. Economically she lives the life of a land-owning peasant, although she is one of the larger landowners in the *bairro*. Most of what is raised on her land is consumed and she sells little. What money she has comes from her brother, who pays her for permission to raise cattle on the hilly parts of her land.

Her brother is a prosperous commercial farmer, yet not wealthy enough to be considered a *fazendeiro*. He raises a number of crops commercially and has some cattle. He is undoubtedly the most urbanized and prosperous of the residents of the *bairro*, and lives in a new brick house with his wife and seven of his nine children. The other two live in São Paulo.

Part of the *bairro* is owned by a wealthy merchant, Sr. Jacob, who lives in the town of Cunha. He is the largest landowner in the *bairro*, even though the buildings of his *fazenda* are located elsewhere. Most of his land is a pasture, but he also plants a considerable quantity of corn. The work is done by the small landowners in the valley, all of whom work part-time for him for cash on a *per diem* basis. There are no longer any resident sharecroppers on his land, although two small unoccupied houses testify that this was not always the case.

There are four small peasant landowners in the *bairro:*

Sr. Manoel has five hectares which he has farmed for many years in addition to working as a fieldhand for Sr. Jacob. He is now 61 years of age, and says that he cannot work as much as he used to any more. He is thus planning to sell half his land. Presently he is only planting some corn, rice, and potatoes for home consumption, although he still plants some beans to sell. He has four children. The oldest is a married son who lives in the neighborhood and helps plant on his father's land. The second son, however, is feeble-minded and can help only a little with the farm work. One married daughter lives in São Paulo, while the youngest child, an 11-year-old adopted daughter, lives at home.

Sr. Benedito is the most prosperous of the small landowners. He has several animals, a plow, and fairly extensive plantings on his own and Sr. Jacob's lands, which he works on a *meeiro* basis. Although he has six children, only one son, 18 years-old, is old enough to do effective farm work. A couple of his daughters go to school nearby, and the family is much more urban-oriented than the others of this peasant class in the *bairro.*

Sr. Estivam has a very small section of land; hardly enough to support his family of six children, especially since none are old enough to work. He works, therefore, as a day laborer on the *fazenda* whenever work is available. This is the poorest family in the *bairro.*

Francisco is only 16 years of age, but supports his mother and young sister by planting corn and beans on the family's six hectares. He also works, from time to time, on the *fazenda* of Sr. Jacob.

In addition to the *fazenda*, and the farm of Sra. Vitória's brother, there are three other commercial properties in the *bairro.* A few years ago a well-off *sitiante* from a nearby *bairro* sought to expand his operations by buying land here. He has now turned this land completely into pastureland for his dairy herds. He thus plants nothing on his lands here and no one lives on the property, although he is currently building a new brick milking shed for his animals.

Sr. José lives in the *bairro* on land belonging to his second wife. One son by his first marriage lives in the house, but they have no other children. He is a vigorous, suspicious man of 57, very urban and commercially oriented, and he has numerous relatives living in the town. He is a member of the dairy cooperative and has eight or ten milk cows.

Sr. Antonio is a widower who lives on a *sitio* of 12 hectares with his only son. The *sitio* is located at the end of the valley and the soil is some of the best in the region. "Anything will grow here," says the owner. On the slope they plant some corn, *"per gasta"* (for consumption), but the rich bottomland is carefully planted with a variety of commercial crops such as beans, tomatoes, and onions. These they sell directly in Guaratinguetá and Paratí. They once owned their own truck, but when it began to wear out they found it more profitable to rent one. The work requires a considerable amount of labor at various times during the year and when necessary they hire day laborers from this and nearby *bairros*.

In these two case studies, the basic processes by which the *caipira* neighborhoods are being dissolved can be seen. In *Sítio* the residents are forced to work on the *fazendas*, because of demographic pressure on limited lands. In Varzia de Vitória, a much larger *bairro*, the land is almost entirely owned by commercial farmers, and the few *caipira* who are left, with the exception of Sra. Vitória herself, are dependent upon the nearby *fazenda* of Sr. Jacob for their livelihood.

The Social Structure of the Rural Zones in Cunha Today

Traditionally, it may be recalled from Chapter III, the social structure of rural Cunha consisted of a series of interlinked *caipira* neighborhoods, tied together by bonds of kinship and mutual economic aid. These could be found throughout

the settled parts of the *município*. Some of these were inhabited by *sitiantes*, relatively free of control by the elite, while
others were dominated economically and politically by the
fazendeiros, the landed elite. The *caipira* lived and worked on
the *fazendas* as *parceiros*, sharecroppers.

The pattern of *bairros*, named localities, still exists in Cunha.
The "neighborhood" as a social organization, however, is
declining in importance as the need for cooperative labor
disappears under the new economic conditions of the region,
and as the people turn more and more to the *sede* as the
center of their social life. An indication of the shift is a decline
in importance of the local neighborhood chapels. These are
gradually either becoming important established churches, such
as in the Methodist zones, or are being abandoned. Some of
the older chapels are slowly being allowed to fall into ruin.
The Vicar of Cunha estimated that in 1965 there were 56 rural
chapels, but only 26 of these were equipped for services. The
number of *vendas*, however, seems to be gradually increasing,
indicating an increasing commercial interest on the part of the
rural population. The *vendas* are frequently owned by local
landowners or by one of the town businessmen. In 1965 the
shopkeepers were often young men, sons or other relatives of
the owners, and usually much better educated than the folk
who lived about them. They thus formed a true group of
"culture brokers."

A great change, moreover, has taken place in the style of
life of the rural people themselves. The traditional *caipira* of
a generation ago, whether *parceiro* or *sitiante*, was minimally
articulated with the urban society. He was wholly illiterate,
dressed in rags, was characteristically barefoot, and lived in
a house of wattle-and-daub on the corn and beans he grew
himself. Apparently, according to the literature, this was the
style of life of the great majority of the rural people.

Poverty of this degree, as a general rule, is today found
only among the *parceiro* class or among the *lavradores*, the

rural field hands, particularly among the *lavradores ambulantes*: field hands without regular employment. It is usually, moreover, found among the older people, as the majority of young people would prefer to leave the region rather than live under these conditions. Today, the majority of *sitiantes* and rural workers, *camaradas*, while still poor, have a somewhat higher standard of living than the former *caipira*.

The *sitiante* of today lives a very different life from that of the *caipira sitiante* of the past. The modern *sitiante* is essentially a commercial family farmer, producing crops both for subsistence and the market with his own labor and that of his family. His income is usually sufficient to at least buy new clothing for his family and sometimes, though rarely, may be enough to enable him to live in town.

The *bairro* of Rochedo is a modern *bairro* of *sitiantes*. It is a single, narrow valley, some two and a half kilometers long and is entirely occupied by small landowners. There are no big landowners and no sharecroppers in the *bairro*. For this reason Rochedo is considered one of the most traditional regions in Cunha. The nine families who live in the *bairro* each have enough land to live on and all of them produce a few commercial crops for sale. Six of the nine families belong to one extended family and the father of this family owns the local *venda*. The other three families are related to each other as well. All nine families are reasonably prosperous, although none has more than fifteen hectares of land.

The people of Rochedo, however, are culturally not *caipira*. They are all commercial in orientation. Although Rochedo is a true *bairro* of *sitiantes*, the people who live there say that they have not attended a *muterão* in years, so that the most important and characteristic of the traditional rural institutions no longer exists here. A couple of the more active farmers who need more land than they own to plant, rent land from their neighbors on a cash basis. Thus it can be seen that the Cunha *sitiantes* have come a long way from the cooperative *caipira* of the past and are very different from the *parceiros* of the *bairro* of Sítio. They are transitional between peasant cultivators and commercial farmers.

Perhaps the basic reason for the elevation in the standard of living in rural Cunha has been the opportunity for rural exodus. The resident of Cunha no longer must live at a near subsistence level, for if things get too bad he has an alternative. He can leave the *município*. Many have done so, as will be seen below.

The *caipira* who stay generally do so for one of four reasons: (1) He owns a bit of land which he is reluctant to abandon and he is able to supplement what he can produce by working part-time elsewhere. (2) He is too old or too timid to try to start life anew in the cities. (3) He is able to make a reasonably good living by sharecropping. (4) He lives on one of the traditional, paternalistic *fazendas* and accepts the life.

The first is well exemplified by the *parceiros* of Sítio who, despite a relatively low standard of living, preferred to stay on their traditional lands. For the second there are a great many examples. The most interesting is an ancient Negro called Zé Sertão. Zé's memories go back to the time of slavery, and despite his 102 years his mind is still sharp. As a young man he traveled widely and even lived for awhile in Rio de Janeiro but he always came back to his home region, Cunha. He has outlived three wives and no one is quite sure how many children. He is now too old to work but lives with a granddaughter. He has become so much of a local institution that his few wants are easily satisfied by the *bairro* residents.

The third pattern is exemplified by a small *bairro* in the southeastern part of the *município*. The *bairro* has eight resident landowning families and one landless laborer. The head of the landless household, the father of an enormous family, says that he can make a better living hiring out in turn to the other families, than some of the eight *sitiantes*.

Each of the three patterns mentioned, however, generally implies a breakdown of the traditional neighborhood *caipira* form of mutual aid. For the most part, traditional *caipira* ways of life are only found on the old traditional *fazendas* which, despite economic pressures, have managed to maintain the basic economic pattern of corn and bean production. A few of these great old estates still exist and a few of the traditional landowners still live in Cunha, although most of them now are old men.

One of the last of the traditional landowners is Joaquim Luís dos Santos, who owns the Fazenda Santos in the southern part of the *município*. The exact size of the *fazenda* is obscure, but it is undoubtedly over 1,000 hectares. The *fazenda* was one of the great slaveholding plantations, and was one of the few regions of Cunha where coffee was actually produced. The original "great house" is still occupied and is truly enormous— one of the largest buildings in Cunha. Sr. Joaquim is the grandson of the original founder of the *fazenda* and is related to several important people in the city of São Paulo. He is very well educated and holds a university degree, as does his wife, who is much younger than he. They have no children, however. He owns a house in Taubeté but prefers to live in the great house of his parents where his wife is the local schoolteacher.

Large areas of the *fazenda* are planted in corn and beans and the hogs of the *fazenda* are locally famous for their size and quality, though exact data on production could not be obtained. Thirteen families of sharecroppers still live on the *fazenda* and largely keep the traditional ways of life. Mutual activities are performed constantly by the *parceiros,* both for each other and for the work of the *fazenda.* This was the only area in Cunha where the author actually saw the local people engaged in road repair. Sr. Joaquim said that about ten or twelve *muterões* a year were held on his land, but only one or two of these were sponsored by him. He continually oversees the work being done on the *fazenda,* but does little of the work himself.

Few of these *fazendas* still exist, however. It has been noted that the important rural elite of Cunha tended to leave the *município* after the end of slavery. Their land was either sold to commercial farmers, especially the *mineiros*, or abandoned to the *caipira*. In addition the Brazilian system of partible inheritance means the fragmentation of the large holdings as well as the small.

One case—the most important in the *município*—will illustrate this point. *Capitão* Ricardo Aliandro Calmón arrived in Cunha as a young man in the middle of the nineteenth century from one of the cities in the lower Paraíba Valley. He apparently had some financial resources and was able to buy considerable land and a number of slaves. He planted food crops, mainly corn and beans, and sold these to the coffee *fazendas* and cities of the valley. As he prospered he reinvested in land until he was the largest landowner in the *município*. His holdings consisted of dozens of square kilometers, most of which were undeveloped forest. With time, thousands of hectares were cleared for farming and later pastureland. Eventually other vast tracts were sold to the lumber company. At his death it is said that he owned about 7,500 ha., but the actual total may have been considerably more. His holdings were divided among his ten children, and each became a major landowner in his own right. His sons especially continued his practice of investing in new lands. At the present time each of the surviving sons, in their late fifties and sixties, is a wealthy *fazendeiro*. One of them is the largest landowner in Cunha. The family has great pride and cohesiveness. All of its members live closely together in a single *bairro*, their lands radiating out from this center in all directions.

Most of Ricardo's children have their own families and some are quite large. These children in turn have their own children, so the total number of descendants is now over 100. Thus, as the direct descendants of the Captain pass on, the great *fazendas* will be broken up and probably the unity of the family, which currently makes it such an economic force in the region, will also disappear.

Thus the trajectory of cultural forces in Cunha tends to favor the emergence of a class of resident, commercially astute, rural bourgeoisie. This group differs from both the peasant and elitist slave-owning land owners of the traditional society. The earlier great landlords were planters. They watched over and organized the work of their people, but did not themselves do agricultural work. Their orientation was to urban activities, especially politics, and they were very interested in education. The new rural middle classes, on the other hand, work their own land with their own labor and that of their families, as well as their fields hands. Their primary interests lie with their rural commercial activities, and their attitudes are not elitist. They are true commercial farmers.

The continuing breakup of the large estates will tend to further fragment the *caipira* neighborhoods. Since the smaller holdings can support fewer workers, more and more of the necessary work will be done by the landowning family itself. Several important Cunha rural *fazendeiros* have no share-croppers at all, hiring all the labor they need. The increase in number of *fazendas* of moderate size has had an effect on the kind of farming undertaken in the region. It should be noted that cattle raising on a large scale requires extensive land holdings. Therefore as the big estates are divided this industry must take on new forms. More and more economic forces tend to push the agriculturalists of Cunha to the mixed "Minas type" of farm wherein cattle raising, hog raising, milk production, and agriculture are all combined. This allows greater flexibility to the farmer, as he can concentrate on the most profitable product at any given time.

Thus it can be seen that both classes of the traditional *caipira* society are disappearing. Both the great landowner and the peasant are being replaced by a rural middle class. The modern Cunha *fazendeiros*, including some of the wealth-

iest of them, usually do a large part of the farm work themselves, with the aid of their families. The fragments of the
peasant culture, however, still provide a plentiful source of
cheap and available labor and it is common for landowners
with even moderate holdings to have a *caipira* family or two
on his land. The end result of the division of the large estates
will be further breakdown of the *caipira* society, as it is difficult for the social unit of the neighborhood to function
interspersed with commercial resident farmers.

Thus the peasantry still exists in Cunha, but in a social
system which is less and less his own. He has become a member of a new rural lower class, in what is essentially an agricultural region of a commercial-industrial complex. He is
becoming a landless, illiterate day laborer for various large
and small commercial farmers who do not greatly need his
services anyway. It is just such a social position that many
of the peasantry have fled, preferring to be a part of an urban
lower class in the factories or construction work of the cities.

Rural Exodus

Rural exodus, the migration of the country people into the
cities due to demographic and economic pressures, has become one of the major social movements of modern Brazil.
Many studies have been made of the patterns of such migration,
with special stress on the selective nature of such exodus—that
is that the younger and more vigorous tend to be the ones
to leave (Williamson, 1965:5). This can be seen in Cunha,
where the peasants who stay tend to be elderly.

Cunha is located near São Paulo, the greatest industrial
metropolis in Brazil. Thus, as the large and relatively poor
rural population experienced increased difficulties in the *municipio*, they migrated on an exceptional scale. The web of
social and familial relationships which link the *bairro* residents
is so strong that they will usually leave only under severe
economic pressure or when the neighborhood structure itself

has severely weakened. Thus in Sítio, which is one of the most conservative, though poorest, *bairros* in the *município*, only two members of the family had left for the city, despite severe overpopulation in the *bairro*.

Nevertheless, rural exodus from Cunha has been extensive. This can be seen from demographic statistics of the *município*. Rural population figures for Cunha are given in the table below:

1890	c. 19,400
1920	c. 26,500
1934	20,706
1940	19,414
1950	19,086
1960	18,895
1965	c. 18,000

While figures before 1934 are perhaps not too accurate, those after 1934 do show a slowly declining rural population. Cunha, however, is a rural region with an enormously high birth rate. The real growth of the population is considerable. Since the decade of 1930 the number of registered births over deaths in Cunha has ranged from 500 to 700 per year. Between the years 1940 and 1960, while the population of the whole *município* increased only about 2,000 and the rural population actually decreased slightly, the registered population increase was 13,190. It is safe to assume that at least eleven thousand people left the *município* during these years— a municipal exodus equal to half of its present population. There seems, moreover, to have been some regular pattern to this movement, as will be seen below.

Kinship is of primary importance in discussing patterns of rural-urban migration. Such migration tended to follow family lines, as is shown by a number of factors. The extended family in Brazil tends even in cases of rapid horizontal mobility to still have some functions of protection and mutual service.

This is shown by the Cunha data. A young man, for example, would become established in one of the interior cities. In time he would have a job and home, and perhaps would have married a girl from the city. Knowledge of his success would embolden others of his family to come to the same city. For a time his home would become a base of operations for his relatives who, with his help, would start households in the same neighborhood, and a small colony of people from Cunha would soon develop. During important local holidays often hundreds of people would come in from these colonies in the Paraíba Valley to visit their relatives and partake in the *festas*.

By 1965 this migration had been going on for more than a generation, and colonies of Cunhenses had developed in several cities in the Paraíba Valley and elsewhere. The most important of these extended in Guaratinguetá, Aparecida do Norte, Lorena, Piquete, Cruzeiro, Taubeté, and São Paulo. Methodist Church records show that members of this faith tended to settle in Taubeté and Santo André. The cities of the Paraíba Valley seem to have attracted more people from Cunha than the capital city of São Paulo.

Analysis of census materials for the town shows that 155 children of urban Cunha families, excluding students, have left the *município*. Where these live may give some idea of the patterns of rural exodus, and this is shown below.

Guaratinguetá	55
Aparecida do Norte, Lorena, and Taubeté	51
The rest of the Paraíba Valley	21
The city of São Paulo	30
Interior cities in the state of São Paulo	6
Minas Gerais	9
Rio de Janeiro	33

From the available data it seems that few people migrated to the city of Rio and the old isolated rural *municípios* of the valley, such as Areias and Bananal, despite strong historic ties between Cunha and these cities.

Thus the family connections of Cunha spread throughout
the whole Paraíba region and became enormously complex,
especially since many people from Cunha married into extended families in the valley. The Cunhenses usually remembered all of their urban relatives and were not averse to using
their relationships to obtain various services when necessary.
Such services ranged from free medical care, if the relative
happened to be a doctor; a place to stay overnight, if the rural
relatives were vacationing; or active help and political influence in finding a job in the city.

The services were not all one-sided. The relatives remaining
on the land, especially if they were landowners, offered not
only a temporary vacation spot, but for many a type of insur-
ance policy—a home to return to if the individual should fail
in the city. There were a few cases of this in Cunha. The most
notable was a young man who had left his *bairros* to seek work
as a truck driver in São Paulo several years ago. After some
years in the capital he fell victim to the recession, lost his job,
and returned to his old neighborhood. He was loaned a new
house entirely rent free by his relatives in the *bairros*, and was
allowed to plant some corn and raise a few chickens on their
lands. It was very unusual to see this highly urban and literate
family living as peasants in the country. The man expressed a
desire to return to the city when things improved, but there
was a general feeling in Cunha that it was better to be without
a job in the country than in the city, since at least food was
available cheaply in the rural zones.

The greatest rural exodus in Cunha apparently took place
in 1957 with the large-scale changeover from agricultural to
animal products. Which was cause and which was effect is hard
to say. Under Brazilian law a sharecropper has many rights to
his own crops but a landowner has many ways of freezing
commercial returns on a peasant's land and letting inflation do
its work. This, the author was told, was responsible for much
of the rural exodus in Cunha in the past few years. The great
extent of this exodus must change the picture of what is hap-

pening to the people of Cunha. Their society has changed from one of simple commercialization to one of commercialization and urbanization. At least 40 per cent of the people born in the *município* do now in fact live outside Cunha, and the evidence is that most of them now live in the cities and towns of São Paulo State and hold some kind of urban jobs. This situation has also eased the pressure on land and has meant increased commercial opportunity for those who have stayed behind. It seems possible that the exodus of the Cunhenses has contributed more to the development of the state than any of its products. The movement also has changed the make-up of the community. Extended family structures, instead of being confined to the network of neighborhoods and *bairros*, are now spread over much of the state of São Paulo and extend even into Minas Gerais. The family is rare in Cunha today that does not have a few relatives working at urban occupations in some of the cities of the state. The extent of the urbanization process is thus made clearer; Cunha is linked to the cities by social and family bonds as well as economic and political ones.

Chapter VIII

A Changing Society: the Urban Zone

The town—and the village as well—is in essence the concentration of a group of people in a small area with the aim of establishing close intra-group contact. Such contact is necessary for certain social activities requiring the constant cooperation of many people: industry, trade, administration in its various aspects, education, and the dissemination of information, together with the forms of housing and recreation corollary to them. The more intensively and extensively such activities are conducted, the more important and characteristically urban the town becomes. Its pace quickens, its whole tone of life grows more intense, and all this finds expression in the town's appearance, its physical form.

(The Indonesian Town, Dutch Scholars, 1958:63)

The most dramatic change which has taken place in Cunha in the past quarter of a century, and one which very much reflects the new social and economic conditions of the people, has been the exceptional growth of the *sede* of the *município.* Traditionally, it has been pointed out in Chapter V, the town of Cunha served, as in most Brazilian communities, as an organizational and commercial center for the municipal landed elite. For the majority of the *caipira* peasantry the *sede* served no functions at all, religious, political, or commercial. The tremendous recent growth of the town, therefore, both in size and the variety of services offered, reflects the changes in the rural zones. The expansion of a class of urban-oriented commercial farmers coupled with their increasing monetary wealth, has brought about a great expansion of services offered in the town to meet their demands. In addition, the *sede* serves as an operational center for the expanding state bureaucracies. These factors in turn have produced a notable increase in economic opportunities within the town itself which in turn has stimulated the town's growth.*

Population figures for the town of Cunha, including urban and suburban zones, are as follows:

1940	975†
1950	1,508†
1960	2,693†
1965	3,934

†Data from the national censuses for each year, I.B.G.E.

The 1940 figure of about one thousand inhabitants for the town seems traditionally to have been a fairly stable one so that the really rapid expansion has taken place within the past two decades. The population increase compares not unfavorably with that of many larger Paulista communities.

Examination of the patterns of occupations in the town of Cunha will help clarify the basis of this growth. Table VIIIA compares the occupations of the heads of households in Cunha for the years 1945 and 1966. Two factors are most notable, a more than threefold increase in the number of civil employees

* In order to determine the actual extent of this growth, a complete urban census was carried out under the author's direction with the cooperation of many of the local people and the support of the *Instituto Brasileiro de Geografia e Estatística* (I.B.G.E.). In all, eighteen individuals, all local people including students, teachers, and others, worked on the census. The questionnaire was six pages long and one was filled out for every family in Cunha and its suburbs. Emphasis was placed upon standard of living, occupation, kinship, demography, and population movement, although there were questions on religion, politics, and education as well. In general the response was very good; only about 3 per cent failed to answer, and for these the data were obtained from other sources. Certain kinds of data, however, proved very difficult to obtain. In general questions on economics and income proved worthless, since many of the local people, fearing tax increases, gave obviously incorrect answers. A great deal of valuable information was obtained, however, and much of the statistical material in this and subsequent chapters comes from this census.

in the town, at all three levels of government, and a great influx of rural landowners into the town: an increase in 1966 over six times the number in 1945. The two factors are related, for it has been the development of public services, with the consequent increase in the number of civil service positions which has attracted the *fazendeiros* and *sitiantes* into the *sede*. The new urban population then puts further pressure on the public and private sectors for further services and the result is a snowball effect where the two elements reinforce each other. Notable, however, is the fact that the increase in the number of public employees is nearly double the number of private jobs, a fact which reflects the growth of governmental bureaucracies in the town which was detailed in Chapters V and VI.

Table VIIIA. Changes in Patterns of Occupations in the Town of Cunha: 1945–1966

Occupations	1945* Households		1966 Households		Percentage Increase
	No.	%	No.	%	
I. *Rural*	114	35.5	325	44.7	185
Landowning	31	9.7	222	30.5	616
Landless	83	25.8	103	14.2	24
II. *Urban*	207	64.5	402	55.3	94
Professional	8	2.5	14	1.9	75
Civil Employees . . .	31	9.7	119	16.4	284
Commerce and Industry	106	33.0	168	23.1	59
Other Urban	62	19.3	101	13.9	63
Total	321	100.0	727	100.0	126

* Data from Willems, 1947:26-34.

The change and the growth of the *sede* can, therefore, be seen as due to the increasing importance of the town as the social, political, and economic center of the *município*. While

in a sense it can still be said that the town is still an administrative center for the local elite, the nature of that elite has
changed considerably and it has grown considerably in size.
The way of life of the rural people is becoming more and
more involved with the activities in the town. The whole region, in a sense is becoming urbanized. The rural neighborhoods of the *caipira*, and even the *fazenda*s are no longer able
to satisfy the ambitious and economically active rural bourgeoisie of Cunha. They want services which can only be furnished by the town.

Industry in Cunha

Although the economy of Cunha is essentially rural and
based upon food production, there are some minor industries
which have contributed to the economic growth of the region
and the town. The cornmeal factory has already been noted.
It is the only important transformative industry in the town
of Cunha itself, and employs half a dozen men. In addition,
there is in the rural zone a minor distillery for the production
of *pinga* (*aguardente* or *cachaça*), the Brazilian sugarcane
rum. The production of this factory is small and is almost all
happily consumed in the local bars and *vendas* of Cunha. "This
is the real stuff," say local bartenders, "made from pure sugarcane, none of these artificial chemicals here." Meanwhile they
sell it under several different brand names which command a
higher price.

The other major industry in the town of Cunha itself is the
construction industry. The investment by both the state government and rural property owners in new urban buildings
and homes has created a great expansion in employment opportunities for builders. The great majority of the town laborers make their living as *pedreiros*, masons. In addition there
is one family in Cunha which is actually set up in business as
a construction company, planning and building homes and
other structures with the aid of local labor. They have quite a

good reputation and have been called upon to put up major buildings as far away as Paratí and Guaratinguetá. The expansion of this industry has had interesting effects upon the town's class structure, as will be described in the next chapter.

There is one extractive industry in Cunha which is of sufficient size to be worth noting. This is the lumber industry. Cunha lies in the mountains of the *Serra do Mar* and the coastal escarpment of Brazil receives tremendous rainfall. The whole region, therefore, was once covered with a mixed hardwood rain forest containing many species of very valuable trees. Over the years there have been numerous attempts to exploit this resource and the forest has now been restricted to the most isolated sections of the region. Several earlier experiments failed, the last and largest having been an attempt to lumber out the basin of the Funil River in the north of the *município*. The work required considerable capital investment in road construction and heavy equipment, and the mill once employed some eighty men. Irregular markets and high transportation costs, however, pushed the company into bankruptcy and the area was abandoned, leaving several large wooden buildings and a huge diesel engine decaying in the forest.

The existing company has a different philosophy. The wood is cut in the *sertão*, but is then shipped to a large sawmill located on the main highway to Guaratinguetá. The major operations of the company are thus carried out in an accessible location using hydroelectric power supplied by a local power plant. The company was founded by an Italian immigrant in 1952. Originally he brought all his skilled labor from Italy. Brazilians were soon trained to do the work at much lower wages, however, and today the only Italians in the company are the owner and manager. The operation of the company is very paternalistic, there are some twenty full-time workers and the owner takes care of them, giving them housing, electricity, and running water, *gratis*. He pays them fairly well and expects good work in return. As a result the labor turnover is low and many fathers are training their own sons to take over their occupations.

The company owns about 2,893 hectares of virgin forest in the southwestern corner of the *município*. Over 70 per cent of the wood cut is the *Gruuixana*, or *Grumixama*, the Brazilian Cherry. Other rarer fine hardwoods such as cinnamon and cedar are cut on special order. The company says that it makes an effort to cut only the mature trees so that the forest can regrow later. The actual lumbering is done by members of some thirty families who live in the region. The workers are divided into specialized teams, some for cutting and others for hauling, while others are paid by the day for less specialized tasks such as road maintenance. In addition each family is given a plot of company land on which to grow crops and raise a few livestock. The company also maintains a school and brick factory for the workers' families, so that here too the paternalism is apparent.

The lumber is sold to the British-Brazilian owned *Linhas Corrente, S.A.*, the largest lumber company in Latin America. Since this company effectively fixes prices on hardwoods, the Cunha firm has no recourse but to accept them. They sell a base of 100 cubic meters of *Grumixama* wood a month. Other woods are sold to various organizations and individuals, but the rarer trees are difficult to find and market with any degree of reliability and so make up only a small percentage of the total. The company formerly produced 2,000 sacks of charcoal per month, but finally decided to minimize this aspect of their business. The price was very low with regard to the difficulty of preparation and transportation, and the charcoal kilns were destroying all the young trees that would later develop commercially for lumber. Thus they now produce only about 200 to 300 sacks a month on their lands. Considerable charcoal production, however, apparently still goes on in some other areas, which may have serious effects for the future of this industry in Cunha. Despite its importance in certain regions of the *município*, however, the lumber industry has had little effect on the development of the town itself. Cunha is an administrative and commercial rather than industrial center.

Commerce in the Town of Cunha

A study of the number of commercial enterprises in the town of Cunha at the present time offers a considerable contrast to the list of those available in 1945. Table VIIIB compares the two. The great expansion of commercial services offered is immediately noticeable. Not only has the number of commercial houses more than doubled, but the number of specialized shops has greatly increased. In these cases sometimes several commercial activities are used in the same building under the same owner, or the owner of a large building may lease shops to several different people. Many of the new enterprises reflect the growing commercial prosperity and urbanization of the municipal population. The existence of shops selling (bottled) gas stoves, radios, sewing machines and other appliances, many of them requiring electricity, would have been unheard of in the Cunha of 20 years ago. More significant is the development of garages for the growing number of cars, jeeps, and trucks in the region, as noted in the last chapter, and the opening of a commercial bank. Also of interest are the opening of a cinema, tailor shops, hairdressing shops, and a stationery shop, hints of the middle-class affluence characteristic of many Paulista cities and towns. This is not to say by any means that the majority of the population, especially the rural population, can afford these things, but some can. The existence of these shops locally means that more than just a handful of the local *fazendeiros* can afford a few of the amenities of the metropolitan life style. This is something which has not been true in Brazil throughout most of its history.

Commercial activity in Cunha is predominantly locally owned since there are as yet no chain stores in the town. With the exception of the bank, which is a branch of a large São

Table VIIIB. List of Commercial Activities in the Town of Cunha

Shops—General	Number in 1945*	Number in 1966
General stores (*Armazem*)	7	16
Cloth shops	—	4
Furniture and appliance shops	—	2
Stationery shops	—	1
Hardware shops	—	3
Pharmacies	3	2
Shops—Food		
Bars and food (*sêcos e molhados*)	21	26
Fruits and vegetables	(?)	3
Butcher shops	2	4
Bakeries	(?)	3
Crafts and Services		
Leather workers and shoe repair shops	(?)	5
Tailor shops	—	3
Barber shops	3	5
Women's hairdressers	—	2
Locksmith shops	—	1
Repair shops	—	2
Blacksmith shops	—	1
Garages	—	3
Car wash	—	1
Other		
Gas stations	—	2
Saw mills	—	2
Brickyards	2 or 3	2
Hotels and pensions	2	3
Commercial banks	—	1
Bus companies	1	1
Other transportation	(?)	9
Cinema	—	1
Cornmeal factory (*fecularia*)	—	1
Cooperatives	1	2

* From Willems, 1947, Map opposite p. 6.

Paulo firm, and the dairy cooperative, which is controlled from Guaratinguetá, all town commerce and industry is owned by residents. This may seem an exception to the general thesis of increasing intermunicipal activity, but actually reflects the ability of Cunha's businessmen to operate in the national economy. Whether this ability will be maintained in competition with the larger cities of the Paraíba Valley once the new road is completed, remains to be seen. One indication of this growing competition is an interesting gentleman known far and wide in the region as *o propagandista* (the advertiser). This man, wearing a clown's outfit and makeup and pulling a little cart, is paid by a few businessmen in the valley to wander throughout the streets of the Paraíba towns playing on a small portable tape recorder a commercial message interspersed with much loud band music. Local businessmen don't seem too concerned, however, as they have made no effort to counter his message.

Much of the commerce in the *município* is carried on at a very small scale by the owners of the rural *vendas* and wandering *mascates* in the town and rural zones. A few residents of the town make a living in this way, but, as has been pointed out in Chapter VII, the most prosperous *mascates* come from outside Cunha. On the other hand, almost every household in the town engages in commerce of one kind or another, at least during the major religious festivals. Relatively few, however, are prosperous enough to have their own shops (see the list of occupations, Chapter IX). From the census and information from many informants, there are some fourteen families which tend to dominate the commerce of Cunha. Each of these families maintains more than one commercial enterprise and in all they comprise 27 households. It is these commercial families, together with the industrialists who make up the urban commercial elite, those who have major capital invested in the town and are able to control a good share of its finances. Most of them, in addition, can afford to protect their interests by becoming involved in local politics.

An interesting fact is the predominance of people of non-Portuguese extraction among this commercial elite. The town's four most important commercial families are all of non-Brazilian origin. Three are Lebanese and one is Italian. Of the fourteen families who make up the majority of the important businessmen in Cunha, six are non-Portuguese in background, as are seven of the local families of professionals. Thus despite the fact that the rural folk and the smaller shopkeepers, craftsmen, and rural businessmen almost all have Portuguese surnames, the town's commerce is dominated by people of non-Luso-Brazilian extraction.

The leading example is the Nacib family, one of the richest in Cunha. Jafra Nacib and his wife arrived in Brazil over fifty years ago from Lebanon. All but one of their five children were born in Cunha, where they had opened up a small shop selling cloth. As the community prospered, so did they, and gradually they invested in new enterprises in Cunha and elsewhere; a bakery, a couple of bars, homes to be rented both in Cunha and Guaratinguetá. They also invested in land and purchased one of the better *fazendas* in the *município*. As their children reached maturity each of them, in turn, was given one of the family enterprises to operate. One of the sons, however, rebelled against the small-town life, trained as a lawyer with the support of his family, and set himself up in practice in São Paulo. The remaining four married, built fine houses, and remained in Cunha. The aggregate wealth of the family has been estimated at no less than a billion *cruzeiros* (about $500,000.).

The family remains a cohesive unit, however, and no member makes a serious decision without consulting the others. They are very decidedly separated from the rest of the community, who tend to think of them as "profiteers" and "Turks." The family recognizes this enmity and accepts it, its members considering themselves a class above most of the rest of the community. They prefer to keep their social contacts and friendships in the big cities, although they have a few friends among the professionals in Cunha. All the children of the family have been educated outside the *município*. They are very interested in local politics, however, and contribute considerably to campaigns, thus keeping themselves a firm part of the controlling political elite.

The Growth of the Town

Physically, as can be seen from the maps, the town has expanded enormously. The traditional *sede* held some 250 residences, most of them dating back to the nineteenth and even the eighteenth century. There was little new construction between the end of the nineteenth century and 1940. Emilio Willems in 1945 noted 272 buildings, including 264 homes. Of these he termed only 33 of them "modern" in style. In March of 1966 there were in Cunha and its suburbs 984 structures. Of these 803 were private homes, of which 713 were occupied. Most of the unoccupied homes were closed because the owners lived elsewhere, either outside of the *município* or in the rural zones. A few were being held as investment capital by the local businessmen and some were shut down because of their ruinous condition.

According to the local residents, the great boom in construction began in 1957 and is still going on, although it has slackened considerably since 1963. Despite the reduced rate of construction about 25 new houses were completed during the year the author was in Cunha. In addition, when the census was completed in March of 1966, there were 28 homes and 3 public buildings in construction.

Spatially the town has expanded in all directions as can be seen instantly by comparison of the two maps of 1945 and 1966. The original "compact edifice" clustered around the two Catholic churches and the city hall on a half-dozen major streets. Only this center was supplied with lights and water in 1945 (158 and 83 houses respectively). Since that time the

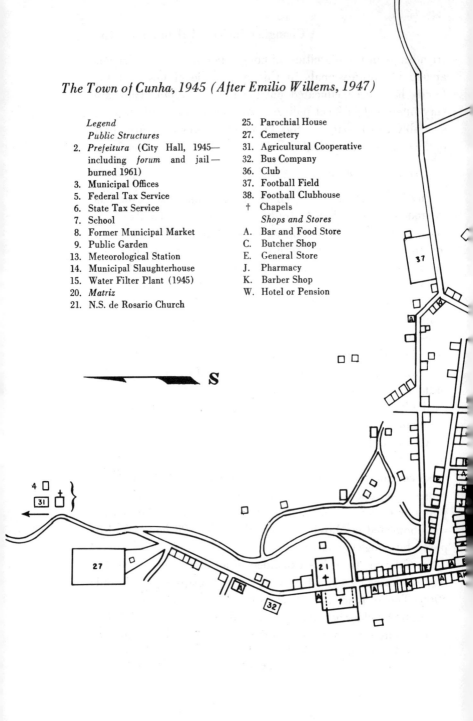

The Town of Cunha, 1945 (After Emilio Willems, 1947)

Legend
Public Structures

2. *Prefeitura* (City Hall, 1945—including *forum* and jail—burned 1961)
3. Municipal Offices
5. Federal Tax Service
6. State Tax Service
7. School
8. Former Municipal Market
9. Public Garden
13. Meteorological Station
14. Municipal Slaughterhouse
15. Water Filter Plant (1945)
20. *Matriz*
21. N.S. de Rosario Church
25. Parochial House
27. Cemetery
31. Agricultural Cooperative
32. Bus Company
36. Club
37. Football Field
38. Football Clubhouse
† Chapels

Shops and Stores
A. Bar and Food Store
C. Butcher Shop
E. General Store
J. Pharmacy
K. Barber Shop
W. Hotel or Pension

S

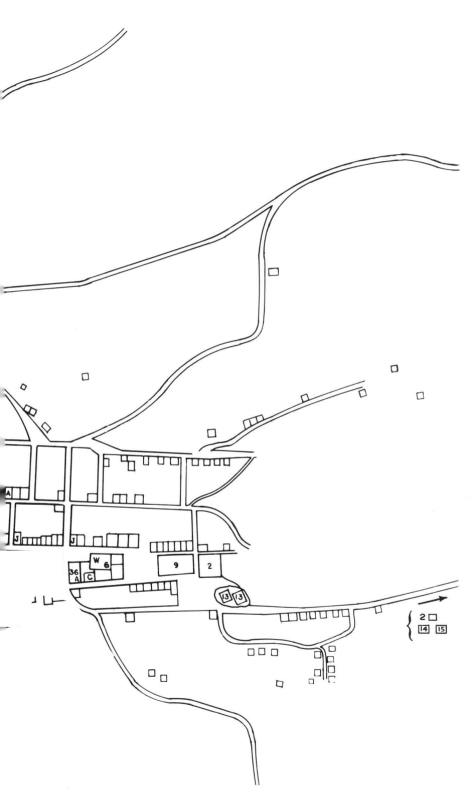

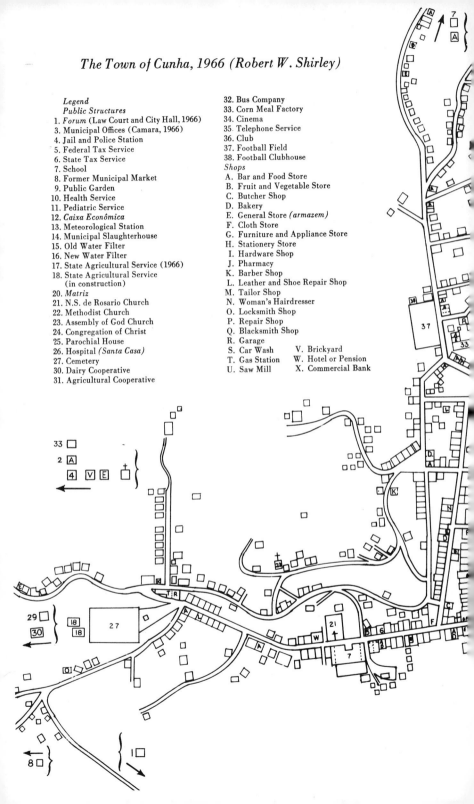

The Town of Cunha, 1966 (Robert W. Shirley)

Legend
Public Structures
1. *Forum* (Law Court and City Hall, 1966)
3. Municipal Offices (Camara, 1966)
4. Jail and Police Station
5. Federal Tax Service
6. State Tax Service
7. School
8. Former Municipal Market
9. Public Garden
10. Health Service
11. Pediatric Service
12. *Caixa Econômica*
13. Meteorological Station
14. Municipal Slaughterhouse
15. Old Water Filter
16. New Water Filter
17. State Agricultural Service (1966)
18. State Agricultural Service
    (in construction)
20. *Matriz*
21. N.S. de Rosario Church
22. Methodist Church
23. Assembly of God Church
24. Congregation of Christ
25. Parochial House
26. Hospital *(Santa Casa)*
27. Cemetery
30. Dairy Cooperative
31. Agricultural Cooperative

32. Bus Company
33. Corn Meal Factory
34. Cinema
35. Telephone Service
36. Club
37. Football Field
38. Football Clubhouse
Shops
A. Bar and Food Store
B. Fruit and Vegetable Store
C. Butcher Shop
D. Bakery
E. General Store *(armazem)*
F. Cloth Store
G. Furniture and Appliance Store
H. Stationery Store
I. Hardware Shop
J. Pharmacy
K. Barber Shop
L. Leather and Shoe Repair Shop
M. Tailor Shop
N. Woman's Hairdresser
O. Locksmith Shop
P. Repair Shop
Q. Blacksmith Shop
R. Garage
S. Car Wash   V. Brickyard
T. Gas Station   W. Hotel or Pension
U. Saw Mill   X. Commercial Bank

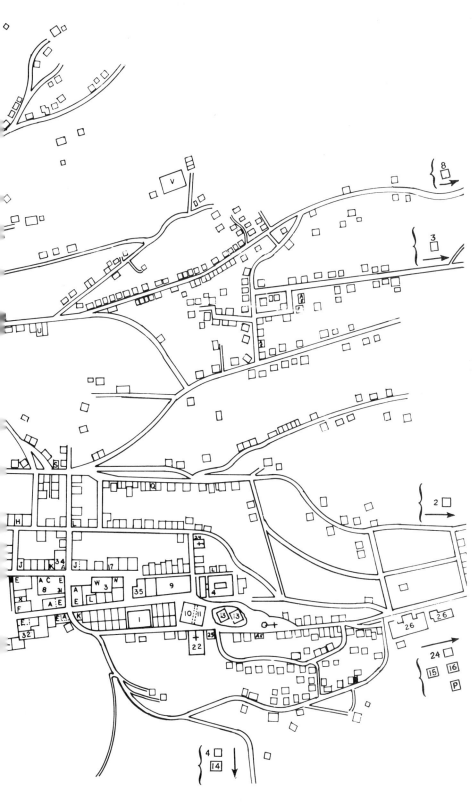

city limits of the *sede* have enlarged considerably, hundreds of new homes have been built, and several new urban neighborhoods have opened up.* A number of these new *bairros* or sections which have been built, especially those which have been built along already important and established streets, consist of well-built and modern brick homes and are, like the center, supplied with water and electricity. On the other hand some of these new "neighborhoods" are little more than collections of shacks strung along a path where live many of the urban poor and some *caipira* families who happen to live within the boundaries of the town.

The largest of these new *bairros*, "Cajurú," which occupies the hill opposite the town center, now has 84 houses. In 1945 there was only one house in the same area. One interesting fact is that half of the households in this *bairro* belong to a single extended family. Over a period of years a large portion of one rural neighborhood moved into the town. Its members tended to settle next to each other. Many of them found urban jobs or purchased small shops and bars. At least one family became fairly well off, they may be considered a part of the commercial elite, but the majority are in the lower middle brackets. Cajurú itself is a respectable *bairro* with no really fine houses but no poor ones either, and supplied, for the most part, with lights and water. The sheer size of the family has given them a certain influence in the town's politics and this has helped in the search for local jobs. Relatively few of the family have left the *município*. One could say that this represents a case of rural exodus wherein the urban site was Cunha itself: an example of colony formation within the *sede*.

* In Brazil, sections of a town or city are also called by the Portuguese word *bairro*. This term in the urban setting, however, should not be confused with its meaning in the rural areas of Brazil where the social significance of the "neighborhood" is much greater than it is in the towns. The urban "*bairro*" is also a named locality, but the "community" of the townsmen is not the *caipira* "neighborhood" (though aspects of this may exist) but the whole town itself.

A great deal of construction has gone on in the town center as well. The majority of buildings in the center have, in fact, been either remodeled or rebuilt. On the Rua Dr. Casimeiro de Rocha, the main street of the town, all but four of the twenty-eight fronting houses have been rebuilt and modernized. Both Catholic churches have been remodeled since 1940 and three new Protestant churches have been built in the same time.

As a general rule the new or rebuilt houses are very different in style from traditional Cunha homes. Stylistically the traditional urban home of better quality in Cunha had colonial Portuguese origins. The walls were usually made of *taipa* (packed mud), bricks, wood, and wattle-and-daub. The floors were of wooden planks. In the urban zones the roof was generally made of curved "colonial" tiles and was peaked so that the ridge of the roof was parallel to the street. The house almost always fronted directly on the street, touching its neighbors on either side so that the town gave the appearance, according to Emilio Willems (1947:8), of a single structure. These houses were generally long and narrow and appeared deceptively small from the front. Often the front of such a house held a shop, bar, or office.

In the 1940s a "chalet" style of construction was briefly popular and a dozen or so examples still exist. The most popular type of home built today, however, is in the "American" style (*estilo americano*). This type of house is separated from nearby houses and is usually set back slightly from the road. It often has a small porch in front, or sometimes even a front yard. The ridge of the roof is set at right angles to the street and, characteristically, one half is set lower than the other. Modern homes almost always use the flat "French" tiles which are now manufactured locally. In 1945 they were brought in from the Paraíba Valley and were hence a sign of wealth. The walls of the house are invariably made of brick and in the better houses are plastered and painted. The floors are of brick or cement which, in finer homes, are inlaid with wood or tile. The Cunha city hall now furnishes finished plans for such houses for a nominal fee. A few large, modern houses have been built with flat roofs and large view windows. Some of these are rather impressive but they are exceptional and belong for the most part to professional people and wealthy business-men.

A major change has also taken place in the type of residence of the poorer citizens of Cunha which reflects both the increas-ing prosperity of the town and a change in the patterns of labor. The traditional inexpensive house in Cunha, in both the urban and rural areas, is a simple hut, of two to four rooms, generally not much larger than twelve square meters. The walls are made entirely of wattle-and-daub. Sometimes the house is whitewashed but more commonly it is not. The floor is pounded earth and the roof is usually made of *sapé*, although it may occasionally be of tile. The materials for such a house cost literally nothing. The sticks for the framework can be obtained from a nearby woods; *sapé* grows in many valleys in Cunha, and mud is always in excess supply.

The construction, however, requires intensive labor over a short period of time. While the house frame can be built over a period of several days, the actual preparation and spreading of mud on the walls should be done as rapidly as possible, since it dries quickly and rain at any time can ruin the work. Such a house, therefore, can best be built with a great number of workers gathered together for a short time. The traditional *caipira mutirão* is ideal for such work and can frequently finish such a house in a single day.

Such houses are no longer being built in Cunha. It is, in fact, illegal to build houses of wattle-and-daub in the center of town and they are no longer being put up even in the sub-urban zones. During the time the author was in Cunha he never saw a house of this type in construction in either the urban or rural zones. The typical inexpensive house being built in Cunha at the present time has, at the very least, brick walls and a tile roof. It is, moreover, usually "American" in style. Unlike the better homes, however, the poorer houses use mud rather than cement mortar and are frequently left unpainted. Such houses require an initial monetary outlay for bricks and tile, but at the same time do not need intensive group labor for construction. One man working full or even part time can put up such a house over a period of several months. Furthermore, the raw materials can be purchased bit by bit as the owner has the money.

It therefore seems likely that labor and economic patterns tend to determine the housing style in Cunha today. The decline of the rural cooperative labor patterns make it increasingly difficult to organize the intensive labor necessary to build the traditional wattle-and-daub house, especially in the urban zones. Even the raw materials for such a house are increasingly difficult to find near the town, whereas brick and tiles are made locally. The ultimate result is a rise in the quality of urban housing since brick buildings are considerably more substantial than the traditional ones.

The result of the new construction and new styles has been to change the character of Cunha from that of a compact colonial *"Cidade"* to that of a sprawling, almost "suburban" type of town. There are still sharp zonal differences in Cunha, and these may currently be even more severe than those noted by Emilio Willems in 1945 (1947:12-13). As in 1945, the center is the focus of commercial and public activity. It includes the main road through the town from the school at the north to the weather station at the south, as well as the old central plaza in front of the *matriz* and two streets parallel to the main one. Most of the shops and bars are located here and almost all public and professional offices. There are a few other small commercial areas, especially along the roads to Guaratinguetá and Campos Novos de Cunha.

Most of the new *bairros* of the town are residential. These show distinct class differences. The majority of the old urban Catholic elite still lives in the center. Most of the best homes are still located here and many of them have been rebuilt. The wealthy rural *fazendeiros* moving into the town, however, have established high quality residential neighborhoods which are supplied, as is the center, with electricity and running water. Probably the finest of these is the "Alto de Cruzeiro," which runs along the main road south of the center. Fifty per cent of the residents of this *bairro* are Methodist *fazendeiros*.

By contrast there are several zones in the town which are distinctly squalid. These are usually located in the low-lying areas, the houses are of the poorest quality, and they are usually without water or electricity. The residents of these neighborhoods usually have menial jobs. The majority of the new residential areas seem to have a somewhat intermediate status. The homes, while small and not elaborately equipped, are of brick, and many of them are painted and supplied with the town utilities.

There is, therefore, considerable variation in home values. A small house in one of the poorer districts may be worth only a few hundred thousand *cruzeiros* in contrast to a value of forty or fifty million for some of the finer homes in the center. Land and building values in the center of town have soared. Homes worth Cr. $20,000 fifteen years ago now are valued at Cr. $10,000,000 which represents a tenfold increase of real value.

The Development of Urban Services

Urban services in Cunha have developed very extensively during the past few years, and are an essential factor in understanding the pattern of social change and urbanization. As was noted in Chapter VI, many of these new services have been given to the *município* by the state government which has also given an economic boost to the town through the public institutions it maintains there. The most important of these, the educational system, will be dealt with in a later chapter.

Electric power is one contribution which the state has made

to Cunha which makes a tremendous difference to the "urban" quality of life. One needs only live for awhile in an interior town without electricity to see what a sharp difference in life styles prevail. Cunha did have electricity in 1945, supplied by a private generator owned by a businessman who lived in Guaratinguetá. Emilio Willems says the following about the service: "The electric lighting was installed more than 20 years ago and is of small amperage, giving off light with force equal to that of a kerosene lamp, thus making it difficult to read or work at night" (1947:13). At that time only 158 houses were wired for electricity. In 1958 the state government installed a hydroelectric plant, utilizing one of the numerous waterfalls in the *município*, and the system now supplies up to 180 kilowatts at a nominal line voltage of 210. At peak hours, however, the system cannot supply all of the needs of the town and the voltage may drop somewhat. Breakdowns are fairly frequent and the townspeople are looking forward to linking up with the national network of the São Paulo Canadian-owned electrical company, *The Light,* within the next few years. At the present time 681 households are supplied with electricity in Cunha.

Several services have been set up by the state government to improve the health conditions of the town. The old water-filtration plant supplied 83 houses with running water in 1940. The rest of the townspeople obtained water from a half dozen public fountains located in various parts of the town. These are presently all abandoned since the majority of the houses, 611 of them, receive running water directly from a new water-filtration plant built in 1958. Outlying *bairros* still utilize public faucets, and a few families in the poorest zones of the town still obtain their water from nearby streams. The filtration system is far from perfect, however, and many residents prefer to refilter or boil their water before drinking it. Epidemics of intestinal disease tend to break out, especially among children, during the dry season of the year.

In addition the state contributed to the construction of a sewage network which was laid out in Cunha a few years ago. It now links most of the houses in the center of town and is being extended in several areas. The state also built a new municipal slaughterhouse in 1957 and the former one was torn down so that the private residences could be built on the site. The new building is a large brick structure with a cement floor and all its interior walls faced with tile. Its construction has greatly improved the quality and sanitation of meat slaughtered and consumed in the town.

There was no telephone service in Cunha in 1945, according to Emilio Willems (1947:22), since the only line had been cut in the revolution of 1932 and had not to that time been restored. There was, however, a newly installed telegraph line. The telephone service has now been restored and in 1966 there was a modest network in Cunha with a total of 93 instruments. There is no rural service, however, and there is only one line linking both the towns of Cunha and Paratí with Guaratinguetá and the major urban networks of Rio de Janeiro and São Paulo. Service to these cities is slow and erratic. A call to São Paulo may take from half an hour to half a day. This problem, coupled with the absence of any rural service, sharply limits the usefulness of the telephone in a town where, in fact, no house is more than a fifteen-minute walk from any other.

Medical service has strikingly improved in Cunha in the past twenty years. In 1945 there was only one doctor and one acting (i.e., not formally trained) dentist in the *município*. The great majority of the rural people sought medical aid from local *curandeiros* (faith healers) rather than the doctor (Willems, 1947:118). The general lack of trained physicians may partly explain the prominence of pharmacists in Cunha. Even at the present time many people, especially rural people, come directly to a pharmacist for their prescriptions, completely bypassing the doctor. The pharmacist in turn will listen to the "patient's" symptoms and prescribe something that he thinks will be helpful, such as a vitamin tonic or penicillin injection and he will seldom lose the opportunity for a sale.

There were three pharmacists in Cunha in 1945. One of them was so esteemed that one of the town's streets was later named after him. Another, still active, was de facto chief of the P.S.P. political party and uses his occupation to advance himself politically. He wins friends and votes by giving away free samples. The other active pharmacist now in Cunha is a young man just out of the university who took over his father's business upon the latter's death a few years ago. He is, one should add, the pharmacist for the P.D.C. party.

Both do a thriving business, although the older man has more old customers. The clear success of antibiotics, available without prescription in any Brazilian drugstore, in curing many serious diseases, has demonstrated the value of modern drugs to even the most backward and isolated rural regions and has brought about a vast expansion of the Brazilian pharmaceutical industry. One of Cunha's most famous *curandeiros*, living in the rural zone, has done extensive reading in pharmacology to take advantage of the demand for modern drugs. It is said that some of the pharmaceutical companies send representatives to him every year with literature, gifts, and free samples, and his prescriptions, excluding narcotic drugs, are generally honored by the local pharmacists. Thus, not only is folk medicine still practiced in Cunha, but it actually is adopting the trappings of urban medicine. The widespread fear of the licensed physician, which was common among many of the *caipira* peasantry, is rapidly declining, and while many of them cling to their folk traditions, the urban medical service in Cunha is rapidly expanding.

There are now three fully qualified medical doctors in the town, and each has an extensive practice. One of them in fact maintains a practice in both Cunha and Rio de Janeiro by commuting every week between the town and the city. The other two live in Cunha, practice full-time there, and are very enthusiastic about the small-town life. A health service and a pediatric clinic were established some years ago by the state government and are now housed in their own building. Each service is headed by one of the town's full-time physicians who spends his mornings treating clinic patients and his afternoons in private practice. Early every morning groups of poor *caipira* men, and women, frequently with small children, line up in front of the clinic's office patiently waiting their turn. The state government pays for the services of the doctors, four assistants, and two inspectors. The local health service, though not really up to the needs of the entire *município* of over 20,000 people, is still a moderate-size operation and has many functions. It inspects sanitary conditions in shops, bars, and even private homes in the urban zone, and also carries out a yearly inspection of all the schools in the *município*. It has considerable discretionary power to close down conditions that might prove dangerous, though the regulations are not very stringent. The state also supplies a pickup truck and driver to serve as an ambulance and for inspections and other services in the rural zones.

One of the greatest improvements in health facilities in Cunha was the opening of a hospital, or *Santa Casa,* in 1955 by the Catholic Church. It opened in that year and almost immediately closed again due to political disputes between the vicar who built it and the town administration. Two years later the old priest left and the new priest who replaced him, the current vicar, devoted considerable effort to settle the disputes and reopen the hospital. He was successful in 1958. Since that time he has devoted major effort to keeping it supplied and running smoothly. It now has twenty-eight beds and a staff of about a dozen, including four nuns who serve as nurses. Two of the town's physicians act as clinical directors, but the third, a qualified surgeon, had an altercation with the nuns and no longer enters.

The *Santa Casa* performs many important services, including maternal and infant care. Various emergency drugs, such as snake antivenom, are kept constantly on hand. Individuals who are seriously ill, however, are generally taken to Guaratinguetá if at all possible, since the local hospital lacks extensive diagnostic and testing equipment and neither of the two resident physicians care to make serious use of its surgical equipment. Nevertheless the hospital is very crowded. Maternal care alone takes up much of its usable space. A new maternity home, which was being built by the society of St. Vincent de Paul, had to be abandoned due to lack of funds. A new hospital wing is stalled in midconstruction for the same reason.

There is now in Cunha for the first time a professional dentist. Dental work in the region in the past has been in the hands of acting dentists without adequate equipment or formal training, a fact which may in part explain the incredibly bad state of the teeth of most of the population. An elderly man or woman in Cunha with all or even most of his normal teeth, is a rarity, especially among the poorer residents. It seems likely that poor diet combines with a lack of professional care in this regard. Unbelievable as it may seem in a land which is famed for the quality and quantity of its dairy products, the conventional rural diet in Cunha contains little calcium. At least this was so in the past, although things may be improving among the younger generation. Most residents seemed pleased that the town finally had a fully qualified dentist, although this was usually accompanied with complaints about the cost. There is, in addition, still one other acting dentist in Cunha who has no formal training. But since his fees are lower than those of the professional, he still gets considerable business. Finally, it should be noted that the state pays for free dental inspections and care for the school children in the town.

In this way local health facilities have developed impressively within the past few years in Cunha, but still lag behind the growing needs of an increasingly urbanized and sophisticated population. It should be noted that this development has had two bases. There has been, on one hand, an increasing demand for urban rather than folk medicine on the part of the rural population, combined with, on the other, a growing interest and capacity on the part of the state government and the Church to meet this demand.

Movimento: The Town as Center of Social Action

There has been considerable discussion about the forces which are bringing about the rapid growth of the towns and cities of Brazil. While the services just listed above, electric lighting, fresh water, improved health facilities, are not unimportant, they are still only supplimentary to the basic service which the town offers to those who are ambitious and seeking upward mobility; the town is the center of social, political, and economic action. *Movimento* is a Brazilian term for informal social activity of all kinds, and the *sede* is really the center for this. Cunha is a highly social town. It has twenty-six bars and each of these, together with the two pharmacies and a number of other fixed locations, such as the front of the *matriz*, are centers where people continually congregate. The times of greatest social activity are in the early afternoon and the evening, although a few bars in the center of town almost always have some customers.

This informal social activity, which at first glance seems like so much idle diversion and amusement to the North American, actually carries on a great many important urban functions. The importance of politics in Brazilian life has already been mentioned, as has the informal, personal way in which Brazilian political networks are built and maintained. The *panelinha*, the self-maintaining political clique, one of the most important institutions in decision-making processes, is a largely informal organization. The point to be made is that in a highly personalized political system such as that of Brazil, one's social contacts are very important to get ahead, socially and economically. Hence this *movimento*, wandering about, making friends, and gathering information is very important for anyone who has much ambition at all. Brazilians listen to gossip and use it. Part of the job of a *chefe político* in a Brazilian town, if he wants to maintain his position, is to gather as much information as possible and the effective politician is frequently surprisingly taciturn though he misses very little. Many of the bars and other fixed gathering places are actually centers for different cliques and political groups (Willems, 1947:74-76). It was customary in Cunha, more so in the past than today, for the political leader of the town to visit each of the bars and social centers of his supporters several times a week and at these centers basic political decisions were made. Thus what might seem like harmless conversation was actually a game of power, and anyone who wanted to play had to keep in contact with the *sede*.

This point can be made more forcefully, and the recent political changes which have taken place reemphasized, by telling the history of the Social Club of Cunha (*Clube Social Cunhense*). Emilio Willems noted the existence of this club in 1945 (1947:70-73) and it still exists today, but its function has changed considerably since then. Twenty years ago it occupied a large old house in the center of town and according to Alceu Maynard Araújo (1945:113) it was the place where the elite, the *juiz*, *prefeito*, and other political powers of the town, congregated. It had several card and game rooms and was clearly the center for the dominant *panelinha*. But a few years ago the club broke up; it was forced out of its old quarters and bought a much smaller house near the church. At this time about half of its membership left. Adults, and especially the town leaders seldom enter any more and its function as a center of political action is gone. Almost everyone noted that the club was not what it used to be. It has, in fact, become purely a social center for young members of the most urbanized Cunha families. It is important to note that no other location has taken its place as a center for the local elite to congregate, since some important state officials are reluctant even to enter the local bars.

The *movimento* has its important economic aspects as well. There are no office buildings in Cunha and most urban business deals, whether they be the buying or selling of animals, crops, or vehicles, are made in the various meeting points of the town. Negotiations may go on for days or weeks before a deal is settled. Real estate purchase or exchange is often carried out in this way. As a rule, however, only business of minor to moderate importance is carried out in Cunha itself: the buying or selling of a jeep, a *sítio*, a pedigreed bull, or the like. The large-scale commerce in animals and agricultural products which forms the backbone of the *município's* economy is carried on in the cities of the Paraíba Valley and not in Cunha.

On the other hand, for the growing commercial middle classes in Cunha the many small business deals available in town often seem worth the trouble. These people are always on the alert for any kind of a deal that can bring them some profit. A case in point is the astonishing amount of business that goes on around the buying, selling, and trading of vehicles. This has apparently replaced an equivalent interest in the commerce of horses and mules. Almost anyone who can afford it takes part in this exchange and a surprising number can do so. For the average Cunhense of the middle to upper classes, whether he is a *fazendeiro,* shopkeeper, or civil servant, a vehicle, especially a jeep, is more than simply a means of transportation: It is a capital investment to be sold or traded whenever a profit can be made. The activity may take on the aspects of a game of skill wherein the aim is to outwit and make a profit off another, as the author found to his disadvantage. One town resident traded cars six times in the year I was there. At least one individual made a living almost exclusively through buying and selling jeeps. He had no regular used-car lot, but he could always be found during the day at a certain spot in the town plaza.

The purely social activities of the town, though of lesser importance, should not be wholly forgotten. The social club itself is still important in this regard. A billiard table is set up, and ping-pong is played on weekdays. Dances are held weekly, and on special occasions they may draw considerable crowds, although really big social events are held in one of the local hotels. The club is thus a place where young members of the local Catholic urban elite can meet each other. A few young members from less prosperous families were members, especially if their parents were interested in their social advancement. For the most part, however, the poorer citizens of the town held their own social activities and dances in private homes and did not try to enter the club.

Emilio Willems noted that there was in 1945 considerable opposition on the part of religious leaders to the *clube* (1947: 72). The club is not without its critics even now. The opposition of the Catholic Church has declined, although one Catholic *fazendeiro* told the author that he felt these modern dances, such as the fox trot, to be shameful. The major opposition now comes from the Methodists. Most of the Methodist families would not let their young people attend the club. Some of them felt that its activities were improper, and for the most part they were not eager to have their children mix socially with the local Catholics. The diversions of the *clube*, however, are a powerful attraction to the young Methodists, and the local pastor has had to set up a Methodist recreational group in competition. This in its turn has been quite successful.

The most important commercial entertainment in Cunha is the cinema, which first opened late in 1945. This is owned by one of the Lebanese families. The projection equipment is old but fully professional (C. Zeiss), and it has cinemascope lenses. The theater seats about 200. Two films are shown a week and are for the most part old American films rented from an agency in São Paulo. Thus, although the sound system is very poor, no one minds since most of the shows have

Portuguese subtitles. A few Brazilian films are shown, but apparently are not very popular. The audience is made up largely of children of the middle-class families, although a few adults attend. The ticket price of Cr. $200 (U.S. 10¢) effectively excludes the poorest families. In 1965 the cinema was closed for nearly a year over a dispute with the judge over enforcement of the Brazilian censorship laws forbidding children to see most films. The incident was a stunning example of judicial power since the *juiz* with a single writ closed down a major enterprise of the richest commercial family in Cunha. Members of the family were furious but helpless.

The common Brazilian pattern of promenading in the late evening is highly developed in Cunha and starts every evening about 8:00 P.M., going on until 10:30 or 11:00. On Saturdays and Sundays there may appear several hundred people in the streets and on major festival nights this number may reach three or four thousand. Currently on weeknights the activity is greatly reduced, since many of the young people are in school. Promenading has general social functions and serves essentially as a courting ceremony.

Chapter IX

Social Stratification

The problem of class and social stratification is one which has confounded social scientists for thousands of years. The terminology alone is vastly confused, with the same words being used for a considerable range of concepts. The Polish sociologist Stanislaw Ossowski has pointed out that Marx himself used the term "class" in six different senses (1963: 83). In any society there are, of course, differences in the way people look, behave, and are treated, but it is still a difficult matter to extract meaningful "classes" out of the plethora of social information which a fieldworker obtains.

Social classification is essentially, after all, a linguistic problem. Like most classification problems, it is an attempt to reduce the enormous and unmanageable number of variables and individuals which exist in the world down to a workable number of sets or "classes." These classes can then be described and given labels (names), and thus it is made possible to produce a simplified model of the society. This model can then be reduced to words, as in this book, or to numbers for statistical manipulation. But there can be no pretense that the model contains more than a very small selection of the totality of information available in the "real" society (Bertalanffy, 1968:212). The importance and interest of the study thus depend a great deal upon the parameters used in establishing these classifications, and it is generally accepted that these are most scientifically useful if the classes can help predict behavior.

This study, following Dahrendorf (1959), Lenski (1966),

and others, has for the most part accepted the idea that authority and its derivative power are the basis behind major differences in stratification. It is the distribution of these which determine in large part an individual's background, privileges, and opportunities which greatly affect his life style and behavior. However, as Lipset has pointed out (1968), power is an extremely difficult thing to measure in any operational way. There are so many different kinds of authority and power, that to single one out as the only measure of stratification—property, for example, or prestige—is to compromise the facts. As a general community study, this book does not attempt to present a final answer to the problem of social stratification. Instead, it seems most useful in this chapter to examine the stratification pattern in Cunha in several different ways, not to present a single "answer," but to give some concept of the dimensions of the problem and the social dynamics involved.

The problem is made more difficult, as well as more interesting, by the changes which have occurred in the *município* over the years. Formerly, under a patriarchal system of local government and the cartorial state, there existed for each region what was effectively a unimodal system of authority and power. The personalization of politics and *coronelismo* allowed the landed elite to maintain authority over commerce as well as land tenure, thus, as has been shown, allowing the concentration of all of the various strands of authority and power into a few hands, the *panelinha*. In such a case a fairly clear-cut dichotomous class system would develop between the powerful and the powerless, the elite and the masses, the landlords and the peasants.

There would be, moreover, a small bureaucracy which would perform the services necessary to maintain the elite in power, supply it with the goods it needed, and ensure the maintenance of the smooth flow of its commercial activity. This bureaucracy would almost invariably be located in the towns and would normally make up the majority of the town's population as well as supply most of the "urban" jobs.

In the past Cunha, like most agrarian communities, had this kind of social system. An examination of a list of urban occupations in Cunha in 1884, shows that members of a handful of important families controlled all the important political positions and most of the better civil service jobs. In addition there were a few well-defined craft and commercial positions held by nonelite families. The local upper class, moreover, maintained a marked distinction between itself and the rural population. This was most conspicuous in the manner of dress. One old Cunha family had a photograph, about thirty years old, showing the town elite of Cunha at that time. In dark suits and neckties, white shirts with boiled collars, and bowler or silk hats, they looked more like the meeting of an English club than a group of isolated townsmen in Brazil. This in the midst of a population of *caipira* farmers who wore patches on their patches.

In such a case, political power and patronage, landed wealth and commercial wealth, as well as privilege and prestige would tend to be dominated by the same few families. The traditional stratification pattern would thus look like Chart IXA.

In Cunha in recent years, however, a number of alternative sources of authority and power have developed which are independent of the patriarchal system. The bureaucracy now no longer serves merely as "functional" agents of the local elite, but increasingly instead as representatives of the state and federal governments for the protection of private property from local political interests. There are thus alternative, poly-modal, ways of establishing authority over persons or property. The fragmentation of commercial and political power at the very top of the social structure has permitted the development of a growing group of people in the "middle sectors," those *sitiantes* and *commerciantes* who are relatively independent of political and economic control by the local elite, even if they

Chart IXA. "Traditional" Stratification Pattern in Brazil

↑	Ia	The powerful (the Elite)	The rural patriarchate and its political allies
Power, Wealth, Prestige, etc.	Ib	The influential (the Elite)	Professionals and others, often relatives of the above High local officials
	II	The "functionary" bureaucracy with delegated authority	State and local public officials Local businessmen and merchants Local police
	III	Skilled and semi-skilled workers	Clerks, craftsmen, laborers, etc.
	IV	The masses	Sharecroppers Unskilled laborers Paupers Others

NOTE. Horizontal lines delimit rigidity and mobility within the social structure.

in turn have little power over others. This pattern has been accentuated by the fact that for the most part the really poor landless peasants have been permitted, and indeed encouraged to leave the *município*. Thus recent changes have brought out the fact that there are several different systems of stratification in operation. These will be developed below.

Occupations and Social Structure in Cunha

The occupational class system becomes more important, supplanting political classes, in any region where there is a decline in the importance of local politics and increasing commercialization and capitalization (Lenski, 1966:346). Such changes are taking place in Cunha where the state judiciary has taken the defense of private property away from local politicians, and, although political involvement is still an important element, it can probably be said now that occupation, more than any other single factor, is the key determinant of social position. This is especially true since political power is becoming less dependent upon the votes supplied by a rural aristocracy interested in maintaining its power, than by the economic interests of a commercial elite interested in increasing its profits both in the town and rural zones. Local politics is thus no longer the vital thing it once was.

Table IXA is a complete list of the occupations of the heads of households in the town of Cunha. Here the senior adult male in each household is considered the head, though in the absence of an adult male, the occupation of the senior adult female was taken. At one small, neat house on the outskirts of the town, the census taker and I were met at the door by a small, bent, 70-year-old widow. After some minutes of conversation she decided that the questions had really best be answered by the head of the house, her mother. She invited us in, because, at 115 years of age, the old lady was too feeble to leave the warmth of the kitchen. In view of the general pattern of neolocal residence in the region, the social position of the head was a good general indicator of the position of the other members of the household, who were in the majority of cases minor children. Retired people are credited with the jobs they formerly held. Urban and rural agricultural occupations are listed separately.

Urban Occupations in Cunha

Table IXA gives a total of 402 households whose heads have urban occupations, that is jobs not directly connected with agricultural production. The total number of occupations in the town, in actual fact, is much larger than this number would indicate, for many dependents in these households also hold

Table IXA. A List of the Occupations of the Heads of Households in Cunha, 1966

I. *Urban Occupations*

High Officials—State and Federal

Judge 1
Police commissioner (*delegado*) . . . . (1)
District attorney (*promotor público*) . . . . (1)
Director of the *ginásio* (secondary school) 1
Director of the primary school 1
Assistant director of the primary school 1
Federal tax collector 1
State tax collector . . . . (1)
Director of the *Caixa Econômica* 1

High Officials—Municipal

Prefeito 1
Vice Prefeito . . . . (1)
Chairman of the Municipal Council . . . . (1)
Vereadores . . . .(13)

High Officials—Private

Director of the bank 1
Director of the agricultural cooperative 1
Director of the dairy cooperative 1

Professionals

Doctor (M.D.) 3
Dentist 1
Lawyer 2
Chiropractor 1
Pharmacist 2
Notary (C.P.A.) 2
Topographer 1
Priest 1
Pastor 1

Urban Entrepreneurs

Large-scale *comerciantes* 27
Industrialists 4
Builders 3

Urban Occupations (cont.)	
Small Businessmen	
Shop owners	23
Garage owners	3
Craftsmen with their own shops	16
Motorists with their own trucks	15
Rural businessmen	19
Service Occupations	
Public officials (medium)	39
State police	8
Shop clerks	10
Labor—Specialized	
State highway workers (D. E. R.)	26
Motorists	18
Other	27
Labor—Unspecialized	
Government laborers	39
Pedreiros	61
Domestics	29
No occupation	11
II. *Rural Occupations*	
Fazendeiros	
Major landowners	61
Fazendeiros	
Moderate landowners	62
Widows	12
Sitiantes	
Commercial	47
Traditional	13
Retired	4
Lavradores	
With some land	23
Lavradores	
Landless	103

gainful employment. The wives and daughters, for example, of many professionals, *fazendeiros*, businessmen, and officials, often teach in the schools. Laboring families very commonly have several members working, the sons helping their fathers or others, and the daughters acting as servants. There are, in fact, about 65 women who are employed as domestic maids in Cunha. Many farming families have children who work in the town. In addition, almost everyone in Cunha has more than one job. This is especially true among the laboring classes, who will try to earn money any way they can. The state and municipal governments employ many students in minor positions, and many shopkeepers employ them as part-time clerks. In all there are about 250 urban paying jobs in the town which are not held by heads of households. Fifty-seven of these are jobs from the state and municipal governments.

While the great majority of the nonagricultural jobs are to be found in the town, there are a fair number of them in the rest of the *município*. There are seventy-four rural teaching positions, and almost as many rural *vendas*. The various lumber and other companies in the region employ somewhat over one hundred men, but the urban opportunities in Cunha are still decidedly limited, especially at an adequate level of income.

High Officials. These are the official and legitimate leaders of the *município*, in charge of many of the major political and economic decisions in the town. Their history has made up much of the history of Cunha and has been recounted in the preceding chapters. Most of the state, federal, and private officials do not come originally from Cunha and several of them, the *delegado*, *promotor*, and state tax collector, do not maintain residences in Cunha at all, but prefer to commute into town each week. All of the municipal officials, on the other hand, come from local families, since they are locally elected. Most of them do hold other commercial jobs, however, and they are listed here merely for reference. Of these, only the *prefeito*, the *vice prefeito*, and one *vereador* hold urban jobs, the rest of the members of the municipal council, including its chairman, would be considered *fazendeiros* or *sitiantes*. This indeed shows the strength of the rural landowners in local politics, and in fact only a few of the *vereadores* live in the town as they come from widely scattered parts of the *município*.

Professionals. Professionals are those whose jobs require relatively extensive professional education. In addition to those noted here, most of the state officials have professional education though they are listed here under their official occupations. A second Methodist pastor lives and works full-time within the *município*, in the *bairro* of Jericó, but is not included here because he does not have a residence in town. The professionals are included as a separate category because the quality of their education, the nature of their work, and the extensive contact which they have with the people make them very influential and important individuals in the region. Some of them, but by no means all, are deeply involved in local politics, though only a handful of them come from old Cunhense families. As might be expected, this is the most metropolitan and sophisticated group in Cunha and all of them had come to know well some of the great Brazilian cities. One lawyer, in fact, a descendant of one of the few remaining traditional patriarchal families in Cunha, had actually visited Europe and hoped to visit the United States. He was also known as a persistent innovator, the first in town to own a movie projector, television set, and ham radio.

Urban Entrepreneurs. This group makes up the commercial elite of the town of Cunha. They are the fourteen merchant families with twenty-seven households who carry on most of the commerce in the town, as was noted in the last chapter. This group should also include the local small industrialists, those who run commercial enterprises of a moderate scale. The economic links uniting these families are very important to their commercial success and they all maintain multiple enterprises. Over half of these families, moreover, have invested some of their surplus capital in land, either in Cunha or in the Paraíba Valley, and a few of them own thriving *fazendas* in addition to their town enterprises. Almost all of them are, or have been, deeply involved in local politics and a few in state politics as well. The importance of the Lebonese and Italian families in local commerce has been noted, but it is also interesting that of the thirty-four family heads in this group, only six were born in the rural zones of Cunha, the rest come from outside the *município*, or from old families of the town.

Small Businessmen. There are a number of businessmen in Cunha who, if they lack the capital or desire to become active entrepreneurs, do maintain their own enterprises, some of which are moderately prosperous. Included in this group are the owners of small shops and bars, the owners of the *oficinas* (garages), the owners of small service shops, tailors, barbers, leatherworkers, and the like. While a few from this group come from outside the *município*, the great majority come from old Cunhense families. A number of these are former *sitiantes* who sold their lands to buy a shop in town, and so few in this group maintain significant land holdings. Also included in this group are the fifteen families, truck and jeep owners, who make a living primarily in local transportation, including several of the line motorists for the dairy cooperative. Here also are nineteen families who deal in rural commerce, these often supply foodstuffs for the town, though some of them also sell in the Paraíba Valley. It should be noted, however, that the great majority of such local rural business is carried on by the *fazendeiros*, and this list only includes those who have no land. In all of these households of small businessmen, members of the family, for the most part, do most of the routine work and few extra people are employed. In this regard, it should be mentioned that the São Paulo region has never had the high degree of prejudice against manual labor which exists in many other parts of Brazil. Many of these families are well respected in the town and fathers frequently train their sons in crafts and mechanics.

Service Occupations. There are many public officials in Cunha who hold full-time "white collar" jobs for the state and municipal governments, and yet cannot be considered to have positions of major authority. These are school teachers and inspectors, municipal clerks, and justice officials. Among this group can be found many of the oldest families of the town of Cunha; people who have been in the "functionary class" for generations and have sometimes even outlived the elite which appointed them. Of thirty-nine households in the "Public Service" category, only three came from outside the *município*, and over half these officials were born in the town itself. As a group, they are not very prosperous, only a couple of these families own land, but because of their descent and long association with the upper classes of the *município* they have adopted the manner and appearance of the elite and they have relatively high influence and prestige. Many of them come from rural families which were important in the past and had entrenched their positions in the town.

Roberto Benedito Mariano is a case in point. His family has lived in the town of Cunha for generations and he is one of the few residents of the town who was actually born there. (Only about 10 per cent of the heads of households in Cunha stated that they were born in the town itself.) He was appointed as a clerk in one of the registry offices by the late Dr. Salvador because of his connections with one of the powerful patriarchal families in the region. He fought on the Paulista side during the Revolution of 1932, but, unlike many of his relatives, after the war he decided to stay in Cunha. He has held his present position for nearly fifty years and is very proud of his record. He is so well established that he has survived several changes of local administration and is training one of his sons to take over after him. He himself has a secondary education and his son is studying in the local *ginásio*. Sr. Roberto has a high regard for education and would like to have his sons continue, but with his limited income he has been unable to do more for himself or his family.

There are eight households headed by policemen in the town, although this number does not include the twenty or so unmarried policemen who live in the stationhouse. The great majority of the police, including those who have established homes in the town, come from outside the *município*, and half of those who do live in town are retired. One of these retired policemen is the effective head of the Assembly of God Church in Cunha.

Most of the white-collar service jobs in Cunha, therefore, are from various government agencies. There are very few private organizations in Cunha which need full-time educated help and are willing to pay for it. For the most part, local merchants, even the most prosperous, manage their shops themselves with the aid of their families. With the surplus of all kinds of labor in the town the pay for such jobs as do exist is very poor, with a few notable exceptions, and it is difficult to make a living thereby. The actual number of clerks is much greater than the ten listed here, but most of these are young, unmarried, and still living with their parents, few of them are heads of families. Since a fair degree of education is a prerequisite for all of these service jobs, many clerks are also part-time students.

Labor. Of 402 family heads in the town of Cunha with urban jobs, somewhat over half the total, 211, are manual laborers without enough capital to set themselves up in a business of some kind. With very few industries in town, the majority of jobs available, construction, road work, and the like, require relatively few skills. The major exception is a driver's license, which qualifies one for the occupation of *motorista* whether or not one owns a vehicle. Three or four of the group who claimed to be motorists, however, were not regularly employed. There were a large number of men who were working for the State Highway Department (D.E.R.: *Departamento Estadual de Rodagem*) in 1966 on the construction of the new paved road from Cunha to Guaratinguetá. Most of these were skilled motorists and laborers working on a full-time basis and earning relatively good pay (Cr. $15,000–30,000 a week).

Few of the other specialized jobs required extensive training or skills, with the exception of a couple of workers who maintained the telephone service. The rest of the workers in this group make a living as carpenters, painters, bakers, and the like, where the earning power and chances for advancement depended to a large degree upon individual reputation and connections. Many people who claimed special skills were not always able to utilize them and were in actual fact only semi-employed. Others work part or full time with those who have their own shops.

There are a large number of laborers in Cunha without capital, connections, or special skills, who make a living as best they can, usually in construction work of some kind as *pedreiros* (stonemasons). A few of these have good reputations and are in fairly constant demand for this kind of work but most are not. The majority of unspecialized laborers and some of the specialized as well could be classified as only semi-employed and indeed many households have from one to several employable members who have no regular jobs. A few of them work full time for the *prefeitura*, doing extremely simple manual jobs such as street cleaning and roadwork. The extension of the sewage network in town, a contribution of the state government, also gave jobs to many laborers. This is a very active and fluid group and its members seek work whenever and wherever they can. It should be emphasized that many of these, especially the specialized laborers and the *pedreiros* are urban workers and in many ways very different from the rural *lavradores*. As a rule they have more education than the rural workers, and, even though many of them are former farm workers, they tend to be rather scornful of agricultural work. This is especially true of the young people in this category, most of whom have never held a hoe. Many of the laborers in the town said they would rather leave the *município* than attempt to return to the land as poor sharecroppers. This is also a very mobile group, seeking work in many regions. Half of the D.E.R. workers and a quarter of the *pedreiros* had worked at some time or another in São Paulo or the cities of the Paraíba Valley. They returned when work was again available in Cunha, usually due to family ties in the town. Of the unskilled group 85 per cent were born in the *município*, well over half in the rural zones. These workers, poor, geographically mobile, and very urban oriented can be considered a small but authentic working class in Cunha. As a whole, this group, ambitious, moderately educated, aggressive, and socially marginal—in contact with both the rural and urban sectors of the community—furnished some of the most helpful assistants and informants in Cunha.

The Rosário family can be taken as an example of this group. José Salazar Rosário, a dark *caipira*, moved into the town seven years ago from one of the large *fazendas*, where he had been a sharecropper. None of his six children knows anything about agriculture, nor does anyone in the family have any interest in returning to the rural zones. The family is poor, if not destitute, and lives in a small unpainted brick house in one of the poorer sections of town. Several years ago, the oldest son, Benedito, left the *município* completely and settled in the city of Campinas as a motorist. The second son, José Salazar filho, "Salazinho," is able and intelligent and, like his father, skilled in painting, carpentry, and masonry. Although he finished primary school and entered the local *ginásio*, his studies have been hampered by the fact that several times he has had to go outside of the town to find work. He feels his poverty and lack of social position very keenly and is much less resigned than the rest of his family to this. As an adolescent he was apparently extremely aggressive and was picked up by the local police several times. As a result he has learned to hide his feelings and rather left-wing political beliefs behind a stream of wit and skillful banter and is now generally looked upon with amusement by the local elite. He likes Cunha and has many relatives in the town but there have been few jobs available locally for any in the family for the past year, and he is seriously considering leaving Cunha and establishing a home in Campinas where he hopes his brother will be able to help him find a job. The elder Rosário hates to see the family break up but does not want to leave Cunha and thinks it would be helpful if there were two members of the family regularly employed.

A final group of unskilled workers in Cunha includes those households which were headed by women without property or families to support them. These are listed as domestics since for the most part they eked out a living as domestic maids, laundresses, or prostitutes, or any combination of the three. Cunha had its own small *zona*, or red-light district (though in fact it had no lights at all since it was a part of the town without electricity).

There are a few households in the town where the head, due to illness or old age, is simply unable to work at all, and they are supported by neighbors or kin. There are eight professional beggars in the town. One of these is a leper, who is permitted to live in town since his illness has been arrested. (There are a number of lepers living in the rural zones.) He in fact is married and with a family which he supports reasonably well by simply standing in the door of one of the local shops until the proprietor, fearful of the potential loss of business, gives him something to go away.

Rural Occupations in Cunha

The key to the classification of rural occupations is land, its ownership and its use. It should be noted that in classifying rural occupations, the distinction "manual" and "nonmanual" taken to mean "working" and "owning" classes, has less validity in Cunha than in some other parts of Brazil. The *fazendeiro* in Cunha, and in many parts of Southern Brazil generally, does not feel disgraced if he or his family does some of the farm work personally. This is especially true since the changeover from hoe agriculture to ranching, and I have seen some of the largest landowners in the *município* working with their families and hired hands in rounding up and milking the cattle.

There are considerable differences in land ownership in Cunha, however. The basic means by which the different sub-groups were determined was through the amount of land registered, it being assumed that the maximum amount of land which a single family can profitably farm is about 25 to 30 *alqueires* and thus the dividing line between a *sitiante* and the larger commercial producer, the *fazendeiro*. While it is true, as was mentioned earlier, that the landowners of Cunha commonly register only a fraction of their lands, this is a fault in which only the larger landowners can indulge. Thus the smaller registrations probably represent the true holdings fairly accurately whereas the larger owners often have registered only a third to a quarter of what they really control. Registration figures do, however, give a fairly good relative idea of who the major landowners are. There are other complications, however, and kinship is an important one. Some sons of extremely important *fazendeiros* have relatively small holdings but may be expected to inherit considerable tracts in the future. The quality of the holdings is another factor, there are some very highly capitalized smaller *fazendas*, as well as some very under-developed large holdings.

The division of the *fazendeiros* into two groups of major and moderate landowners was done primarily on the basis of registration of land, with 100 *alqueires* (242 hectares) being considered the dividing line, with a number of corrections being made on the basis of other information. The 61 households listed here as "major" landowners represent 34 families who make up much of the landowning elite of Cunha. It must be said in addition, however, that there are a number of important landowners in the *município* who do not keep residences in town and hence are not noted in this census. The *sede* serves as a center; social, economic, and even political; for only a part of the entire region, mainly the portion to the east. Landowners living in the northern areas, around Campos Novos, and those near the Paraíba Valley, are oriented toward the valley cities of Guaratinguetá or Lorena. There are over a hundred major landowners who still live on their *fazendas* or elsewhere in São Paulo, including a few big absentee landlords who were usually keeping the land for speculation.

The 62 landowners listed here as "moderate," while not quite as important as the others, can still be considered fairly prosperous. The majority of them, for example, own jeeps or trucks, and they engage in considerable commercial production. Average registered holdings by this group is around 45 *alqueires,* although the actual ownership is probably considerably more. These are a very commercially active and independent group of people and are, in a sense, along with the *sitiantes,* a rural "middle" class.

The are 64 *sitiantes* living in the town of Cunha. The great majority of these also are commercial producers, and may be considered allied to the *fazendeiros* in many of their interests although they do not have the resources or landholdings to produce on a major scale. At least thirteen of this group, however, are traditional *caipira sitiantes.* These are the local landowning peasantry, still oriented largely toward subsistence production. They may in fact own a fair amount of land, but they remain members of the *caipira* culture in identity and orientation. They maintain their folk beliefs, have little interest in formal education, though they do register their lands, and maintain their social ties in the rural zones. The majority of the real *caipira* remaining in the region do not live in the city if they have enough land on which to live, and most of the traditional *sitiantes* listed here actually live in the rural zones and come to town only to *passar festas*, see the festivals, or to retire. It should be recalled that there are well over a thousand small landowners in Cunha. In addition the majority of the *lavradores*, even in the town, are culturally *caipira*, although 20 per cent of these have worked at one time or another outside the *município*, some in factories in various Paulista cities, returning for family reasons.

One unusually interesting example of the traditional *sitiante* is Dona Maria de Luz Perreira. She is authentically *caipira* in background and of mixed Portuguese-Indian descent. Her former husband died many years ago, leaving her with a large family and moderate holdings in the *sertão*. Her children still live and work on the family lands, but with a few hundred thousand *cruzeiros* she bought a small house of wattle-and-daub on the edge of town. She is now 58 years old, a proud, shrewd, and quick-witted woman. She became very communicative after her suspicions that I was a municipal agent had been allayed and volunteered considerable information, mainly about her mistrust of the cities, and especially urban politicians. Her husband is about twenty years younger than she, a shy, tall mulatto who has been with her for ten years, though when asked if they were married she laughed and said that they were just old friends. The only reason she had moved into the city, she said, was because she was tired and her husband had arranged a job in town.

Almost every *fazendeiro* has a number of dependent families working for him. The larger *fazendas*, especially the more traditional ones which still maintain agricultural production of crops such as corn and beans, may have fifteen to twenty such families. More moderate landowners seldom have more than three or four. The more modern *fazendeiros* who concentrate on cattle ranching and dairy production also get by with little extra labor beyond that supplied by the family and a few *camaradas*. The majority of the landless *lavradores* as well as most of those who have a little land but not enough to live on work as field hands in the *bairros* and *fazendas* surrounding the town. In this way, the *sede* serves as its own *bairro* center, especially as the town offers numerous services unavailable to the rural zones. Though few *lavradores* can afford many urban services, a few are available for the taking. Poor Cunhenses, like most Brazilians, show great ability in maximizing the few resources which they do have. A number of extremely poor houses, for example, are supplied with electricity by their owners, who simply tap on to a neighbor's line, and it was pleasantly suprising to find one of the poorest parts of the town was full of loud radio music most of the day and night.

The majority of *lavradores* who work for a *fazendeiro* tend to live on or near his land where they are usually allowed to plant some crops of their own. Of those living in the town, only about a quarter said that they had a specific *patrão*, and usually this was the owner of one of the nearby *fazendas*. About a dozen of the town *lavradores*, however, actually commuted to work, with the head of the household, and often one or two grown sons, living in the country and returning on weekends while the women of the family stayed at home in town. The majority of the group of *lavradores*, however, claimed that their occupation was *lavrador ambulante*, a wandering field hand. These lived in town mainly because it was the center of transportation and they sought work wherever it was available in the *município*.

Occupations and Political Stratification

Under the patriarchal system, it may be recalled, political power was concentrated in the hands of the *coroneis* who were essentially landed aristocrats. The major change which has occurred in Cunha is the submission of the *fazendeiros* to the authority of the state and local governments. In this respect, it should be noted that no one who lives in Cunha belongs to the powerful Brazilian national, and indeed international, upper classes. Although some land is owned by members of this class, it is kept only for speculation and is not worked. Moreover, since the death of Dr. Salvador no one in Cunha has achieved national prominence in the political sphere. Thus there is no source of political or financial power in Cunha to effectively counter that of the local bureaucratic officials.

The preceding pages have examined the interrelations between power and authority in the bureaucracy (Chapter V), elective politics (Chapter VI), land tenure (Chapters V and VII), and commerce (Chapter VIII). There are, however, other kinds of authority which may have important consequences in the social structure and stratification pattern of a community. One of the most important of these is influence. This is a most complex problem, but it is basic to an explanation of the nature of social elites, the value of prestige, and the importance of family and kinship ties in Brazilian society.

Influence is the ability to control decision-making in informal, indirect, unofficial, and personal ways. It is a form of authority—and political authority in that it appeals to mutual interests—but it is without legitimacy or the backing of direct power (i.e., immediate sanctions for failure to comply). The *panelinha*, as described in Chapter V, can be considered an influence group in that it has no formal organization, but is simply a group of people in high positions with different kinds of authority working together informally to enhance their combined power. Influence is very important when it crosses hierarchical boundaries. Influence that is minor at one level of authority can be tremendously magnified further down on the scale. Influence at high levels is real power when seen from below by those who have none. Here the matter of prestige is very important since high prestige and reputation quite naturally put one in a better position to influence major decision makers.

A great many things may be involved here. I, for example, found that the prestige and minor influence accorded to me as an American *doutor*, could be converted into real authority at the local level. This is surely a common phenomenon in a society such as Brazil where there are very important stratificational differences. A person who can influence a high official has almost as much authority and power as the official himself insofar as the rest of the population is concerned. Thus the professionals, with their very high prestige, their essential services, and their urban life style, which permit them free access to the powerful, may be considered, potentially at least, as people with high influential authority, even if they are minimally involved in politics. The same can be said for the *fazendeiros* and wealthy businessmen who are able to buy their political authority with votes or cash.

The family is another aspect of Brazilian political life where influence can be seen in operation. The Brazilian extended family, the *parentela*, is an extremely important institution, in some ways the most important institution in the country. It is generally true in Brazil that loyalty to one's kin takes precedence over loyalty to almost anyone or anything else. This family solidarity is characteristic of many agrarian societies, but especially those with a colonial history. In situations where historically the governmental and bureaucratic organizations were frequently hostile to the interests of the local population, the family served as the major line of defense. Thus *filhotismo*, nepotism, and other services to members of one's family, while considered crimes in American society, are frequently considered major virtues in Brazil. In Cunha one prominent *político* and *fazendeiro* came in for some rather strong criticism for not helping out his second cousin, who died of poverty and alcohol in one of the rural *bairros*. The Brazilian *parentela* can thus be considered, at least in part, as an influence group, with all members sharing to some degree the authority and wealth of its most important members. This kind of indirect authority can in some cases be converted into power at other levels, and this is a major reason why the inter- linking of households by kinship and marriage is an important factor in stratification. Influential relatives of a powerful man are also powerful.*

Chart IXB summarizes the general pattern of political stratification in Cunha at the present time. At the top are the political elite, who are the major decision makers, and those who have important influence over their decisions. Below them is a group who have no great power or influence over the elite, yet somehow have been able to protect their interests through the courts and other institutions so at least they are inde- pendent of the local *políticos*. Until fairly recently this group was quite small, but it is growing. The great bulk of the popu- lation even today, however, still remains dependent and effec- tively powerless. These may have some ties with the political system through their vote, but they simply vote as directed. In recent years some of these people have found that they have legal rights which can be defended in the courts and have joined the middle group, but most of them have not taken advantage of this opportunity.

Occupations and Economic Stratification

Cunha is a poor region, by São Paulo standards, and wealth in it is thus only a relative matter. The coffee planter and the big industrialist cannot be found in Cunha, and the richest Cunhense landowner could not afford a corner of one of the large *fazendas* of the Paraíba Valley. There are major dif-

---

* João Guimarães Rosa, in *Sagarana*, notes that the fictional political boss of his Minas Gerais region was strongly influenced by his brother, Uncle Laudônio. "For Uncle Laudônio as a youth had studied for the priesthood; then he had spent twenty years in riotous living, and now that he had once more become serious, his summings-up were most impressive" (1966:80).

Chart IXB. Political Stratification

Ia	The powerful (the Elite)	High-level bureaucrats and politicians	
Ib	The influential (the Elite)	Many *fazendeiros* Entrepreneurs Professionals	
II	Independent voters (with some influence in law or politics)	*Commerciantes* Lesser *fazendeiros* Some public officials Some *sitiantes*	
III	Dependent voters	Minor public officials Some *sitiantes* Clerks Laborers Sharecroppers Some of the *caipira* peasantry Others	
IVa	Disenfranchised	Some laborers Some sharecroppers Others	
IVb	Politically isolated	Many of the *caipira* peasantry	

(Left margin, vertical, with upward arrow: Political Power)

NOTE. Horizontal lines delimit rigidity and mobility within the social structure.

ferences in income in Cunha, nonetheless, and there is a group which can be considered a propertied elite in the *município*, even if it has only local importance. These are the families which have sufficient resources to expand their commercial operations and defend their interests in the political arena or in the courts (see Chart IXC). The exact size of this group is difficult to determine since reliable data on income was very

Chart IXC. Stratification by Property

	I	The wealthy (the local propertied elite who have investment capital)	Major landowners Urban entrepreneurs Some professionals and high officials
	IIa	The prosperous (who have moderate capital or good earning potential)	Other professionals and high officials Lesser *fazendeiros* Many small businessmen
	IIb	The comfortable (who have some capital or moderate reliable income) Propertied	Many *sitiantes* Middle range public officials Some small businessmen Police
		Workers	
	III	The moderately poor (who have some reliable income)	Clerks Some lesser public officials Some *sitiantes* (*caipira*) Many specialized laborers Some unspecialized laborers
	IVa	The poor	Some specialized laborers Most unspecialized laborers Most *lavradores*
	IVb	The impoverished	Many *lavradores* Some unspecialized labor Paupers

(left axis: Wealth ↑)

NOTE. Horizontal lines delimit rigidity and mobility within the social structure.

difficult to obtain, especially from the wealthier groups who were afraid of tax complications. One local merchant, for instance, who bragged on one occasion that he maintained a stock of merchandise in his store worth one hundred thousand dollars, later claimed that his income averaged only about seven dollars a week. According to information from several sources, however, including land and other property holdings, this group in Cunha numbers about one hundred households, 14 per cent of the urban total. Since this group makes up only about 5 per cent of the total municipal population, the town thus represents a considerable concentration of the region's wealthy seeking the urban services. None of these families is immensely wealthy, however, and it is doubtful if even the richest Cunha families net much more than a few hundred dollars a week.

In addition there are a fairly large number of households in the town which have a reasonable and relatively stable income from occupations as professionals and public servants, or who have some investments in land or commerce. These number about 250 families in Cunha, or about 34 per cent of the urban total. The great majority of the rural middle class, however, the *sitiantes* and minor *fazendeiros* have not come into the town and thus are underrepresented here. The remaining 52 per cent of the urban households are the workers, either urban or rural, who have almost no capital at all aside from a few tools and a house, which they have usually built themselves on ceded land.

The economic stratification pattern, then, shown in Chart IXC, can give at least four groups. At the top are those who have considerable invested capital, the propertied elite. Below them are a large group who have some invested capital or some other regular and reasonably large source of income, often from the state or municipal governments, which would allow the accumulation of capital with time. Below these are the poor, those who are effectively without property or the opportunity to accumulate it, even though they may own a house and perhaps a dab of land. These too, moreover, can be divided between those who have a regular occupation and source of income, and those who do not. At the bottom of the scale is the large group of semi-employed and unemployed, a few of whom are dependent upon family aid or charity for survival.

Classes in the European or Marxist sense of the term as interest groups (Dahrendorf, 1959:238) tend to be rather weakly organized in Brazil. The intense vertical structuring of the social system between patrons and clients tends to discourage attempts at organization and collaboration within the various strata except, sometimes, at the top. Cunha is no exception to this. The local *fazendeiros* are aware of their own interests and work to maintain these. This was as true in the past as in the present. It is important to see, however, that these interests have changed. In the past, when they supplied foodstuffs to the Paraíba Valley, they were predominantly interested in maintaining control over land tenure and an adequate labor supply. The modern ranchers still need to maintain control over land, which they can do through the courts, but they no longer need a large laboring class. Thus they are coming to realize as a class that their main interests are no longer served by the local municipal government but through pressuring the state and national governments as best they can for adequate returns on their products and improved transportation facilities, etc. The most intense pressures in this regard, however, do not come from Cunha, where the *fazendeiros* are still rather poorly organized, but from other regions of the state, such as the Paraíba Valley, though Cunha unwittingly benefits thereby.

It should be noted in addition, that there is very little organization or class awareness among the laboring people of the town. The massive paternalistic weight of the social structure has prevented any effort of the poor from organizing any kind of pressure or conflict groups, and this is coupled with a general pessimistic belief that it would not do much good anyway.

In dealing with the problem of property and stratification in Cunha, the distinction must be made between property as a resource and standard of living. The two are, of course, inter-related—one must be able to afford a high standard of living —but they are not the same thing. A great deal of information about standard of living was obtained in the census of the town of Cunha. This related to both the quality of housing and possession of town services such as water and electricity. In addition each household was given a score based on the num-ber and approximate value of appliances and other objects they owned (see Appendix C). This score gave a rough idea of the degree of "urbanization" of each household since particular emphasis was placed on such means of communication as radios, television, and newspapers and such "conveniences" as refrigerators and showers. None of these items was con-sidered essential to earning a living. Jeeps and trucks, property important to rural life, were considered separately.

It may be said that families scoring at the top of this scale lead lives which would be considered very comfortable by most American and European standards, with gas stoves, in-door plumbing, electric lights, refrigeration, and even televi-sion. These are the families which can afford urban luxuries and live in homes which value between five and forty million *cruzeiros* ($2,500 to $20,000). There are somewhat over sixty of these households in the town. Another hundred or so families are grouped into a middle range of those who can afford many urban conveniences if not luxuries. At the other extreme, at the zero end of the scale, are over 150 households in the town which have almost no urban facilities at all, with the people living on the outskirts of town in little better than huts of *pau-a-pique*. House values for the professionals average more than thirty times the values for the urban poor, and reveal clearly the economic divisions in Cunha (see Appendix C, part 2).

The urban standard of living scores for the various occupa-tional groups in Cunha are summarized in Appendix C, part 1. It is the urban elite, as might be expected, which scores highest in this regard. Most of the professionals and high

officials of the town score near the top, as do more than half
of the major commercial families. The middle-range public
officials, moreover, seem to prefer to place their somewhat
limited resources, perhaps for status reasons, into an urban
life style rather than capital investment. On the other hand,
the rural families, even the biggest landowners, score compara-
tively low in the number of manufactured luxuries they care
to own. Only a handful of *fazendeiros* score at the top, and
two-fifths of the rural elite have low indices. This shows that
the great majority of the *fazendeiros*, including several of the
largest ranchers in the *município*, prefer to put their spare
capital into land and cattle rather than urban conveniences.
The dozen who do score high in this regard, are for the most
part not the largest landowners per se, but descendants of the
old rural elite who have settled permanently in the town and
devote themselves to town as much as rural activities. Two
former *prefeitos* are included in this group, and these are
politically very active individuals. It can readily be seen,
therefore, that a high urban standard of living is not determined by wealth alone, nor is style of life the only indication
of economic strength.

Occupations and Prestige

Prestige is another complex problem in the social sciences,
and tends to be especially important in anthropology when
dealing with the many so called "prestige economies" such as
in Mexico or the American Northwest Coast. Prestige is important in societies or situations where legal institutions are
weak and authority must, as it were, be purchased. It is important in the *caipira* society where it is earned by careful
attention to one's obligations to others. It is less relevant in
highly stratified societies where social position and power are
well defended by law and the police. It will, therefore, be
dealt with only briefly here.

Prestige can have importance in a stratified society through
the mechanism of influence, as has already been pointed out.

It can be an important motivating factor for individuals for this reason, as well as for itself alone: People do like to be respected. In dealing with the interrelations between prestige and power, therefore, there are many complications. In Cunha many very powerful families were not especially well liked by the majority of the population, as was the case with the Lebanese merchants. In addition there were many politicians in the town who were despised by some and adulated by others.

Hutchenson (1960) has pointed out that in São Paulo the highest prestige tends to go to those in the liberal professions and administrative positions.* The high prestige of certain occupations over others may explain the motivation of a number of individuals to seek jobs in the town rather than in the rural zones. It is very likely an important aspect of the great drive to achieve education on the part of many segments of the town society. In this regard it is interesting to note that the liberal professions and primary school teachers carry very high prestige. This point will be examined in Chapter X.

Although the people of Cunha are very conscious of status, there is, as has been mentioned, little awareness of unity of class among them. "We have no classes here" was a common statement made in the town, even though clearly false. The

---

* The rank order of prestige of some selected occupations according to Hutchenson's findings (1960:31) is given below in parentheses:

Doctor (1)	Bookkeeper, clerk (15)
Lawyer (3)	Traveling salesman (15)
Priest (3)	*Sitiante* (15)
Company director (5)	Contractor (16)
Fazendeiro (6)	Policeman (18.5)
Commercial manager (7)	Mechanic (19)
Factory manager (8)	Salesclerk (21)
Primary school teacher (8)	Motorist (21)
Accountant (10.5)	*Pedreiro* (25)
Civil servant in the middle range (12)	Agricultural worker (27)
Owner of a small commercial	
establishment (12)	

most common division that the Cunhenses make among themselves is *os ricos* (the rich) and *nos pobres* (we poor). There is nothing systematic about this, however, since many families who consider themselves *pobres* are considered *ricos* by others still less well off. There does, however, exist a loose social elite in Cunha made up of the old town families and largely descended from the old rural aristocracy. As has been mentioned, these families tend to concentrate in the civil service and commerce, and have some, though limited, representation in the professions and higher officialdom. A number of outsiders, however, are fully accepted into this group, especially if they have education or an important position.

This social elite is very urbanized and members usually have spent a considerable amount of time outside the *município*. It is aware of its superiority in education and life style and also tends to divide the town into two classes, "the ignorant," and "the civilized." The attitude of this group toward the poorer classes varies a great deal. Many of them, especially the professionals, are warmly paternalistic, and really interested in the well-being of the community as a whole. On the other hand, there are many of the commercial upper classes who feel nothing but scorn for the majority of the Cunha population, especially the *caipira* peasants. "Look at me," said one important merchant, "a man of my education and talents living in this rubbish heap of a town."

The social elite, however, is torn by factions—political, personal, and religious—which frequently have little to do with the economic or social realities of the present time. Some of these divisions were so long lasting that they took on the nature of nonviolent feuds, extending into second generations. The anger around political coups and maneuvers frequently was maintained even after the protagonists were gone. Family and political loyalty kept the memories alive. In former times these might have broken out into real feuds, but active violence is no longer acceptable, beyond occasional acts of vandalism or dog poisoning. The gossip of the town, however, is red hot, and very useful to an anthropologist.

Since the basic division is political, each faction has its own bars, hotels, shops, and pharmacies. The split is not carried to the extreme in Cunha that it has been in some Brazilian communities. There are certain major facilities in town, such as the dairy cooperative, bus line, health service, etc., that ride above politics and operate on a contractual basis and are used by all equally. The commercially active groups, more-over, especially the *fazendeiros*, are coming to realize that they have more to gain by cooperating to protect their joint economic interests in the state than they have by petty squab-bles in the town.

The members of the town social elite, despite their divisions, have managed to maintain a degree of their former prestige, at least among themselves, but they no longer have the power that they used to, either political or economic. Thus their influence, with the decline in the personalistic political system and increasing capitalization of the economy, is diminishing. Social position is more and more becoming based upon capital and commerce. This is very much to the distaste of some of the older group. "It used to be," said the same disgruntled merchant, "in the days of Dr. Salvador, there were many people here who knew about music and literature, who were civilized. Now any barefoot *caboclo* with a few *cruzeiros* in his pocket can come in here, put on airs, and pretend that he's as good as anybody."

The old elite still does maintain its own social circle which tends, though in much reduced form, to center on the *Clube*. The traditional *fazendeiros* are fully accepted members of this group, but some of the more modern ranchers, especially those with few town interests and slight education, who worked their own lands, were not fully accepted socially, even if they were noted as *boa gente* ("good people"). This lack of full social ac-ceptance in the town didn't bother these *fazendeiros* too much, as they were too busy making money and buying cattle and land. Most of them in addition had their own social circles, especially the Methodists. Some of the outsiders, moreover, had no great respect for the old town social elite, calling its members, at least in private, "snobs" and "playboys."

Many of the children of the new rural upper class, moreover, were gradually becoming integrated into the urban social elite. One of the sons of a prosperous Methodist rancher has studied in the *ginásio* of Cunha and at the same time has worked for some years in the *forum*. He is respected by the town officials, especially by the judge who values his services very highly. Somewhat to the suprise of his father, he has little interest in ranching or commerce, but hopes eventually to go outside the *município* to study, preferably in law. Here a family which has been economically mobile in the recent past is becoming also socially mobile in the second generation.

Aspects of Race in Cunha

Racially, in both the social and biological senses, Cunha is an extremely interesting community. As was shown in Chapter II, the original *caipira* population of Portuguese and Indian ancestry was modified by the introduction of thousands of African slaves on the great *fazendas* over the centuries. This means that all three of the parent Brazilian stocks are present in Cunha in considerable numbers. The more Indian-appearing population tends to concentrate in the rural zones which are less developed, especially to the north of the *sede*, whereas the Negro population is found in the more commercial regions and occasionally on the outskirts of the *sertão* where there are still living descendants of settlements of escaped slaves.

In the big cities many Paulistas are proud to claim a little Indian ancestry, since it proves the age of their families. In Cunha, however, the people are very touchy about this and deeply resent any implication thay they might be called "*Indios*." Here again it is partly a matter of class as well as color prejudice, since the urban groups in the town are trying to escape the *caipira* tradition. On the other hand, it is rather difficult to tell to what extent color prejudice against Negros and mulattos exists in the community. In this respect, it should be noted that Brazilians conceptualize race differently than do most North Americans. In Cunha one white informant sharply denigrated and ridiculed all those he called "black" (*negro*). When it was pointed out to him that several of his close friends clearly had some African ancestry his reply was, "Oh, yes, but they're not *black*." On further inquiry, the only "black" he could think of in the town turned out to be the local *cabo*, head of the state police.

In Cunha, as in the rest of Brazil, formal restrictions on the basis of race or color largely do not exist. It may be recalled that Doctor Salvador, the political chief of Cunha for some fifty years, and a federal deputy and senator, was a dark mulatto from Bahia. On the other hand, according to many informants, white as well as dark, a significant amount of prejudice against *gente de côr*, people of color, does exist. Emilio Willems reports that in 1945 the *Clube* did not accept "people of color," although he also mentions that one dark mulatto, the adopted son of an important family, was a member (1947:71). At the present time there are a few colored members of the *Clube* and two or three colored families which seem to be fairly smoothly integrated into the town society. Some of the colored population claimed that there were numerous subtle pressures against them, others were not so sure. "Who can tell," said one colored youth, "if at a party a girl refuses to dance with you, whether it's due to prejudice or just that she feels tired."

In Cunha, as elsewhere in Brazil, color is one factor in determining prestige, influence, and social position, but it is by no means the only factor. Political and economic authority are even more important, and the fact is that the Negro started out at the bottom of the scale in both, as slaves, and the struggle upward has been an extremely difficult one. Table IXB gives some indication of the racial pattern of the town.

Table IXB. Occupations and Color in Cunha

Occupation	White Number	White Per cent	Nonwhite Number	Nonwhite Per cent
URBAN				
High officials	10	100	0	0
Professionals	12	86	2	14
Urban entrepreneurs . . .	32	94	2	6
Small businessmen				
Shop owners	22	96	1	4
Garage owners	3	100	0	0
Craftsmen with shops . .	15	94	1	6
Motorists with trucks . .	14	93	1	7
Rural businessmen . . .	15	79	4	21
Service occupations				
Public officials	32	82	7	18
State police	3	37	5	63
Shop clerks	9	90	1	10
Labor—specialized				
State highway workers				
(D.E.R.)	18	69	8	31
Motorists	13	72	5	28
Other	11	41	16	59
Labor—unspecialized				
Government laborers . .	26	64	13	36
Pedreiros	32	52	29	48
Domestics	11	38	18	62
No occupation	6	55	5	45
RURAL				
Fazendeiros				
Major landowners . . .	58	95	3	5
Moderate landowners . .	55	89	7	11
Widows	11	92	1	8
Sitiantes				
Commercial	42	89	5	11
Traditional	10	77	3	23
Retired	4	100	0	0
Lavradores				
With some land	17	74	6	26
Landless	58	56	45	44

The most notable thing is the very heavy concentration of the colored in the manual occupations, over half in some groups. The sharpest distinction is in the matter of property. The majority of the nonwhite population do not have much in the way of major property in Cunha, either in land or in capital. Only 10 per cent of the property owners in Cunha, whether it be in land or commerce, are colored whereas 40 per cent of the laboring class is nonwhite. Even in the propertied groups, those enterprises which are owned by nonwhites tend to be undercapitalized. In a country where it is said that "money whitens," the majority of colored in Cunha thus remain dark.

Chapter X

Changing Patterns of Education

The school as a separate formal educational institution is one of the key elements of urbanization for both pre-industrial and industrial cities. It might, in fact, be pointed out that a formal educational system is an essential part of the process of social evolution. Among non-urban peoples, including peasantry, education of the young is carried out largely by each family. The division of labor in such societies is minimal, the technical knowledge within the culture is slight and can be learned by observation either by watching adult members within the family or by serving an apprenticeship with a craftsman. Long periods of specialized education are not necessary to maintain the culture, therefore, and literacy is frequently considered something alien and useless.

Schools usually become necessary with the development of urban life. Literacy becomes an essential adjunct to trade and commerce, and to the maintenance of the administrative structures of the agrarian state. In the pre-industrial city, as Sjoberg points out (1960:289-306), the schools are few and are designed to train the experts—priests, merchants, and others with literate skills—necessary to keep the city administration running. In addition the schools serve to give children of the governing landed class distinctive social skills to enhance their authority over the bulk of the population. The great majority of the rural population are deliberately excluded from formal education and the advantages of literacy. Sjoberg says that such schools are thus usually small, and often tightly integrated with the religious structure. They rely heavily upon authority and rote learning rather than experimentation in the form of teaching. These schools tend to favor education of males rather than females and stress the humanities, the "sacred books" of religion and history, rather than the sciences. In short, the pre-industrial school is designed to impart the knowledge and values of the past to those destined to dominate in the future.

An industrial society, however, depends upon the technical skills of its people, its progress depends upon innovation. Lenski says:

In advanced industrial societies, illiteracy and ignorance are handicaps not only for the illiterate and ignorant, but for the rest of society as well . . . . there is good reason to believe that the level of productivity of the economy is closely related to the level of education of the labor force. Hence, the privileged classes have a vested interest in providing educational opportunity for all— a situation radically different from that in agrarian societies (1966:390).

Industrial society, therefore, must have a mass educational system with emphasis upon sciences and experimentation.

The lack of an adequate educational structure is one of industrial Brazil's greatest problems. As Werner Baer has stated, "It [the lag in educational development] will result in severe shortages of trained manpower in the growing industrial sector, possibly leading to reductions in the potential growth rate, and it will also result in higher costs to industry. . . ." (1965:188). The basic problem is, as Charles Wagley has shown (1963:204-5), that the Brazilian educational system is pre-industrial in form while much of the country is becoming economically industrialized. The end result is a staggering educational lag which puts trained people, even poorly trained people, at a premium everywhere. The state of São Paulo, as the most highly industrialized region in Brazil, is coming to realize the problem and recently has begun to put some of its considerable resources into educational activities. Thus this state has the best educational system and the highest literacy rate in the country. Even this system, however, seriously lags behind the need.

Development of Schools in Cunha

In Cunha, the development of the educational system demonstrates more strikingly than any other evidence the spread of urban culture and mass society. Education can be characterized as the single most important service which has drawn the landowning middle classes into the town. Seventy per cent of the Cunha *fazendeiros* and *sitiantes* living in town who stated why they had moved from the country said they did it *"para ensinar os filhos"* ("to instruct the children"). By this generally they meant study in the local secondary school, the *ginásio*, since there are many rural primary schools. In addition, however, there is a widespread and probably valid belief that the *grupo escolar*, the town primary school, is superior to those in the rural zones.

For most of its history the educational system in Cunha followed very closely the "pre-industrial" pattern noted by Sjoberg. Schools were designed for the small town elite, the urban commercial and professional classes, those who could afford to send their children outside of the *município* for further study. The really powerful traditional rural elite, the *coroneis*, also frequently encouraged professional education for their sons—a fact which led many of these young people to remain in the large Brazilian cities, and thus contributed to the decline of the landed patriarchy in Cunha.

Formal education was not a part of the life of the *caipira* society as it was for the townsmen. Formal schooling in fact probably was not necessary for the isolated *bairros*, and a school did not traditionally make up a part of the neighborhood center. Further, there was not much effort on the part of the urban society to supply educational opportunities. In 1884, for example, there were only four rural schools in the entire *município* for a rural population at least as large as it is at the present time. Even today in Cunha some of the more traditional *caipira* families look upon formal education as rather foolish and something for the idle rich. At times among the very poor rural and even town families, the author found that questions about education and literacy were sometimes met with laughter and an attitude that for a poor family a strong back is more important than a strong head. This attitude reflects the sharp separation between the two cultures which existed in the past.

The schools, then, at the end of the last century, were an urban phenomenon. The great majority of the farming population including the *sitiantes* and other minor landholders, seemed to feel that education was unnecessary, although they sometimes encouraged literacy for the clear advantages the literate man has in commerce. For the most part, the schools were by, for, and of the patriarchy. The *Almanach* of 1884 shows that the town in that year had five school teachers. The integration of the school system with the local landed elite is shown by the fact that the school inspector was an honorary *capitão* (captain) and the senior teacher an honorary *tenente* (lieutenant) in the state militia, both sure signs of landed wealth. The inspector was also a *vereador*. At least two of the other teachers belonged to important traditional families. A few *fazendeiros* sought to train their sons in a profession in the expectation that they would return to practice in Cunha.

In 1913 the state government, pushed by Dr. Salvador, built a school building in the town. Previously teaching had gone on in several private homes. In that year there were only four classes, one for each grade, and four teachers— fewer than there had been in 1884. The school system remained very static; even in 1940 there were only four teachers and 145 students in the town of Cunha.

Until 1940, therefore, the traditional pre-industrial pattern was largely unchanged, with the growing *caipira* rural population neither pressuring for nor receiving formal schooling. Increased commercial opportunities, however, and the disasters which befell many *caipira* families over legal ownership of land, made the value of at least some education increasingly apparent to the growing number of commercial farmers. Literacy was important to protect their rights, commercially, legally, and politically. In the town, moreover, the growing group of government workers were among the first to stress local education, since in many cases they were technical bureaucrats and their jobs depended upon their learned skills. Thus there was always the hope that further education might mean further advancement for themselves or their children. These "middle" sectors of the Cunha society began sending their children to school in ever-increasing numbers and began to put increasing pressure on their political representatives to persuade the state government to build and staff new schools.

By 1945 the movement was well under way. At that time the number of urban teachers had increased from four to seven and the number of students from 145 to 255. Every year since then the number of students has gone up, despite, it should be remembered, a stable population size. In 1965 the *grupo escolar* in Cunha had 754 students. This represents a more than fivefold increase in urban matriculation in 25 years. At the present time the resources of the old school are stretched to the breaking point. While there are now twenty teachers instead of four, the old 1913 building has not been augmented and it is so crowded that the school has gone on to three three-hour shifts daily, 8 to 11 o'clock in the morning, 11:15 to 2:15, and 2:30 to 5:30. The *ginásio* occupies the building at night.

The educational explosion has not been limited to the urban zone. Whereas there were four rural schools in 1884, by 1945 this number had increased to twenty, with 601 students. In 1965 there were two additional four-year *grupos* in the *muni-*

cípio, each about the size of the *grupo escolar* in Cunha itself in 1940. The village of Campos Novos had four teachers and 150 students, and the *bairro* of Paraitinga, where the lumber company is located, had four teachers and 140 pupils. There are in addition 66 three-year rural primary schools, each of which has its own teacher. Of these there are 16 "regular" rural schools which have a total of 543 students and there are 50 "emergency" rural schools which have a total of 1,160 students.

The "emergency" schools are important as they reveal some of the lag between the formal educational system and educational demand. These schools are established in the *bairros* only on petition of the *bairro* residents themselves and only if the *bairro* agrees to find space for the school and housing for the teacher, as the state has little money for school construction. In 1966 four more such schools were added. Thus a great deal of rural education in Cunha is at least partly supported locally.

In summary, therefore, there are nominally in Cunha at the present time about 94 teachers and 2,747 students in the primary grades. About 10 per cent of the rural population and 20 per cent of the urban population are in school. This, as will be shown, is a somewhat excessively idealized picture of education in the region but, despite this fact, the figures do show the extent of the dominance of urban middle class ideas of education in the *município.*

While the primary schools have brought urban education to the majority of rural families, the most important educational development in the town was the establishment of the *ginásio,* the four-year secondary school, in 1957. By that year the pressure for creating a secondary school in Cunha was intense. Members of the professional and commercial classes disliked the considerable expense of sending their children to towns in the valley for education beyond the primary grades, and many of the poorer members of the local middle classes who

could not afford secondary education hoped that a local high school might help the advancement of their children. Here too the official state system lagged behind the demand. After several fruitless years of pressuring the state government, a number of town officials, led by the local judge, founded the school with private and municipal funds. Most of the early teachers in the *ginásio* were members of the local community with special skills who volunteered to teach what they could.

The high school opened in 1958 with two grades and 80 students. At the time of the study it had four grades and 194 students. The state took over its administration in 1959 but six years later it still had the atmosphere of a community affair. The only professional full-time teacher brought in from outside the *município* was the director. All the other teachers have regular urban daytime jobs and teach in the *ginásio* at night. Thus the local dentist taught science, one of the pharmacists, English, and the vicar taught Portuguese. While few besides the director himself were fully qualified as secondary school teachers, the quality of education, at least in some subjects, seemed fairly good.

According to many of the residents of Cunha the *ginásio*, more than anything else, has enlarged the intellectual horizons of the community. There had always been a small educated group in the town: judge, physicians, lawyers, pharmacists, etc.; but these in the past had tended to move in their own circles and form their own elite society with headquarters in the club. The *ginásio* for the first time brought these educated adults of the community into constant contact with the young people of many sectors of the population. The result was, it seems, stimulation on both sides. The fact that there are now in Cunha several hundred young adults with eight years of education has definitely increased the awareness of the community with regard to the existence of national and international concerns, even though the level of sophistication is still not very high. One result has been a blunting of social differences, par-

ticularly with regard to manner and language as young people from rural and working families study under the town intelligentsia. In other words, the *ginásio*, probably more than the primary schools, has had an intensely urbanizing effect. One of the local lawyers said to the author, "The old people here, the *caipira*, they don't know anything else, they don't want to change. They're afraid to change. But the young people, that's something different. They know what's going on. The future of Cunha is in the hands of its young people."

There is good evidence that intellectual achievement is honored to some degree in Cunha. The festivities surrounding graduation of the *ginásio* students are the major social events of the year among the urban groups. The graduation ceremony itself is one of the very few events which unites all of the leading citizens of the town, regardless of occupation or party affiliation. The fact that the town elite is so intimately involved with the *ginásio* may partly explain its high importance. This is coupled with the fact that the town's religious leaders, both Catholic and Methodist, are intensely interested in education. The ceremonies witnessed in 1965 were held in the local cinema, the only building large enough to hold all the guests. Almost everyone of importance was there and the vicar, at that time acting director, presided. The degrees were awarded in order of scholastic achievement, with prizes awarded to the first and second place. As a general rule, the girls, though younger, were much more academically successful than the boys, a sharp difference from the pre-industrial pattern. One of these girls, considered one of the best students in town, expressed a real interest in studying medicine in São Paulo, a thing which would have been unheard-of in traditional Brazil.

The founding of the *ginásio*, as well as the flood of new students at all levels, has brought about changes in the structure of the local school system. Traditionally the school was dominated by a few families of the local elite. One family in particular, closely allied with the Catholic Church, had virtual control of primary education in Cunha. Three of its members were part of the school staff, including the director and assistant director of the *grupo escolar*. This family was, therefore, largely in charge of appointment and location of teachers so that, in the past, members of families of the town elite received favorable treatment. This pattern is currently changing. The need for new teachers is vastly greater than the number of qualified or even partly qualified people available in Cunha. Thus many new teachers have been brought in from the Paraíba Valley. These people are often better trained than the local teachers, although frequently they are assigned to the rural zones.

Also important is the fact that the director of the *ginásio* tends to dominate, *ex officio*, the local educational structure. He, however, must by law be a fully qualified professional for the school to continue to receive state aid. He must, in other words, have a university education, and thus has usually been a trained specialist brought in from outside the *município* rather than a member of the local elite. For many years this office was held by a priest, but upon his death in 1965 a new director, more oriented toward the sciences, was appointed. In this way, bit by bit, the educational system of Cunha is moving away from control by the local elite and even by the Church, and becoming a professional system directed by the state and federal governments.

In Cunha, as in all Brazilian communities, the federal government sets standards, chooses textbooks, and gives examinations. Many of the elitist educational elements which remain are part of the national system and reflect the basically preindustrial orientation of the Brazilian educational system. Thus uniforms are required of all students, which puts a strain on the resources of the poorer families. Sciences generally are not stressed and for the most part rate memorization of a standard textbook is the main method of teaching. In addition rural and lower class students are handicapped by a language barrier.

The schools put great stress on learning proper Portuguese, and there are no special classes to help those who have grown up in families where one of the many rural Cunha dialects were spoken. The grading system, moreover, is ruthless. It is not uncommon for half the first year class to fail and have to repeat the year. One rural resident remarked that he had ten years of education, all in the first grade. The director of the *grupo escolar* said that she tried to see that no one passed the first year who did not know how to read the language. While a case can be made for this attitude, it nonetheless puts a burden on the rural and lower-class child. This is, however, a national pattern and not specific in Cunha (Wagley, 1963: 213).

Since education is set by fairly rigid national norms the teacher has little margin for initiative and teaching tends to become a routinization of memorized material from a text. A few skilled teachers, notably the director of the *ginásio* and the vicar, were noted for their ability to liven up the pattern, but even with their help few develop out of such a system a real interest in learning. Instead there develops what Brazilians call *bacharelismo*: the desire to obtain a degree for the sake of having a degree. This is especially important if the degree has economic value.

There are some mitigating factors which show the beginning of a mass educational philosophy in Cunha. Uniforms are required, but shoes are not, and it is usually not too difficult for a poor family to make the uniforms. In addition there is some effort to supply poor children with uniforms and scholastic materials, even though the quantity is far behind the need. Also the *grupo* in Cunha tries to supply, with American aid of powdered milk and flour, a lunch for all their pupils, an important factor in encouraging children from poor families to attend.

The quality of education in the rural schools varies a great deal, depending on the quality of the teacher. In theory every primary-school teacher should have eleven years of education: four primary grades, four years in the *ginásio*, and three years in a teachers' college or *escola normal*. Most school teachers come from the cities and find difficulty adjusting to life in the rural zones. Thus the majority of rural teachers are either very young and lacking in seniority so that they are sent to Cunha by the general inspector of education in Guaratinguetá, or they are people who live in the rural *bairro*, and since they have some education they get the job whether fully qualified or not. These are often the wives of *fazendeiros*. The result is that some of the best as well as some of the worst teachers in the *município* are found in the rural schools. Some *bairros* go to great effort to attract and hold a qualified teacher and not infrequently the finest building in the region is the school. Other schools, however, are falling into ruin. A *bairro* which will not maintain its school properly, however, will rapidly find it shut down by the state.

The *bairro* of Vale do Norte is a good example. This is one of the largest *bairros* in the *município*, yet also one of the most isolated and thus most traditional. The area is occupied mainly by *caipira* landholders and there is relatively little commercial production. Yet the *bairro* has built one of the finest rural schools in Cunha: a neat, whitewashed building on a hill dominating the valley. The building is double, half of it forming a single-room schoolhouse, and the other a house for the teacher. The *bairro* has been lucky in attracting one of the best of the region's new young teachers, Dona Miranda, a friendly, homely woman, raised and educated in the Paraíba Valley, who is married to one of the local rural businessmen. She, although very concerned for the welfare of the children of the *bairro*, is a very urban young woman and has found some difficulty adjusting to the rural conditions of the area. To make her feel more at home, therefore, local residents have donated a gas stove, apparently the only one in the *bairro*, and have gone to considerable effort to make her life comfortable.

They have, for example, planted flowers on all sides of the school building. She appreciates their efforts, but still says that she misses the city life. Rural life in Cunha without electricity, conveniences, or *movimento,* and where most social activity ceases at sundown, is understandably difficult for a young person raised in the vibrant Paulista cities. Fortunately her husband owns a jeep which enables them to visit the town fairly often. The case, however, illustrates some of the problems of rural education in Cunha and the desire of many of the people to obtain it.

School teachers are poorly paid in São Paulo, as seems to be the case everywhere. Cunha, however, is a poor region, and the salary of a teacher, from Cr. $80,000 to Cr. $180,000 a month, seems considerable in an area where the standard daily wage is only Cr. $1,000. Thus there is great interest in obtaining the education necessary to be able to qualify as a teacher, namely the degree of the *escola normal.* This is the least degree which is economically valuable. The new middle classes of Cunha have no scholastic tradition and hence little interest in higher education for its own sake. The lack of industry in Cunha means that a technical education means little; there is not even very much interest in agronomy. But the *normal* degree means that the holder can at any time get a well-paying job with the state government. This is thus the goal of most higher education in Cunha. There are some exceptions. Some families, especially some of the Syrian and Italian merchant families and a few of the *fazendeiros,* are willing to underwrite a university education for their children, but these are few.

Usually the daughters in a family are encouraged to seek the *normal* degree on the theory that the sons will follow their fathers into agriculture or at least will always be able to find some kind of job, whereas a girl cannot. Moreover, a girl so educated is much more likely to marry well, as she can always supplement her husband's income by teaching. Thus even a family with limited resources will go to great effort to educate its daughters before its sons, a fact which has had some interesting social consequences. In some families the wife as a teacher actually makes more money than her husband. It has given the woman economic independence for the first time and an alternative to the traditional pattern of an early arranged marriage. Education, therefore, has great appeal to the more urbanized young ladies of the region. The result has been an increasing sophistication on their part, especially since several have studied in the *escolas normais* of São Paulo or the Paraíba Valley.

Felicia de Castro is the daughter of a well-to-do rancher in the Methodist section of the *município*. She studied for eight years in Cunha, but has just obtained her teaching degree from a state *colégio* in São Paulo. In dress, mannerisms, and speech she is highly urbanized, even *"chique,"* much more than the other members of her family, and she could easily pass for a student from any big Brazilian city. She has no desire, however, to live in the city, but prefers to remain in Cunha with her family and longtime friends. "The city is far too noisy and busy; it's difficult to make friends there," she said. She has been assigned to teach in a rural school some distance from her home, but it is problematical how long she will stay. She is already engaged to one of the young men in town.

The education beyond the primary grades, formerly restricted to a very small elite group, has thus become more and more important in the eyes of the community. In 1945, according to Emilio Willems (1947:23), there were eleven students from Cunha studying in secondary schools in Guaratinguetá and Lorena and two students taking advanced courses in Rio de Janeiro. In late 1965 there were nearly two hundred secondary students in Cunha itself and thirty-eight Cunhenses studying for higher degrees outside the *município*. Of these, fifteen were men and twenty-three were women, most of the latter studying to be teachers. The majority, 60 per cent, were studying in the nearby valley cities of Guaratinguetá and Lorena, but there were four students in the city of São Paulo itself and a few as far away as Minas Gerais. Interestingly, no one, at the time the census was made in 1965, was studying in Rio de Janeiro. The great majority of students outside the *município* came from well-to-do families, but there were a few families of very slender means who were able to support a student outside of Cunha. This was usually done with the aid of relatives living in the city where the student was at school and with whom he could stay.

Because of the clear value of the *normal* degree and the difficulties and expense of sending a child outside of the *municipo* for study, political pressure built up for the creation of an *escola normal* in Cunha. "Paratí already has an *escola normal*," was the cry. "There's a town and a state which knows how to get things done. What's the matter with this administration here? We've got more people than Paratí. What's holding up the state government?" As was the case with the *ginásio*, once again the state educational system lagged behind local demand, and in 1966 for the second time the people of Cunha went their own way and founded a school with municipal and private funds. This time it was the local mayor who organized the school, thus seeking to enhance his political authority. He was aided by the *ginásio* director, who became acting head of the new school.

The ultimate effects of the new *escola normal* on the educational system and patterns of Cunha still cannot be assessed. Much depends upon whether the state government will be willing to take over the costs and administration of it within the next few years, since it is doubtful if the municipal government alone can support the costs of such a school indefinitely. If the school can maintain itself, it will mean that a great many teachers will be brought in from outside the *município*, and this will further increase the trend to professionalization of the school system in Cunha. On the other hand, the new graduates will probably replace many of the teachers now in the local schools who come from outside the community. The major opposition to the new school, as was the case with the *ginásio,* came from the old elite who saw their authority and positions threatened.

The quality of education in such a school is problematical. It may turn out to be merely a boondoggle to get *normal* degrees and state jobs for local people, or it may truly enhance the level of education in the community, as the *ginásio* did. The ultimate decisions regarding the quality of education in Cunha rests with the state government, which can encourage the school and develop it, or can ruin it.

Patterns of Education in Cunha

From the census made in the town and suburbs of Cunha, the number of years of education of each citizen was correlated with a number of factors, such as age, sex, and urban-rural occupation. Further analysis of quantity of education with occupational class was done on the basis of the occupation of the heads of households. Some of the results are tabulated below.

Table XA shows the average number of years of education

Table XA. Average Number of Years of Education

Years of Age	Urban Male	Rural Male	Urban Female	Rural Female	Total Male	Total Female	Total
70+	3.10	1.00	1.07	0.20	2.29	0.85	1.72
60–69 ...	2.20	1.32	2.12	1.25	1.73	1.60	1.67
50–59 ...	3.16	1.54	1.90	1.82	2.23	1.78	2.05
40–49 ...	2.78	1.88	2.08	1.36	2.26	1.68	1.99
30–39 ...	3.56	2.58	3.30	2.44	3.14	2.93	3.00
20–29 ...	3.85	2.96	3.78	3.54	3.48	3.68	3.58
10–19* ..	3.60	3.18	4.04	3.44	3.37	3.61	3.54
Total	3.46	2.60	3.33	2.78	3.02	3.06	3.03

* It should be noted that an average of 50 per cent of these students are still in school.

of all townspeople over ten years old correlated with age, sex, and rural-urban occupation. Table XB shows percentage of

Table XB. Percentage of Total Illiteracy

Years of Age	Urban Male	Rural Male	Urban Female	Rural Female	Total Male	Total Female	Total
70+	42%	50%	66%	80%	45%	80%	59%
60–69	26%	47%	63%	56%	38%	58%	47%
50–59	16%	30%	50%	35%	24%	43%	33%
40–49	27%	25%	39%	44%	26%	42%	33%
30–39	16%	22%	23%	26%	18%	24%	21%
20–29	7%	18%	18%	22%	12%	20%	16%
10–19	8%	11%	10%	13%	10%	13%	12%
Total	10%	20%	24%	25%	17%	25%	21%

total illiteracy among the same group. Table XC shows the percentage with more than a primary education, and Table XD the percentage with more than a secondary education.

Table XC. Table of More Than Primary Education

Years of Age	Urban Male	Rural Male	Urban Female	Rural Female	Total Male	Total Female	Total
70+	16%	0	0	0	10%	0	6%
60–69	3%	0	12%	0	1%	5%	3%
50–59	12%	0	2%	2%	5%	2%	4%
40–49	8%	2%	7%	2%	5%	4%	4%
30–39	12%	11%	15%	4%	11%	10%	10%
20–29	19%	8%	22%	17%	14%	20%	17%
10–19	21%	18%	27%	21%	19%	20%	20%
Total	16%	10%	18%	13%	13%	14%	13%

Certain anomalies exist. As has been noted, because of the high number of people who repeat years, the number of years of education is not always an accurate record of an individual's final educational accomplishments. Moreover, the number of functional illiterates is considerably higher than appears from Table XB. Individuals who claimed they were literate yet had

Table XD. Table of More Than Secondary Education

Years of Age	Urban Male	Rural Male	Urban Female	Rural Female	Total Male	Total Female	Total
70+	5%	0	0	0	3%	0	2%
60–69	0	0	8%	0	0	0	0
50–59	8%	0	2%	2%	3%	2%	3%
40–49	7%	0	4%	1%	3%	4%	3%
30–39	7%	3%	8%	3%	5%	5%	5%
20–29	6%	2%	11%	3%	4%	8%	5%
10–19	3%	3%	5%	1%	2%	3%	2%
Total	5%	1%	7%	2%	3%	4%	4%

not attended school were arbitrarily given one-half year of education in the ratings. Many of these people, while legally literate and able to vote, can do little more than sign their own names. The tables of illiteracy show only those who could not even do that. Thus in fact the educational system in Cunha is not as good as might seem from either the tables or figures on the total number of students. A great many children, especially in the rural zones, are or have been students in name only, attending school only when convenient. Many of these learn little more than a minimal literacy.

Accepting, however, the somewhat over-optimistic nature of the study, certain interesting points can still be made. Most important, the tables offer convincing evidence that the people of Cunha are better educated now than they were in the past. This is especially true of those who have rural occupations. Even the rural lower classes, the field hands and sharecroppers, who live in the town are better educated now than in the past. Thus of this class only 30 per cent of the young people are illiterate in contrast to 80 per cent of the older people. The 10- to 20-year-olds, in addition, have an average of two years of education, whereas their parents and grandparents have only a few months' average education.

The high average education for urban males of all ages is

due to the presence in the town of a highly educated group of professional men. As a general rule, however, young people in Cunha tend to be distinctly better educated than their elders. This is largely an urban phenomenon, however, since frequently the older people were raised in the rural zones. The new emphasis for the younger women to obtain the *normal* degree is reflected in the tables. Traditionally the women were consistently more poorly educated than the men, and the charts show this among the older women. On the other hand, the young females of Cunha are actually somewhat better educated than the males.

Education in Cunha is also correlated with class and occupation. The best educated group in Cunha are the professional families. Extensive formal education is, in fact, a prerequisite for admission into this group. In this class the men average eleven and a half years of study and the women nine years. These families also greatly stress education for their children and can usually afford to pay for it. All but one of the 21 young people in these families had finished or were studying in the *ginásio,* and nearly 70 per cent have had some years of higher education as well.

Among the commercial families, some stress education for their children while others do not. As a general rule, the families most interested in education are those of Lebanese extraction. These families began as traders and peddlers and with time they have become economically well-to-do. Almost without exception these families have encouraged their children to study to the maximum of their ability, and their descendants have entered the professions on an important scale. They have thus, in a sense, played a structural role in Brazil similar to that of the Jewish people in the United States, and have suffered some of the same opprobrium as a result. "Those Turks, all they think about is making more and more money off the backs of us poor folks. Thieves. They think they're better than the rest of us because they've robbed us," are all comments that have been made about the Lebanese and even Italian businessmen of Cunha.

Interestingly such expletives are seldom used against the professional people of Lebanese descent. The anger against the "Turks" is directed mainly against those who make a profit. There are doctors, lawyers, and *fazendeiros* of similar origin in Cunha who are smoothly integrated into the local society. Their background is never referred to and they are largely accepted as old Cunhenses. Perhaps the most popular physician in Cunha is a *moreno* of partly Lebanese origin. The author was, in fact, considerably surprised on analysis of the census material to find out how many of the local elite were of foreign extraction. It seems that hostility is based more upon economics and occupation than upon actual origin. This may be one of the motivating factors which makes these families stress professional education.

The state and municipal officials and civil servants tend to put considerable emphasis upon education. Several of the state officials with temporary appointments in Cunha actually prefer to live in the Paraíba Valley and commute to their jobs in Cunha, partly because they regard the Cunha school system as inadequate. Many of these have professional educations and among this group the majority of young people are studying for advanced degrees. The civil servants at the intermediate level, the clerks, secretaries, police, and teachers, are also interested in education. Many of them, especially the children of politically influential families, are themselves students. Since these are families of trained bureaucrats, education is important to them, yet they generally are not wealthy enough to send their children outside the *município* to study. Thus, while 50 per cent of the young people of this class have some secondary education, only 10 per cent have studied further.

The laboring classes frequently do have an interest in education, but more often than not feel it an unattainable ideal. Their main concern for themselves and their children is earning enough live and there is little interest in devoting several years to study, even if the ultimate economic advantages are known to be considerable. The young people of these families must frequently work to make ends meet, and if they leave the *município* it is more often to find work than to study. There are some notable exceptions. One widow with very slender resources has managed to put her only daughter through *escola normal,* and another laboring family has two children studying outside the *município* for advanced degrees. These cases are few, however, and can only be done in families where there is fierce determination to get ahead. In general it can be said that while education is one key to social mobility in the state of São Paulo, this is not the case as yet in Cunha. The bureaucratic structures are still too traditionally organized. Appointments are still based largely on family connections rather than ability, although this is gradually changing. The opportunities for the moderately well educated are slight in Cunha and highest training, as for lawyers or physicians, is beyond the reach of most youth of the region.

Among the rural families only a very small number of *fazendeiros* have shown any interest in educating their sons beyond the primary level. There is, however, considerable interest among these families in training their daughters to be teachers. Of the families of *fazendeiros* who live in town, nearly 20 per cent of the girls between the ages of 10 and 29 years have gone beyond the secondary school stage, but only 6 per cent of the boys have done so. Of those *fazendeiros* who live in the rural zones, none of the sons have studied beyond the *ginásio* level, but 10 per cent of the daughters have. The least educated group in Cunha are the rural field hands, the *lavradores.* Fifty per cent of them are totally illiterate and only 3 per cent have entered the *ginásio.* Many of these are *caipira* families with little interest in the urban school system.

Table XE briefly summarizes the relationship between education, illiteracy, and occupational cases in Cunha.

Table XE. Education of Occupational Classes in Cunha
(*Ten years or older*)

Class	Average Number of Years of Education			Percentage of Illiteracy
	Male	*Female*	*Total*	
Professional	11.45	8.70	10.00	0
High-level officials	7.75	8.10	7.95	0
Important commercial families	4.29	4.73	4.50	5
Intermediate public servants .	4.55	4.46	4.50	2
Small businessmen	3.20	3.78	3.46	10
Specialized labor	3.36	2.66	2.83	23
Unspecialized labor	2.20	2.02	2.10	34
Fazendeiros				
Major landholders	3.65	4.60	4.12	4
Moderate landholders . . .	3.30	3.55	3.45	8
Sitiantes				
Commercial	2.91	2.74	2.82	14
Traditional	2.22	1.94	2.10	25
Lavradores				
With land	2.06	1.57	1.82	31
Without land	1.37	1.31	1.34	50

It may be said that the educational system in Cunha has come a long way from its original pre-industrial origins. Formal education is an aspect of urban identification, so that it is difficult for any individual to relate to any of the other urban systems without some prior contact with the educational system; that is, in the form of literacy. Education is thus the key to entrance into or manipulation of the urban bureaucratic structures. Thus the fact that the number of people in the schools of Cunha has increased from one per cent in 1940 to 13 per cent today reveals the extent of the transformation which has gone on in Cunha.

This growth, however, has largely been only an expansion in literacy. The basic problem is that the change is still in its preliminary stages. The great rural majority, landed and landless alike, have shown little interest in technical education to improve their agricultural production. They have merely been content with sufficient education to defend their commercial and political rights. Cunha has yet to produce one professional agronomist, although some of the young people have some interest in this. As a general rule, therefore, the educational system in Cunha does not reflect the realities of Cunha life. The majority of rural people still learn their occupations the traditional way—in the family. The schools are still largely geared to urban leisure activities rather than rural professional activities, and until this changes, the educational system will not truly reach the majority of the people in Cunha. Until this system begins to train agricultural specialists for the rural areas, Brazil's agriculture cannot properly serve a dynamic industrial society.

Chapter XI

Religion and the Churches of Cunha

The full role of "religion" in any community is an immensely complex matter. Whole books could be devoted to it and there is no space here to examine all of the rich and multifold aspects of the *caipira* religious tradition. This discussion will concentrate, as in other parts of the book, upon social dynamics to show what effect the rapid changes which have taken place in Cunha have had on religious expression in the region, and on the organization of churches within the *município*. The fundamental change which has taken place in the pattern of religious life in Cunha is an increasing orthodoxy of worship and belief at the expense of the local "folk" elements. As in the case of politics, economics, and education, the rural people are in increasing contact with the metropolitan institutions in religion as well. There is increasing contact with the formal national churches of Brazil. The notable growth of Protestantism within the *município* has only encouraged this contact.

There are four formally organized churches in Cunha, each with its own house of worship and each officially linked to the large national and international religious organization of the same name. These are, in order of importance, the Roman Catholic (*Igreja Católica*), the Methodist (*Igreja Metodista do Brasil*), the Assembly of God (*Assembléia de Deus*), and the Christian Congregation (*Congragação Cristã*). The last two are very small in Cunha and will be considered together as Pentecostal churches. There are also a handful of Spiritualists in Cunha, but they are not formally organized.

Church History and Organization

Roman Catholic. The Parish of Cunha is a part of the Roman Catholic Diocese of Lorena. Formal authority from the Vatican is vested in the bishop. Since the bishop rarely visits Cunha, most matters pertaining to the Church are decided by the vicar. Membership rolls are not kept for the Catholic Church, as they are for some of the Protestant sects, but in Brazil almost anyone who is not formally a member of another church is automatically considered a Roman Catholic.

In discussing the religion of the people of Cunha it is important that we distinguish between orthodox and heterodox members of the Catholic Church. Traditionally in the past, the formal Catholic organization located in the *Matriz* and headed by a priest was nominally the church of all the people of the *município*. In actual fact, however, it served mainly as the religious organization of the town, the urban part of the "folk" society. The peasantry, the *caipira*, had only occasional contacts with this formal system, usually, as has been shown in Chapter III, at the times of the *bairro* festivals. During most of the year the local *bairro* chapels were left largely to themselves, and an extensive local folk religious pattern developed, being made up of a combination of Catholic, Folk Portuguese, and African elements, as was examined in Chapter III. What is important to note is the fact that only in the town did the people have any continuous direct contact with the full panoply of the Catholic Church. The rural zones were largely on their own, and this isolation probably was partly responsible for the very early success of Protestant Missions in the region.

The early history of the parish is in a sense the history of the town of Cunha. The two developed together. The original chapel erected in this region was built over 250 years ago on a site about 8 kilometers south of the present *sede*. By the beginning of the eighteenth century, a small settlement had grown up around this church, but the site was unsatisfactory and the first regular vicar sought another location for a new parish church. This would be nearer to the crossroads and to his brother's property which extended close to the present town-site. According to legend (Willems, 1947:14), an image of the Virgin Mary disappeared three times from its place in the chapel and was found on the site of the present *matriz*. This disappearance was declared a "miracle" and the priest and his *fazendeiro* brother determined that a great new church should rise on the site. Many local landowners contributed the labor of their slaves to the construction, and after some years the enormous *matriz* was completed. In 1749 the village which had grown up around the construction site was named the parish of *N.S. de Conceição*. This village grew up rapidly and soon became the obvious urban center for the region. The separate parish of *N.S. de Remédios* in Campos Novos de Cunha was organized and put in the hands of the vicar of Cunha. At present the priest says mass there the last Sunday of each month.

After the construction of the *matriz*, the formal Catholic organization in Cunha remained static for a great many years. The number of active priests in the *município* was actually reduced in 1915 from two to one, as the church records show that traditionally the vicar had an auxiliary.

Thus, in religious matters the rural people were left very much on their own. As has been noted, the *bairros* as well as the larger *fazendas* had their own chapels, but it was fortunate if the priest arrived more than once a year. Thus, Stanley Stein noted the following about slaves in nineteenth-century Brazil: "Sometimes . . . (the slaves) are baptized. But most of the time they are born, live and die without having had any contact with the representatives of the Divinity" (1957:199). In the absence of a priest, local religious matters were handled by a chaplain or *curandeiro*. The result was that the traditional religious system in Cunha came to have the same kind of dual nature that so many other systems had in the colonial society, with the urban element dominating the structure, but with the majority of people involved mainly in their own local sphere of interest.

Under these conditions the number of local chapels steadily increased to the present total of about sixty. Of these, only twenty-six are in active use; that is, have regular religious services performed in them. Over the years five chapels were built in the town for various special ceremonies, but all but one are now closed. About ten years ago the Church began to expand its field of operations. New parish houses were built in both Cunha and Campos Novos, and the *matriz* was remodeled. Most important of these was the construction and staffing of the hospital, as was noted in Chapter VIII.

Methodist. The first Protestant Church to proselytize in Cunha and still by far the most important is the *Igreja Metodista do Brasil,* the Methodist Church. This church has in fact become so important that the terms "Methodist" and "Protestant" are synonymous in the eyes of many local Catholics. Non-Catholics are either Methodists or atheists, by this view. In 1965 there were two parishes and three congregations in the *município.* The largest and most important parish was located in a *bairro* called "Jericó," which was the site of the original mission, and is located about 40 km. from the town. This congregation had, in 1966, 380 regular members and an estimated 1,500 *afiliados* (affiliated members). It also operated a small mission church in Paraibuna near the *sertão.* The parish of Cunha-Cume has 206 members in two congregations; one in the town and one in the *bairro* of Cume, which lies about 15 kilometers from the *sede.* There are many affiliated members of this parish as well, but since this includes the intensely Catholic urban zone, the number is much smaller than in Jericó.

Both parishes are part of the Brazilian Methodist Church, a national organization with many thousands of members throughout the country. This Church was founded largely by American missionaries in the last century and its structure and general outlook still reflect American influence. Thus each parish is considered essentially independent and Church policy is largely determined by local and regional elected councils. In most considerations the Church shows a highly urban orientation, with emphasis upon education and hard work, a fact which has limited its appeal largely to members of the middle classes. The Methodist Church is highly organized. Each parish has its own full-time professionally trained pastor who is sent by the national church organization, and is always someone from outside the region. The pastor is responsible to both the parish and the bishop, and has little to say in where he is to be sent. It seems that in the church, as well as in the courts, Cunha was used frequently as a temporary (one is tempted to say "hardship") position for those professionals on their way up.

Although Methodism was introduced into the São Paulo region by American missionaries in the last century, the first missionary to enter the *município* of Cunha was a Brazilian, who had been sent out by the Methodist Church already established in Taubeté. These early Protestants avoided the town which, at that time, was openly hostile to their work. Instead, the first Protestant Church in Cunha was established in Jericó in an area where the local great *fazendeiro*, the *Capitão*, was sympathetic. This man and his family played a vital role in the development of the Methodist Church in Cunha.

It should be noted that Protestantism in Brazil usually appeals to certain peripheral classes. It is seen as one of the ways by which an aspiring individual or group may seek to attain position or articulation into the national life. Thus, in the Brazilian Protestant Churches there is usually intense dedication to a rigorous ethic. As T. Lynn Smith has pointed out (1963:526–28), "Protestantism in Brazil is still largely a missionary activity with emphasis upon proselytizing." Therefore, there are few established communities of persons born into the Protestant faith.

Cunha is an exception. In Cunha, the lack of articulation of the rural people with the town's political and economic structure was due not so much to social factors as to physical isolation. By converting first the great landowners in the area around Jericó, the early Methodist missionaries created essentially a subcommunity which was almost entirely Methodist. Hence, in this region one encounters a situation which is very rare for Brazil. Here the local elite is Protestant, and the few unconverted Catholics form a poor, rather outcast subclass. The result is that the Methodist congregations in Cunha have an entirely different character than most Protestant groups in Brazil, and are very different in structure and ethic than the Pentecostal Churches in Cunha.

The first Methodist Church was constructed in Jericó in 1901. In that year the congregation finally separated from Taubeté as an independent parish with its own pastor and about 60 members. At that time the congregation was still a fairly small mission activity, and few important local people had yet joined. The pastor during the 1930s was, in fact, an American missionary. The early years saw a very rapid increase in the number of members. It is important to note that many of these members were large landowners, some of them sons of the local *capitão*, who joined the Church, although the head of the family himself never became an official member. It is said that the sons joined because the most attractive girls of the area were members.

As the region prospered, so did the congregation. Most of the Methodist landowners belong to one of five or six extended families, all of whom are interrelated through marriage. It is generally believed that in Cunha the largest fortunes in the *município* are to be found among the Methodist *fazendeiros* of Jericó and Cume. In the 1920s the size of the congregation reached stability. At this time the general missionary work was finished and the whole region was solidly Methodist, as is shown by the Church records. These show that entrance of new members by means of conversion rather than profession of the family faith had nearly disappeared. Since 1923 the number of members has fluctuated between two and four hundred. A great many members left between 1957 and 1960, due to the general rural exodus as the *fazendeiros* changed over to meat and dairy production, but the number has recently gone back up again due to natural population increase.

Jericó, itself, has grown. The original Methodist chapel, which also served as a schoolhouse, was supplemented a few years by the construction of a large new church built along American lines. And a few years ago a new school building was built which also houses a new cooperative. The village has its own electricity and running water supply. The local parish has plans for creating a separate town around the church, and thus establishing a true Methodist community, but with the increasing influence of Methodists in Cunha urban society the interest in this may decline.

The establishment of the Methodist congregation in the town of Cunha has a long history which reflects changing patterns of belief and authority. According to local Methodist leaders, the *sede*, stronghold of the Catholic Church and the urban Catholic elite, had always been fiercely hostile to Protestant proselytizing. Three early attempts were made to found a Methodist Church in the town and were met with what Emilio Willems (1947:68) calls "a violent reaction." He says that once, "Only the intervention of the *delegado* prevented the evangelists from being lynched." Local Protestant leaders claim that the trouble was instigated each time by local priests.

For many years the Methodists, while economically strong and directly linked with the Paraíba Valley in the sale of their crops, were isolated from the political and social activity of the *sede*. Importantly, the state judicial system protected them, partly because the judge, for many years, was a Presbyterian and was himself occasionally pastor in the Jericó Church.

The effort to build a Methodist Church in the town of Cunha was successful in 1957. The new church, with 160 seats, was built on a hill near the weather station and dominates Cunha visually, especially since it was constructed, like the one in Jericó, with a steeple along American architectural lines. A full-time pastor was appointed from Taubeté and the parish was separated from Jericó. This success was due to a combination of circumstances. Some local residents attribute the lack of Catholic opposition to the vicar, who at that time was a European and somewhat more tolerant than earlier priests had been. In addition, the fact is that by 1957 the economic and political powers of the Methodist *fazendeiros* was too much to resist. They were supported by both the state judiciary and the local political chief who hoped, thereby, to earn their support. The Methodists' political power has developed with their economic strength. Several have been *vereadores* and one was even elected *vice-prefeito* (vice-mayor) in 1959. The local Catholic elite saw that an urban church would probably bring many of the Methodist landowners into the town which would greatly aid its development. Thus, they authorized construction.

Since the church was built, only one incident has taken place. In 1963 a group of Catholic youth, inflamed by a heated theological exchange, carried over loudspeakers, between the pastor and a visiting priest, invaded the new church, ostensibly to attack the pastor. They were met by a group of Methodists and a "free-for-all" was only averted by the intervention of the Catholic vicar. The youths were arraigned in court and forced to pay for damages. At the present time, an arrangement has been worked out between the two churches, and relations are fairly good. The Methodists, secure in their own organization, do not openly proselytize, and the Catholics, in turn, leave the Methodists alone.

Pentecostal. The two Pentecostal churches have a very

different history and form from the Methodist. They more nearly approach the traditional model for Protestant churches. They are still mission-oriented and have not yet developed strong support or organization. Members are mostly aspiring people of the lower and lower-middle urban classes. Neither congregation is yet a parish and there is no full-time Pentecostal pastor in Cunha. They, therefore, are unregistered and do not appear on any official statement of censuses.

The larger and better organized of the two sects is the Assembly of God (*Assembléia de Deus*). This sect claims to have some forty members in the town and a total of about 160 in the whole *município*. Four small rural chapels exist in Cunha, as well as the church in the town. The Cunha branch is a mission of the Assembly of God Church in Guaratinguetá. It, in turn, is an offshoot of the Mother Church of Belém, one of the largest branches of the Brazilian National Assemblies of God Churches. The Cunha church is too small, as of yet, to support a full-time pastor and until that happens it must remain a congregation of the church in Guaratinguetá. Church matters in Cunha are, therefore, in the hands of lay members and most local services are performed by them. A pastor does come up from the valley from time to time to officiate at baptisms and other important ceremonies. The congregation is currently awaiting the official appointment of a pastor of their own.

The Assembly of God Church has been in Cunha for twenty years, according to local members, but the actual church building in town is only five or six years old. Growth of this group in Cunha, therefore, has been very slow, especially when contrasted with the very rapid development of Pentecostal churches in some other parts of Brazil. The fact that the Assembly does not have a full-time pastor or regular church organization in Cunha may partly explain this fact. It may also help explain the indifference of the powerful Catholics to having these churches in town. Proselytizing is subdued in the urban zone. There is another separate mission of the Assembly of God in the northern part of the *município*. This claims some 80 members.

The *Congregação Cristã* is the smallest church in Cunha. It is also the most precariously organized. Only a handful of families belong, and these are devoted, but extremely poor. More than any of the other churches in Cunha, it appears to be locally organized and run. It seems to have been created less because of mission activity of some larger church than because a few families of the same general beliefs decided to get together. There are two *cooperadores* who take care of the tiny church and hold services. Occasionally an elder from a larger Church of the same name in Pindamonhangaba will arrive for baptisms and is nominally responsible for the operations of the church, but the organization of this group is very loose. The church was built two and a half years ago and now has about a dozen members. It does not have members in the rural zones.

As a general rule, the Pentecostal churches appeal to poorer members in the community. These churches generally have appealed to factory workers and other lower and lower-middle class groups in Brazil, a fact which explains their enormously rapid growth. The development of the Pentecostal congregations in Cunha follows a more typical pattern for Brazilian Protestantism than the Methodists (Wagley, 1963:248–49). Thus its members are poor, hard driving, puritanical, and intensely devout, whereas the Methodist farmers of Cunha are rich, shrewd, and worldly.

The Role of the Church in the Community

Roman Catholic. Brazil is a Catholic country and Cunha is a Catholic *município*, and despite Methodist expansion in the past few years, there is still no real threat to the Catholic hegemony. In the town census about 85 per cent of the population stated at least nominal affiliation with the Roman Catholic Church. Only three people denied any kind of religious affiliation. Despite strong Methodist influence in the rural zones, three quarters of the *fazendeiros* are Catholic. The town officials are almost all Catholic. All but one of the professional class, the Methodist pastor himself, are Catholic, and the local schools are organized and run almost exclusively by Catholics. Thus, it can be seen that the urban life of Cunha is still overwhelmingly Catholic, even if the Protestants have a strong foothold in some rural areas. No one who has witnessed one of the great religious festivals in Cunha, where up to 3,500 people fill the streets in a procession which may take hours to pass, can doubt the enormous influence the Catholic Church exercises.

The spread of Protestantism has apparently not cut seriously into the urban orthodox Catholic population, and the Methodist Church does not seek to do this. An analysis of baptismal records in the *Matriz* shows that since 1909, when the records begin, there has been a gradual increase of about 30 per cent throughout the *município* in the number who annually receive this important sacrament. It seems, therefore, that Protestantism has made its major inroads among nonorthodox folk in the rural zones, rather than those who form an active part of the urban Catholic organization in Cunha. This is supported by statements made by the Methodists themselves. The author remembers a few elderly Methodist *fazendeiros* describing with considerable animation the dances and other folk festivities that they had taken part in or witnessed as children. "But we haven't had doings like that around here for years and years," they said. On the other hand, many of the Pentecostals, are ex-Catholics who had left the formal Church. These, in fact, make up the group who most heatedly oppose the Catholic Church in Cunha.

The Catholic Church is deeply involved in many aspects of Cunha life. Aside from purely religious matters, its most immediate and direct concern is the operation of the *Santa Casa*. The Church is largely responsible for the building, staffing, and operations of this hospital, though there has been a certain amount of state aid. The building was put up by a former vicar, a European. There was some debate whether or not to allow Protestants to enter, and construction was only started when the discussion was settled in the affirmative. The current vicar considers the *Santa Casa* his major responsibility and devotes his and the parish's resources accordingly.

To understand the role of the Catholic Church in Cunha, it is necessary to understand the intense interweaving between the formal Catholic organization and the urban society. The school system is largely a branch of the Church, and, in fact, is shown as such in the organizational chart of the parish. The vicar teaches in the *ginásio* and for many years its director was a priest. Moreover, the primary school is dominated by conservative urban Catholic families. There are six religious fraternities which carry out the activities of the Church. One of these is made up of adult men, and this group forms the "elders" of the Church. They are generally drawn from the very highest levels of the local elite, both urban and rural. The Catholic leadership is much more urban in its structure than the Methodist. In short, the formal Catholic Church is, in Cunha, the "establishment" religion.

While the Catholic Church does a great deal of charitable work, especially in the realm of health, there is a widespread feeling, even among the Catholics, that the Methodist Church does more in this regard. This may be largely due to the fact that the Methodist pastor did most of such work himself, whereas the Catholics left it in the hands of a separate society, the Society of Saint Vincent de Paul. Nonetheless, the Methodist pastors had built up a strong backlog of goodwill among the poorer residents of the community.

A very strong strain of anticlericism runs through Cunha, even where it does not lead to a formal break with the Catholic Church. There are a great many people in Cunha who insist that they are devout Catholics, but who never attend mass or have any other links with the formal Church. Frequently these are people, no matter from which class, who still believe in the folk traditions. Others come to oppose a certain priest for political reasons. It is, perhaps, inevitable that a religion which is so bound up in the activities of the urban elite should become involved in politics. At any rate, this has frequently been the case in Cunha. It is not uncommon for a priest to become openly involved in political battles, much to the anger of the opposing factions. This has meant that any vicar runs the risk of offending some group in the region no matter what he does. The former vicar, the European, is a case in point. Among many groups, especially the poorer classes, he is condemned as "a snob who had no interest in the people." Members of the traditional upper class, however, praised his learning and energy. There were a few Catholics in Cunha, strongly devout in their daily behavior, who said that all priests were "fools" or "hypocrites," and who refused to attend mass even though they gave extensively to the religious ceremonies of the town.

Methodist. The Methodist Church in Cunha is decidedly more rural in orientation than the Catholic. The 1965 census lists a total of 83 Methodist families in town. Of these, 54 are occupied in agriculture. Exactly half that number are classified as *fazendeiros*, although many of these are members of the Jericó rather than the Cunha parish. Thus, about a quarter of the rural upper class in the town are Protestant. Of the remaining 27 rural families, 12 are *sitiantes*; the rest are workers.

Few of the Methodist families who have urban occupations belong either to the local elite or to the very poor. Thus, while there are ten Methodist families in commerce, only one of these can be considered important. Only two heads of families have civil service jobs, but several young members of the church have some kind of state employment. There is a tendency for young members of the Methodist rural families to seek some kind of urban employment as clerks or teachers. There are none in really high-level bureaucratic positions, however, or in the influential professional groups, with the exception of the pastor himself. On the other hand, there are few Methodists among the very lowest levels of Cunha society. Only one of the fifty families belonging to the semi-employed group is a Methodist, although there are a few rather badly off rural families. As a general rule, the very poorest elements of Cunha society come from the peasant class and these tend to believe in the folk-Catholic religion. Those who join the Methodist congregation are usually commercial farmers, and by that fact, a cut above the rural poor.

The Methodists are very active in charity and not just among their own coreligionists. Social aid is one of the pastor's most important jobs, and both parishes have jeeps which are used a great deal for service in the rural zones. Much of the organization's activities is devoted to supplying special urban services for the Methodists, due to the fact that most urban services in Cunha are dominated by the Catholic community. Thus, there is a very strong emphasis upon social activity for Methodists to counteract the appeal of the club and cinema. In addition, each congregation has a Sunday School which had a total of 449 students in 1965. The Methodists are not opposed to sending their children to the public schools, despite their Catholic influence, but they apparently feel that a little supplementary work is necessary.

Pentecostal. The two Pentecostal churches have somewhat different orientations. The Assembly of God Church had 13 families in the town. These, like the Methodists, show a largely rural orientation. Six families have rural occupations and four are *fazendeiros.* There are no really wealthy members of the Church, however. The head of one of the remaining seven families is a soldier, and the rest are all laborers. A main concern of this church is proselytizing. It is by far the most aggressive Protestant sect in Cunha, as can be seen by the fact that they have four rural missions. This activity may be expected to increase in the future, especially if the region gets a full-time pastor. This in turn may create some trouble with the Catholics in the town. The six families who make up the *Congregação Cristã* are all laborers or minor civil servants. This church takes on few social services, as it has no real resources. Importantly, they have no support and do not recruit in the rural zones.

This description should give some idea of the role of religion in Cunha. There are several important dynamic factors to consider. In the traditional agrarian pre-industrial society the church is a major service organization. It is responsible for the health, education, and welfare of its people. In such a society, the peasant supplies the economic base, and the elite the political control while the religious system integrates, motivates, and organizes. As the community develops, more and more of these functions are put into the hands of specialized bureaucracies, and this is clearly happening in Cunha. Church influence over the schools is decidedly waning as educational specialists come in and take over from the priests. In the matter of health, the Church still keeps an important role, but even in the *Santa Casa*, final medical decisions are in the hands of trained physicians. This leaves the Church predominantly active only in social aid and charity work—the adjudication of structural inequalities—and in value indoctrination.

In the folk culture the religious system had an enormous series of important functions which are being assumed by specialized urban structures. It has already been shown how in matters of health, the faith healer is being replaced by urban medicine. Most significantly, the great festival cycle, the most impressive aspect of the folk religion, is on the decline. It would be an overstatement to say that it has disappeared, but the characteristical *caipira* elements have diminished sharply. This has been especially true since the 1950s. Many folk elements noted in Cunha by earlier writers are no longer seen. The traditional Christmas festivities, the *folia de Réis,* was only performed in 1965 at my own request. The famous *moçambique* dances are still performed, but whereas in 1945 there were 45 companies, there are at the present time only three or four.

Much of the decline was attributed to the former vicar who was a European and highly urban-oriented. He seems to have been well educated, urbane, and a hard worker, but profoundly opposed to the folk tradition, and he forbade any expression of it in the town. The *caipira* society was already disintegrating and this official discouragement was the deathblow to many folk activities. The European priest alienated much of the population by his actions and he soon found his congregation declining. Even today the poorer classes remember him with some anger. The present vicar said that the decline was so severe that when he first came to Cunha only two old women attended his first mass. Current weekly attendance is several hundred.

The present vicar has rebuilt his congregation by deliberately encouraging the festival system. Processions are organized by the Church and are carried out with great ceremony. Nevertheless, the tone of the festivals seems to have changed. Time after time the author heard statements to the effect that, "This is nothing like it used to be in the old days." The festivals have, in part, the effect of skilled recreations rather than popular celebrations. They have become urban rather than truly "folk" activities. Thus, the author noted that the Cunha town band was performing from a score taken from an article on the music of Cunha which Alceu Maynard Araújo published from his field work in *município* in 1947. In addition, even though the priest goes to some effort to invite various folk groups to perform in town, they are sometimes met with widespread indifference. The urban Catholic Church thus finds itself in the position of propping up a dying folk tradition and is transforming what is left of it along more orthodox Catholic lines.

Former hostilities have declined so far in Cunha that the

two established churches, Catholic in most of the *município* and Methodist in part of the rural zone, are finding more and more agreement. The conflict between the folk society and commercial farmers has been decided in favor of the latter, and the two church organizations are each too powerful to be eliminated by the other. Thus there is a general acceptance of the Methodists entering the town, although they are not fully integrated into the urban society as of yet. One prominent Methodist once told the author that the real division in Cunha was not between Catholic and Methodist, but between rich and poor. One example is the attitude of the local elite toward the two Pentecostal Churches. The Churches were tolerated, but many of the important Catholics claimed that they did not even know of the Pentecostal's existence. Even the most profound Catholics would admit that there were many *boa gente* (good people) among the Methodists, but would generally dismiss the Pentecostals as "crackpots."

Finally, mention should be made of the ecumenical movement in Cunha. The initiative on this matter has come entirely from the Roman Catholic Church, and was generally met with suspicion by the Protestants as an attempt to take over ground that had been lost to the Catholics. In 1966 the Catholic Church was making a real effort to create some dialogue between the two organizations. The Pentecostal churches, as usual, were excluded. Thus, for the first time in Cunha's history the vicar actually spoke to the Methodist congregation in its own church. The next week a Catholic Professor of Theology from Recife came to enhance the movement by giving Biblical conferences in the *Matriz*, to which the Methodist pastors were invited. While a few "diehards" on both sides were shocked, the great majority of the people in Cunha felt that at least some cooperation among the churches would be constructive.

Chapter XII

"São Paulo Cannot Stop"

Paulistas are a willful crowd. They are proud of their city and their state and are strongly determined that the social and economic forces that have made their city the most prosperous in Latin America will continue. The plantation days are over in this part of Brazil and are not about to return. São Paulo is a center of energy and enterprise where an alert and progressive landed elite permitted and encouraged the development of industrial capitalism with startling results. *"São Paulo não pode parar,"* the Paulistas say, "São Paulo cannot stop." And indeed it is clear that the Paulistas will not willingly allow the economy of their state to collapse. Whether their prosperity and expansion can continue, however, in view of the increasing problems of the rest of Brazil is a difficult question to answer, but São Paulo hasn't stopped yet.

And Cunha, lost in its green mountains, is still enmeshed in this massive change, even if it is only fitfully remembered by the busy politicians, bureaucrats and industrialists who run the state. It will continue to be a small cipher in the statistics of some department's data on cattle production, a day's stop on the part of an important politician seeking to be elected governor, and a temporary appointment on the part of an ambitious young official, anxious to be promoted to better jobs. There is little doubt that Cunha will be more and more involved in the busy Paulista life, and as long as the forces which drive São Paulo as an industrial center remain active, Cunha will be swept along.

Two themes have run concurrently through the narrative of

this report of the changes occurring in Cunha. One of these is the end of a tradition, and the other is the ascendency of the commercial metropolis. The first, the tradition, is dying in Cunha in all aspects. Even the great old rural patriarchs, the *coroneis*, are almost all gone now. The few remaining traditional *fazendeiros*, overseeing their sharecroppers planting corn and beans on their estates, are almost all old men, and the historical old form of the *fazenda* with its big house and many peasants' huts will soon be a thing of the past. The traditional town, with its small, aristocratic upper class and family controlled bureaucracies, is also changing almost beyond recognition as rural landowners move in seeking urban services. Urban sprawl has come to Cunha.

The town, no doubt, will remain and even prosper; there seems little likelihood that it will disappear. It is a municipal, religious, and commercial center, and improved transportation will probably lead to its increasing importance, perhaps at the expense of the *bairro* centers. The new road to Guaratinguetá, though it may drain off a few services, should in actual fact quicken its activities. Its traditional functions, on the other hand, as the political and organizational center for the rural patriarchate, a tradition some two hundred years old, have changed enormously. It is now the commercial and educational center for a large number of commercial ranchers in the region, most of whom work their own lands, and an organizational center for the state as well as local bureaucracies.

And what of the *caipira* culture with its great elaboration of ritual and belief, as well as the rich tapestry of Portuguese folk tradition in the town and rural zones which has in the past made Cunha appear so much a pocket of seventeenth century Brazil in modern São Paulo? What of the *moçambique*, the *cangada*, the *muterão*, and the *baile de roça*, the dances in the field? Interestingly, it seems that many of these practices actually increased the year after this study was made. In the long run, however, it seems very doubtful if these can survive the combined impact of economic change and mass society. The shift from agriculture to ranching has already driven many of the *caipira* out of the *município,* and whose who remain are increasingly commercially rather than traditionally oriented. In addition, radio and television have had a profound impact on the old patterns, one which can be expected to continue in the future. With the improvement of education and communication many people in Cunha today, especially in the town, feel nothing but scorn for the old way of life which they are trying strenuously to escape. Bits and pieces of the old traditions may remain in Cunha, the *moçambique* dances have already been presented by a São Paulo television station, but the *caipira* culture is dying.

With the decline of the old way of life comes a new, and Cunha is more and more integrated with the industrial urban metropolis, São Paulo. The basic change has been economic, with new commercial opportunities completely overturning the production base of the region to cattle ranching and dairy farming. This is likely to continue, although a few specialty crops such as fruits and wine could profitably develop in Cunha if the demand and skills were available. In Cunha, the impact of industrial urbanism has been more balanced and, perhaps, more benign than in many regions. Frequently the effects of intense commercial demand have produced a form of "factory in the field," with extremely efficient specialized production of commodities and the development of a wage earning "rural proletariat" (Mintz, 1953–54). This in fact represents an even further extension of the industrial urban process on rural regions.

In other sections of São Paulo something akin to this has happened. The Paraíba Valley, a much richer region, has some huge commercial estates which may employ over a thousand workers and produce on a large scale, rice, milk, meat, and even paper (Long, 1947:63). In Cunha this form of *latifundismo* has not taken place, and the probable explanation is that the region, with its poor roads and hilly terrain, is not rich enough to merit the huge private investment necessary to create such a commercial enterprise. Without extensive commercial pressure from big financial interests, local bureaucratic organizations of the judicial and marketing systems tend to treat everyone equally and have protected the rights of the smaller as well as larger commercial landowners. The result has been that the economic effects on Cunha were diffused and a great many landowners have been able to join the commercial economy without subsequent annexation.

How long this pattern can continue is doubtful. The breaking up of large and small holdings by the Brazilian inheritance pattern makes life increasingly difficult for the very small landholder. Should the industrial boom continue, as seems likely, these small *sitiantes*, or at least their children, are likely to continue to seek work in the towns and cities. It is the more productive farmers, moreover, who can afford to buy the extra land, and it is to be expected that if the commercial opportunities for the products of the *município* continue to grow, the more efficient producers will gradually force out the less efficient. Any such change will be irregular and slow, however, especially since the existing institutions, such as the courts and cooperative, protect the less efficient small producer from takeover. Another possibility is that the improved roads and increasing opportunities will make it worthwhile for large-scale producers to move in and dominate the region. This could well happen should the cooperative fail for any reason.

In view of the tremendous diversity of Brazil, it is hazardous to extrapolate from one community to the national scene. Nevertheless, the study does shed light upon some points. Significantly, it suggests the extremely important role which the metropolis plays in determining rural change. Change must come from the cities. The old patriarchal agrarian structure is very stable and changes only in response to external stimuli. The urban centers supply such stimuli at the most basic level through commerce, but they can effect the rural zones in other ways as well. If the influence is purely from the commercial side the end result is a renewed colonialism with a small agrarian ruling class, such as exists in so many countries of Latin America. But if the metropolitan governments have sincere interests in the development of an entire state or nation they can offer aid and protection to the working rural population to stimulate production. Cunha has developed the way it has because it is a part of the political and legal structure of the state of São Paulo, as well as being increasingly integrated economically. The state government has been willing to contribute aid to the *município*, partly to gain the political support of the rural areas, and partly to insure the production of goods needed by the cities.

It must be admitted, however, that this aid has still been rather haphazard. Agricultural and dairy production could be increased considerably if the state were to send agronomists and other experts into the region with some degree of authority and funds for livestock improvement and the like. This, though in part promised, has not yet been done, possibly due to a lack of trained manpower. It seems likely that for the foreseeable future, therefore, agricultural improvement will be undertaken only by the individual *fazendeiro*, perhaps with some advice from the state or, more likely, the cooperative.

The future of Cunha, and indeed all of rural Brazil, lies in the continued development of its industrial cities. With the decline of a dependent agrarian economy and the rise of industry, Brazilian cities are losing their old nature as places of parasitic consumption of luxury goods by the landed rich, and are becoming actual centers of production. The industry of the cities can potentially supply the goods necessary to raise the general standard of living and absorb the excess labor of the rural population. The evidence shows in São Paulo that this is happening in fair degree, but the process still has a long way to go. It is, however, in the cities that the ideas, the planning, and the research must come, if Brazil, urban as well as rural, is to develop the way it should, and can. It is the leaders of the metropolitan centers who must take the initiative in the development of the rural zones as well as of industrial production. Only in this way can the country's agriculture develop to serve the nation rather than a small elite.

Nor is the situation entirely one-sided. The increased prosperity of Cunha's middle-class farmers and ranchers has expanded the opportunity for Brazil's industry. The number of manufactured goods in the region has expanded enormously over what it was twenty years ago, when only a few of the town elite could afford such things. The *caipira sitiante* owned practically nothing that he couldn't make for himself. Even his clothing was patched and repatched. The modern commercial rancher, on the other hand, not only buys cloth and clothing, but jeeps and trucks, sewing machines and many other items, most of them built through Brazilian industry. Distribution is important here. It is better to have several hundred moderate producers who can afford Brazilian-made jeeps than half a dozen *latifundistas* who can afford imported Cadillacs.

Continued development is vital to the region. Should the industrial economy fail, not only would commercial demand cease on both sides, but the opportunities for rural exodus and city employment would be destroyed. It may be recalled that 40 per cent of the potential municipal population now lives in the cities of the Paraíba Valley and São Paulo. If this potential population were still living in the *município*, traditional agriculture would probably be maintained owing to cheap labor costs, but the soils would soon be exhausted and the standard of living fall to subsistence levels or below. The people in the cities, moreover, like the laborers in the town, are no longer *caipira*. They have been exposed to the cities and generally would not want to return to the land and the way of life of a poor peasant, even if they knew how. Cunha, for the first time in its long history, is no longer able to revert to subsistence peasant agriculture should the commercial economy decline, as it always has reverted in the past. Truly São Paulo cannot stop now. The new rural middle classes can be encouraged by Brazil's cities to greater production and improved technology, or they can be dominated and impoverished through failures and monopoly in the marketing systems. Brazil is a rich country; its chances for balanced development are greater than that of any nation of Latin America. These basic decisions and planning must be made by the national elites for the development and integration of the country as a whole as local control and isolation wane. The end of this tradition is at hand, and while there are things to mourn in its passing the future cannot wait.

Notes about the Literature on Cunha

Cunha was the site of the first community study ever made in Brazil: Emilio Willems' *Cunha: Tradição e Transição em uma Cultura Rural do Brasil* (1947). This monograph had a notable impact on Paulista intellectual life. It focused the attention of the urban intelligentsia upon the peasantry of their own state and described the folk culture in considerable detail. It soon became the standard work on the subject. It is still widely quoted in many fields, from history to literature, and may be considered a classic of Brazilian sociology.

The work came out in 1947, when interest in community studies, stimulated by Robert Redfield's work (1930, 1941), was just coming into full development. Within a few years several other such studies were completed in Brazil (Wagley, 1964; Harris, 1956; Pierson, 1948; Leeds, 1957), but it should be noted that the methodology of the community study approach (Arensberg and Kimball, 1965) has never found great favor with Brazilian social scientists. They generally prefer a broader based sociological approach to the intense focus of the community study. Thus Nelson Werneck Sodré, in his preface to the 1961 edition of *Uma Vila Brasileira*, praised it as a "masterly book" yet conceded that he prefers to use "different methods and analytical criteria" (Willems, 1961:8). In point of fact, the majority of Brazilian community studies have been written by non-Brazilians.

It is instructive in the methodological sense to compare Emilio Willem's study with my own, even though I do not consider this a "restudy" in the sense of Oscar Lewis's work on Tepoztlan (1951). I would say that I found his *Cunha* to be a well-balanced and unusually insightful work. Predictions that Willems made, in the book and in private conversation, have been confirmed repeatedly by the present research, and it is safe to say that most of the key economic and social changes were foreseen by him. The only serious flaw in Willems's work, in the opinion of this author, was its failure to fully and systematically delimit urban-rural connections, and hence the full nature of the community structure. While the study does a fine job of describing the way of life of the *caipira*, it gives only a few hints about the social structure of the neighborhoods, a fact which was noted by Charles Wagley in his review of the book (1951).

The failure to stress the "urban" quality of the town (see Harris, 1956) may have been partly responsible for the poor reception which the book found in Cunha itself. I have noted in the text how proud the Cunhenses are of their town and how touchy they can be about any hint of a rustic background. Over and over I was told how the work was full of "lies" and errors, although when I asked which specific passages were wrong I could find no one who could cite any. Perhaps it is the fate of the student of community to disturb his community. The problem may be demonstrated by the actions of one of the town leaders. He had actively tried to suppress the publication of the book when it first came out and told me that the first edition was "nothing but lies." He was pleased with the second edition of the book (1961), however, which I lent him and found it to be "much better and more accurate" than the first. The two books are almost identical.

Emilio Willems's work did stimulate a considerable revival of interest in the *Caipira Paulista* culture, an interest augmented by the fact that several of his students studied with him in Cunha. Many of them later became very prominent in Brazilian letters and social sciences; they included Mario

Wagner da Cunha, Alceu Maynard Araújo, Carlos Borges Schmidt, and Gioconda Mussolini. All of them continued their research and writing on Brazilian folk cultures, and one of them returned to Cunha for a year's study.

The later research in Cunha by Alceu Maynard Araújo was much more restricted in scope than the work of Willems. It was ethnographic, rather than theoretical, and concerned mainly with folk religion and folk lore. By way of compensation the wealth of detail and meticulous descriptions make books such as his *Folclore Nacional* (1964) valuable sources of data for all kinds of folk beliefs and actiivty. *O Ciclo Agrícola* (1957), Alceu Maynard Araújo's major publication on his research in Cunha, ties in agricultural production and the amount of labor needed during the various times of the annual agricultural cycle with the yearly round of religious celebrations. He shows that the major holidays occur during "vacant" periods in agricultural work. These are all important for students of the *caipira* culture and Brazilian folk religion.

Many other articles have been written about Cunha by Pierre Monbeig (1949 and 1957), Carlos Borges Schmidt (1943, 1946, 1950a, 1950b, and 1951), and Emilio Willems himself (1949a and b). The most important of them, however, is the one written by Mario Wagner Vieira da Cunha (1944) on population growth and settlement in the *município*. This essay, although very short, is based on research carried out in the municipal archives before their destruction in 1961 and is of considerable importance in studying the early history of the region.

Appendix B

Public Finances in Cunha, 1945-1963

The three tables in this appendix show *official* federal, state, and municipal receipts and expenditures for the years 1945 to 1963, as far as figures were available in 1965. Both are given in gross amounts and corrected for inflation. The first and third columns show actual receipts and expenditures for each year shown, according to the statistics of the state. The second and fourth columns are the same, corrected for inflation according to figures furnished by the Fundação Getulio Vargas (1965).* In these the first year in each column represents "100."

As was noted in the text, federal expenditures, although increasing rapidly, are still less than half of federal tax receipts. In general, municipal expenditures just about match their receipts, and state expenditures tend to exceed receipts. The commanding role of the state in government finances is clear, although the *município* until recently was not far behind. It is important to note that there has been a continual increase in *real* (inflation-corrected) income and expenditures in all segments except federal receipts. Large jumps in receipts are probably due to new taxes as well as improved methods of collection. There is constant effort on the part of the federal and state governments to weaken the taxing powers of the *municípios*. Unfortunately, certain key expenses were not available at the time of the study, especially for those of the state government in recent years. Current state expenses in

* Fundacão Getulio Vargas, "Indices Econômicos Nacionais—1965." *Conjuntura Economica*, various issues.

Cunha should be running in the billions of *cruzeiros,* since the construction of the state highway alone is said to be a project of that magnitude.

A. Public Finances in Cunha—Federal

Year	Federal Receipts (*Amounts in \$Cr.*)		Federal Expenditures (*Amounts in \$Cr.*)	
1945	149,692	100	—	
1946	202,645ᵉ	117	—	
1947	—		—	
1948	—		—	
1949	—		—	
1950	305,258	121	—	
1951	169,688	74	—	
1952	204,049	63	—	
1953	283,237	75	—	
1954	338,952	74	—	
1955	476,459	84	—	
1956	573,485	84	—	
1957	767,610	97	154,078	100
1958	789,847	87	131,662	74
1959	1,060,795	84	272,614	111
1960	1,316,478	80	605,002	190
1961	2,007,660	99	1,141,176	292
1962	3,412,074	103	1,556,266	242
1963	4,419,122	78	2,127,185	194

B. Public Finances in Cunha—State

Year	State Receipts (*Amounts in \$Cr.*)		State Expenditures (*Amounts in \$Cr.*)	
1945	485,976	100	405,711	100
1946	570,825	102	581,049	125
1947	549,033	81	623,343	109
1948	—		—	
1949	—		—	
1950	1,154,011	141	—	

Year (cont.)

1951	1,470,249	161	—	
1952	1,777,597	168	2,680,296	303
1953	1,972,378	162	3,389,216	332
1954	2,417,490	163	3,060,089	246
1955	3,445,394	188	3,865,453	251
1956	4,371,005	197	4,095,281	222
1957	5,227,243	204	5,668,972	264
1958	5,993,476	220	8,047,590	326
1959	6,982,475	170	10,702,166	312
1960	27,212,266	512	15,543,299	350
1961	36,569,862	559	—	
1962	52,746,792	512	—	
1963	90,772,223	495	—	

C. Public Finances in Cunha—Municipal

Year	Municipal Receipts (Amounts in $Cr.)		Municipal Expenditures (Amounts in $Cr.)	
1945	128,999	100	137,596	100
1946	148,751	100	140,136	89
1947	160,079	89	162,354	84
1948	268,333	143	337,440	168
1949	—		—	
1950	824,272	380	953,168	411
1951	1,154,399	477	1,061,011	410
1952	1,602,358	570	1,350,088	450
1953	1,234,128	383	985,369	284
1954	2,158,363	550	1,507,549	358
1955	2,214,344	455	2,088,922	400
1956	2,584,512	434	3,340,921	531
1957	3,478,199	507	3,372,170	461
1958	3,689,834	471	3,317,362	396
1959	5,403,726	496	4,838,288	415
1960	—		—	
1961	8,537,821	492	8,158,431	440
1962	19,148,990	672	17,102,042	561
1963	—		—	

Appendix C, Part 1

Standard of Living Scale

The "urban" quality of the standard of living was determined for each household by assigning points on the basis of the approximate value of certain key manufactured possessions. A high score was accepted at 30 or above, and a medium score at 14 to 29. These items are as follows:

Item	Total Number in the Town	Points Assigned
Radio	396	1
Wristwatch	326	1
Newspaper subscription . .	98	1
Electric shower	184	2
Phonograph	53	2
Bicycle	26	2
Sewing machine	270	5
Gas stove (bottled)	163	5
Telephone	93	5
Refrigerator	101	10
Television	54	20
Passenger car	8	30
(excluding jeeps or trucks)		

In marginal cases, house values were also taken into consideration. Zero scores were assigned only to households with a house value of less than Cr. $500,000 ($250).

Occupations and Living Standards in Cunha

Occupation	Standard of Living Score			
	High	Medium	Low	0
URBAN				
Professionals	11	3	—	—
High officials	16	3	1	—
Urban entrepreneurs	15	12	7	—
Small businessmen				
Shop owners	2	7	14	—
Garage owners	1	1	1	—
Craftsmen with shops	—	4	11	1
Motorists with trucks	3	4	8	—
Rural businessmen	1	2	16	—
Service occupations				
Public officials	10	8	21	—
State police	1	2	5	—
Shop clerks	—	3	7	—
Labor—specialized				
State highway workers (D.E.R.) . . .	—	—	21	5
Motorists	—	3	10	5
Other	—	3	20	4
Labor—Unspecialized				
Government laborers	—	—	20	19
Pedreiros	—	1	30	30
Domestics	—	—	6	23
No occupation	—	—	3	8
RURAL				
Fazendeiros				
Major landowners	12	23	26	—
Moderate landowners	—	12	50	—
Widows	1	—	11	—
Sitiantes				
Commercial	—	4	43	—
Traditional	—	—	10	3
Retired	—	—	4	—
Lavradores				
With some land	—	—	17	6
Landless	—	—	40	63

Appendix C, Part 2

House Values

Approximate values were obtained for every house in Cunha. Although the amount reported was frequently inaccurate, especially for the finer houses, the results are still of some interest and are listed here. Although the exchange rate at the time of the study was Cr. $2,000 to one United States dollar, in view of the low cost of construction in Brazil comparable values in the United States would be two or three times the value noted here. The best houses in Cunha were valued at about Cr. $40,000,000 for a modern, well-built *sobrado* (two story house) with all possible urban facilities. Only a handful of the professional and commercial families had homes of this quality. The poorest house in Cunha was a single room lean-to of *pau-a-pique*, occupied by a single elderly woman who was no longer able to work. She said that her shack was worth about Cr. $10,000 (5 dollars). The average value of a house in the town was estimated at about Cr. $3,100,000.

House Values

Occupation	Average House Value in Cr. $1,000,000
URBAN	
Professionals	12.6
High officials	7.7
Urban entrepreneurs	
Commerce	10.2
Industry and construction	7.0

Occupation (cont.)

Small business

    Shop owners 3.6

    Garage owners 3.6

    Craftsmen with shops 3.4

    Motorists with trucks 2.8

    Rural businessmen 3.9

Service occupations

    Public officials 4.0

    State police 3.5

    Clerks 2.7

Labor—specialized

    State highway workers (D.E.R.) 1.4

    Motorists 1.9

    Other 1.3

Labor—unspecialized

    Government laborers 1.0

    Pedreiros 0.9

    Domestics 0.4

    No occupation 0.4

RURAL

Fazendeiros

    Major landowners 9.1

    Moderate landowners 3.6

    Widows 3.3

Sitiantes

    Commercial 2.6

    Traditional 2.0

    Retired 3.0

Lavradores

    With some land 0.9

    Landless 0.7

Glossary

agregado: a tenant farmer or sharecropper. In Cunha it often refers to one who works for more than half the crop, paying often only 20 per cent of the crop. See *meeiro.*

agricultor: anyone who practices agriculture.

alqueire: a measure of land, in São Paulo equal to 2.42 hectares.

Alta Paraíba: the "high Paraíba" region to the south of the main Paraíba Valley.

armazém: a general store.

bacalhau: dried codfish, an important food in the interior of Brazil. In colonial times especially, it was a major source of protein in the diet of the slaves.

bacharelismo: the desire to obtain a degree from a school or university (*bacharel*) simply for the sake of having such a degree.

bairro: literally "neighborhood" or "district." In Cunha a named geographical region with known boundaries. The term "neighborhood" is used in this study to refer to the social unit which the term *bairro* implies.

caboclo: a backwoodsman, hillbilly.

caipira: a backwoodsman or rustic. More specifically in this study a member of, or an adjective pertaining to, the "folk" culture of Southern Brazil, of mixed Portuguese-Indian origin.

caipira Paulista: the variant of this culture which developed in the state of São Paulo.

caixa econômica: a state-run savings bank.

camâra municipal: the municipal council chambers, meeting place for the *vereadores,* the legislative body of a *município.*

camarada: literally "comrade." In Cunha, usually referring to a paid field hand or ranch worker, as opposed to a *parceiro* who works for shares.

Caminho Velho: literally "old road." In this study it refers to the old colonial road from Minas Gerais to the port of Parati which passed through Cunha.

capitão: captain; often an honorary title.

Capitão-mor: the "greater captain," in Colonial Brazil, the local representative of the Portuguese crown and leader of the state militia. Usually also the largest landowner.

chefe político or *chefe:* a local political chief or "boss."

chique: chic, stylish.

cidade: a city or town; more exactly a concentration of population which has the political rights of the center of a *município,* with an elected town council, *prefeito,* etc.

cidade morte: literally, "dead city"; specifically, a term used by the writer Monteiro Lobato to refer to the isolated cities of the Paraíba Valley.

colégio: college, the three years of study after *ginásio.*

comarca: a legal district, presided over by a *juiz de deréito.*

comerciante: a trader, merchant, or business man.

congada: a festival of the *caipira* culture wherein mock battles between "Christians" and "Moors" take place.

cooperativa: a cooperative.

cooperativa agrícola mista: a cooperative dealing with mixed agricultural production.

cooperativa de laticínios: a cooperative of milk producers.

coronel: colonel; in this study, referring to the purchased rank in the state militia, hence an honorary title for a wealthy landowner.

coronelismo: the system of rural politics wherein the *coroneis,* the local landowners and political chiefs, would exchange the votes under their control with state and national politicians in return for political support and favors.

cruzeiro: the Brazilian monetary unit (Cr. $). At the time this study was made it was worth about 2,000 to the U.S. dollar.

curandeiro: a curer, faith-healer.

delegado: a district commissioner of police.

doce: literally "sweet"; also a common kind of Brazilian dessert or snack, usually made of fruit or coconut.

doutor: "Doctor," a title of respect usually accorded to anyone with a university degree.

escola normal: "normal school," a college which grants a teaching degree.

a favor: literally "at the kindness of" or "at the patronage of"; here referring specifically to the practice in rural Brazil of allowing people to live on one's lands rent free.

fazenda: literally a commercial operation ("making"); hence any commercial establishment, ranch, or plantation on a large scale employing workers beyond the owner and his family.

fazendeiro: an owner of a *fazenda,* hence a commercial rancher or planter.

festa: a religious festival or feast.

festeiro: the individual who organizes and sponsors a *festa.*

folia dos Réis: "frolic of the Kings," a traditional *festa* in Brazil held on January 6th.

fôrça pública: the "public force"; in São Paulo the paramilitary state police.

forum: the building which houses the law courts and other offices of a *comarca.*

ginásio: a secondary school, in the Brazilian educational system, supplying the four years of education after primary school.

grupo escolar: a "scholarly assemblage," a primary school.

interventor: "one who intervenes," specifically someone who is appointed by higher authority to replace an existing, usually elected, official.

juiz de deréito: a "judge of law," an important judicial official, trained as a lawyer and appointed to a *comarca* by (in São Paulo) the state supreme court.

juiz de paz: a justice of the peace, a locally appointed judicial official.

latifúndio: a very large landed estate.

lavrador: any agricultural worker, especially one who works on the land himself. In this study it usually refers to someone who works for others. See *camarada, parceiro.*

mascate: a traveling peddler, salesman.

matriz: the "mother church," the main church of a (Catholic) diocese or parish.

meeiro: from *meio*—half, a sharecropper who works on half shares, paying 50 per cent of the crop to the landlord.

mineiro: a native of, or adjective pertaining to, the state of Minas Gerais in Brazil.

minifúndio: tiny landholdings, too small to work profitably.

moçambique: a festival dance of the *caipira* culture characterized by the use of long sticks with which the dancers strike at each other in rhythm with the music.

moreno: "brunet," someone with a dark complexion.

movimento: "movement," action in the widest sense, social as well as political.

município: a municipality, the smallest Brazilian division of local government, corresponding roughly to a county.

muterão: in the *caipira* society a cooperative gathering to render mutual aid and a concentration of labor for house raising or agricultural work; a "bee." Properly, a *muterão* should end with a feast and dance, sponsored by the one who called the group together. According to Octavio Ianni, this is the most important feature of *caipira* culture.

onça: the Brazilian jaguar (*felis onca*).

P.C.: Partida Comunista, the Communist Party.

P.D.C.: Partido Democrático Cristão, the Christian Democratic Party, one of the important parties which supported Janio Quadros.

P.S.P.: Partido Social Progresista, the Social Progress Party, one of the major political parties in Cunha and São Paulo. It was the personal party of Adhemar de Barros.

panelinha: literally a "little pot." This is one of the basic political institutions of Brazil. It is an informal group of political insiders "held together in common interest by personal ties and including a roster of all key socio-politico-economic positions," according to Anthony Leeds.

parceiro: a sharecropper. See *agregado, meeiro.*

parentela: the Brazilian extended family, kindred.

patrão: "patron," a political or economic "boss" or benefactor.

pau-a-pique: wattle-and-daub construction.

paulista: a native of, or adjective pertaining to, the city or state of São Paulo in Brazil.

pedreiro: a bricklayer or stonemason; in Cunha a term frequently reserved for an unskilled urban laborer who often can find jobs only in construction.

pinga: a "drop," euphemism for the Brazilian sugarcane rum, *cachaça.*

político: a politician or anyone deeply involved in politics.

prefeito: the chief administrative officer of a Brazilian *município,* corresponding roughly to the term "mayor."

prefeitura: a city hall, the administrative offices of a *município.*

promotor público: "public prosecutor," a local district attorney.

Santa Casa: "Blessed House," a hospital run by the Roman Catholic Church.

sapé: a Brazilian grass (*Imperata Brasiliensis*) used for thatching roofs of poor rural houses.

sêca: a dry spell, drought, especially during the Brazilian winter, the months of June, July, and August.

sêcos e molhados: literally "drys and liquids," a grocery store, usually in combination with a liquor store and bar. In fact in Cunha these are for the most part bars, in combination with a small liquor and grocery store.

sede: the center of a *município* or diocese. See *cidade.*

sertão: the backlands of Brazil, any remote wilderness regions.

sesmaria: in Colonial Brazil a land grant from the Portuguese crown, often of a square league in area (c. 36 square km.).

sítio: a small family farm, usually with adequate land to supply the owner and his family with a living and worked by them.

sitiante: the owner of a *sítio;* hence a small-scale farmer who works his own land with the aid of his family. He may produce commercially but not on the scale of a *fazendeiro.* A *caipira sitiante* is one who still follows the customs and forms of the *caipira* culture but owns enough land to work on.

taipa: a form of construction used in Colonial times utilizing very thick walls of packed mud. This was reserved for very large constructions, as opposed to the *pau-a-pique* technique.

tenente: "lieutenant," also sometimes used as an honorary as well as military title.

usina: any factory, mill, or processing plant. In Cunha, any location where milk is shipped or processed.

venda: a small rural general store.

vereador: a municipal councilman, one of thirteen in Cunha.

vigário: the vicar, a priest in charge of a parish.

Bibliography

Part A, Documents

ALMANACH Administrativo, Commercial, e Industrial da Provincia de São Paulo (1884). Organizado por Francisco Ignacio Xavier de Assís Moura, Editores Proprietarios Jorge Seckler & Cia.

ARQUIVO DO ESTADO DE SÃO PAULO (1803). (Unpublished). Censo de Ordenança de Cunha.

COMMISSÃO CENTRAL DE ESTATÍSTICA (1888). *Relatório* Apresentado ao Exm. Sr. Presidente da Província de São Paulo, São Paulo, Le Roy King Buckwalter.

(D.E.E.S.P.) DEPARTAMENTO DE ESTATÍSTICA DO ESTADO DE SÃO PAULO. Various years. *Anuário.*

O ESTADO DE SÃO PAULO (journal). Various issues.

(I.B.G.E.) INSTITUTO BRASILEIRO DE GEOGRAFIA E ESTATÍSTICA
(1920). IV Recenseamento Geral do Brasil.
(1940). V Recenseamento Geral de Brasil.
(1948). Sinopse Estatística do Município de Cunha.
(1950). VI Recenseamento Geral do Brasil.
(1960). VII Censo Demográfico, preliminary information.
(1964). Anuário Estatístico do Brasil.

SECRETÁRIO DA AGRICULTURA DO ESTADO DE SÃO PAULO: Divisão de Economia Rural. Various years. (Unpublished). Estimativa das Safras do Estado de São Paulo.

(S.N.P.A.) SERVIÇO NACIONAL DE PESQUISAS AGRONÔMICAS (1965). *Boletim #12:* Levantamento de Reconhecimento dos Solos do Estado de São Paulo.

(T.R.E.) TRIBUNAL REGIONAL ELEITORAL DO ESTADO DE SÃO PAULO. Various years. *Boletim Eleitoral.*

276 Bibliography

Part B, Maps

(I.B.G.E.) INSTITUTO BRASILEIRO DE GEOGRAFIA E ESTATÍSTICA (1960). Carta do Brasil ao Milionésimo.
(I.G.G.E.S.P.) INSTITUTO GEOGRÁFICO E GEOLÓGICO DO ESTADO DE SÃO PAULO.
(1943). Carta Hipsométrica do Estado de São Paulo.
(1954). Folia Topográfica de Taubeté.
(1963). Mapa Geológico do Estado de São Paulo.
(Unpublished) (a) Mapa do Município de Cunha (1945).
(b) Folia de Cunha
(c) Folia de Cruzeiro
(d) Folia de Guaratinguetá
(e) Folia de Ubatuba
(S.N.P.A.) SERVIÇO NACIONAL DE PESQUISAS AGRONÔMICAS (1965). Mapa dos solos do Estado de São Paulo.

Part C, Books and Articles

AB'SÁBER, AZIZ NACIB (1950). "A Serra do Mar e a Mata Atlantica." *Boletim Paulista de Geografia*, 4:60–69, São Paulo.
AMADO, JORGE (1965). *The Violent Land*. (Translated by Samuel Putnam.) New York: Alfred A. Knopf.
ANDERSON, NELS (ed.) (1964). *Urbanism and Urbanization*. Leiden: E. J. Brill.
ANDRESKI, STANISLAV (1968). *Military Organization and Society*. 2d ed. Berkeley and Los Angeles: The University of California Press.
ARAÚJO, ALCEU MAYNARD (1945). "Notas Colhidas em Cunha" (Unpublished).
——— (1957). "O Ciclo Agrícola." *Revista do Arquivo Municipal* (da Prefeitura de São Paulo). Vol. 159, Ano 23:1–155. São Paulo.
——— (1964). *Folclore Nacional*. 3 vols. São Paulo: Edições Melhoramentos.
ARENSBERG, CONRAD M., and SOLON T. KIMBALL (1965). *Culture and Community*. New York: Harcourt, Brace and World.

Bibliography 277

BAER, WERNER (1965). *Industrialization and Economic Development in Brazil.* Yale University: The Economic Growth Center. Homewood, Illinois: Richard D. Irwin.

BAKLANOFF, ERIC N. (ed.) (1966). *New Perspectives of Brazil.* Nashville, Tennessee: Vanderbilt University Press.

BEALS, RALPH L. (1953). "Social Stratification in Latin America." *The American Journal of Sociology,* LVIII:327–39.

BELLO, JOSÉ MARIA (1966). *A History of Modern Brazil: 1889–1964* (Translated by James L. Taylor). Stanford, California: Stanford University Press.

BENDIX, REINHARD, and SEYMOUR MARTIN LIPSET (1966). *Class, Status, and Power: Social Stratification in Comparative Perspective,* 2d ed. New York: The Free Press.

BERTALANFFY, LUDWIG VON (1968). *General Systems Theory: Foundations; Development; Applications.* New York: George Braziller.

BOTTOMORE, T. B. (1964). *Elites and Society.* New York: Basic Books.

BOULDING, KENNETH E. (1968). *Beyond Economics: Essays on Society, Religion, and Ethics.* Ann Arbor: The University of Michigan Press.

BOXER, CHARLES R. (1964). *The Golden Age of Brazil: 1695–1750, Growing Pains of a Colonial Society.* Berkeley and Los Angeles: The University of California Press.

CALDEIRA, CLOVIS (1956). *Mutirão: Formas de Ajuda Mútua no Meio Rural.* Brasiliana. Vol. 289. São Paulo: Compania Editôria Nacional.

CALLOW, ALEXANDER B., JR. (1966). *The Tweed Ring.* New York: Oxford University Press.

CAMARGO, JOSÉ FRANCISCO DE (1966). *Êxodo Rural no Brasil: Formas, Causas e Conseqüências Econômicas Principais.* Temas Brasileiros, Vol. I. Rio de Janeiro: Conquista.

CANABRAVA, ALICE P. (1951). *O Desenvolvimento da Cultura do Algodão na Provincia de São Paulo: 1861–1875.* São Paulo. n.p.

CANDIDO, ANTONIO (1964). *Os Parceiros do Rio Bonito: Estudo sôbre o Caipira Paulista e a Transformação dos seus Meios de Vida.* Coleção Documentos Brasileiros. Rio de Janeiro: Livraria José Olympio Editôra.

DAHRENDORF, RALF (1959). *Class and Class Conflict in Industrial Society*. Stanford, California: Stanford University Press.

——— (1968). *Essays in the Theory of Society*. Stanford, California: Stanford University Press.

DEFFONTAINES, PIERRE (1938). "The Origin and Growth of the Brazilian Network of Towns." *Geographical Review*, 28:379–99.

DUTCH SCHOLORS (1958). *The Indonesian Town: Studies in Urban Sociology*. Published for the Royal Tropical Institute. The Hague and Bandung: W. van Hoeve.

FERRAZ, MARIO DE SAMPAIO (1939). "Cunha." Published by *O Estado de São Paulo* (newspaper), 14 de Março.

FIGUEIRDO, EUCLYDES. n.d. *Contribução para Historia da Revolução Constitucionalista de 1932*. São Paulo: Livaria Martins Editôria.

FIRTH, RAYMOND, and B. S. YAMEY (1964). *Capital, Saving and Credit in Peasant Societies*. London: George Allen and Unwin, Ltd.

FOSTER, GEORGE M. (1953). "What is Folk Culture?" *American Anthropologist*, 55:159–73.

FURTADO, CELSO (1962). *A Pre-Revolução Brasileira*. Rio de Janeiro: Editôra Fundo de Cultura.

——— (1963). *The Economic Growth of Brazil: A Survey from Colonial to Modern Times*. (Translated by Ricardo W. Aguiar and Eric Charles Drysdale.) Berkeley and Los Angeles: The University of California Press.

——— (1965). *Diagnosis of the Brazilian Crisis*. (Translated by Suzette Macedo). Berkeley and Los Angeles: The University of California Press.

GOUROU, PIERRE (1959). *The Tropical World*. (Translated by E. D. Laborde.) London: Longmans.

GRAHAM, LAWRENCE S. (1968). *Civil Service Reform in Brazil: Principles versus Practice*. Institute of Latin American Studies, The University of Texas. Latin American Monographs, No. 13. Austin and London: The University of Texas Press.

GREENFIELD, SIDNEY M. (1968). "The Município, The Community, and the Study of Contemporary Brazilian Society." (Unpublished manuscript.)

GRUPO DA GEOGRAFIA DAS INDÚSTRIAS (1963). "Estudos para a

Geografia das Indústrias do Brasil Sudeste." *Revista Brasileira de Geografia;* 15, No. 2:2–155.

HARRIS, MARVIN (1956). *Town and Country in Brazil.* New York: Columbia University Press.

HERRMANN, LUCILE (1948). *Evolução da Estrutura Social de Guaratinguetá num Período de Trezentos Anos.* Revista de Administração (de Universidade de São Paulo). II, 5–6:3–326. São Paulo.

HONEY, JOHN C., et al. (1968). *Toward Strategies for Public Administration in Latin America.* Syracuse, New York: Syracuse University Press.

HUTCHINSON, BERTRAM (director) (1960). *Mobilidade e Trabalho: Um Estudo na Cidade de São Paulo.* Rio de Janeiro: Centro Brasileiro de Pesquisas Educacionais, I.N.E.P. Ministério da Educação e Cultura.

IANNI, OCTAVIO (1963). *Industrialização e Desenvolvimento Social no Brasil.* Rio de Janeiro: Editôra Civilização Brasileira S.A.

JAGUARIBE, HELIO (1968). *Economic and Political Development: A Theoretical Approach and a Brazilian Case Study.* Cambridge, Massachusetts: Harvard University Press.

KAPLAN, ABRAHAM (1964). *The Conduct of Inquiry: Methodology for Behavioral Science.* San Francisco: Chandler Publishing Company.

KUZNETS, SIMON SMITH, et al. (1955). *Economic Growth: Brazil, India, Japan.* Durham, N.C.: Duke University Press.

LAMBERT, JACQUES (1967a). *Latin America: Social Structures and Political Institutions* (Translated by Helen Katel). Berkeley and Los Angeles: The University of California Press.

——— (1967b). *Os Dois Brasis.* Brasiliana, Vol. 335. São Paulo: Companhia Editôra Nacional.

LEAL, VICTOR NUNES (1948). *Coronelismo, Enxada e Voto: O Município e o Regime Representativo no Brasil.* Rio de Janeiro: n.p.

LEEDS, ANTHONY (1957). *Economic Cycles in Brazil: The Persistence of a Total Culture Pattern, Cacao and Other Cases.* Ph.D. Thesis, Columbia University, New York City. Ann Arbor: University Microfilms.

——— (1964). "Brazilian Careers and Social Structure: An Evo-

lutionary Model and Case History." *American Anthropologist,*
No. 66, Part I:1321–47.

LEFF, NATHANIAL H. (1968). *Economic Policy-Making and Development in Brazil, 1947–1964.* New York: John Wiley & Sons,
Inc.

LENSKI, GERHARD (1966). *Power and Privilege: A Theory of Social
Stratification.* New York: McGraw-Hill Book Company.

LEWIS, OSCAR (1951). *Life in a Mexican Village: Tepoztlán Re-
studied.* Urbana, Illinois: The University of Illinois Press.

LIPSET, SEYMOUR MARTIN (1968a). *Revolution and Counterrevolu-
tion: Change and Persistence in Social Structures.* New York:
Basic Books.

——— (1968b). "Social Class." *The International Encyclopedia
of the Social Sciences,* Vol. 15:296–316. New York: The Free
Press.

LIPSET, SEYMOUR MARTIN, and ALDO SOLARI (1967). *Elites in Latin
America.* New York: Oxford Universitiy Press, Galaxy Books.

LOBATO, MONTEIRO (1959a). *Cidades Mortas,* Obras Completas de
Monteiro Lobato, 1.a Série, Vol. 2. São Paulo: Editôra Brasiliense.

——— (1959b). *Idéias de Jéca Tatú.* Obras Completas de Monteiro Lobato, 1.a Série, Vol. 4. São Paulo: Editôra Brasiliense.

LONG, ROBERT GRANT (1949). *The Middle Paraíba Valley of
Brazil: A Study in Land Utilization.* Ph.D. Thesis, Northwestern
University. Ann Arbor: University Microfilms.

LOPES, JUAREZ RUBENS BRANDÃO (1967). *Crise do Brasil Arcaico.*
São Paulo: Difusão Européia do Livro.

LOPREATO, JOSEPH (1967). *Peasants No More: Social Class and
Social Change in an Underdeveloped Society.* San Francisco:
Chandler Publishing Company.

MARCONDES, J. V., and T. LYNN SMITH (1952). "The Caipira of
the Paraitinga Valley, Brazil." *Social Forces,* Vol. 31, No. 1:
47–53.

MINER, HORACE (1965). *The Primitive City of Timbuctoo,* Revised
Edition. Garden City, New York. Anchor Books, Doubleday and
Co., Inc.

MINTZ, SIDNEY W. (1953–1954). "The Folk-Urban Continuum and

the Rural Proletarian Community." *American Journal of Sociology*, 59:136–43.

MONBEIG, PIERRE (1949). "Evolução de Generos de Vida Rurais Tradicionais do Sudeste do Brasil." *Annales de Geographie*, Ano. 58, No. 309:35–43, Paris.

———— (1952). *Pionniers et Planteurs de São Paulo*. Paris: Libr. A. Colin.

———— (1957). *Novos Estudos de Geografia Humana Brasileira*. São Paulo: Difusão Européia do Livro.

MORSE, RICHARD M. (1958). *From Community to Metropolis: A Biography of São Paulo Brazil*. Gainsville, Florida: University of Florida Press.

MOSCA, GAETANO (1939). *The Ruling Class*. (Elementi di Scienza Politica) Edited and revised by Arthur Livingston. Translated by Hannah D. Kahn. New York: McGraw-Hill Book Company.

MYRDAL, GUNNAR (1963). *Economic Theory and Underdeveloped Regions*. London: University Paperbacks, Methuen & Co., Ltd.

OBERG, KALERVO (1965). "The Marginal Peasant in Rural Brazil." *American Anthropologist*, No. 67:1417–1427.

OSSOWSKI, STANISLAW (1963). *Class Structure in the Social Consciousness*. (Translated from the Polish by Sheila Patterson). London: Routledge & Kegan Paul.

PEN, JAN (1966). *Harmony and Conflict in Modern Society*. (Translated from the Dutch by Trevor S. Preston) London: McGraw-Hill Publishing Company Ltd.

PIERSON, DONALD (with the assistance of Levi Cruz and Others) (1948). *Cruz das Almas, a Brazilian Village*. Washington, D.C.: Smithsonian Institution. Institute of Social Anthropology, Publication No. 12.

POLANYI, KARL (1957). *The Great Transformation*. Boston: The Beacon Press.

PRADO JUNIOR, CAIO (1967). *The Colonial Background of Modern Brazil*. (Translated by Suzette Macedo) Berkeley and Los Angeles: The University of California Press.

REDFIELD, ROBERT (1930). *Tepoztlán: A Mexican Village*. Chicago: The University of Chicago Press.

———— (1941). *The Folk Culture of Yucatan*. Chicago: The University of Chicago Press.

282   Bibliography

REDONDO, GARCIA (1895). "O Municipio de Cunha e a Cultura da Vinha." Separate from the journal *Correio Paulistano*, São Paulo.

RICH, JOHN LYON (1951). "Problems in Brazilian Geology and Geomorphology Suggested by Reconnaisance in the Summer of 1951." *Geologia*, No. 9. São Paulo.

RIGGS, FRED W. (1964). *Administration in Developing Countries: The Theory of Prismatic Society*. Boston: Houghton Mifflin Company.

ROSA, JOÃO GUIMARÃES (1966). *Sagarana: A Cycle of Stories*. (Translated by Harriet de Onís) New York: Alfred A. Knopf.

RUELLAN, FRANCIS (1944–1945). "Interpretação geomorfológica das relações do Vale do Paraíba com as Serras do Mar." *Boletim Geografico*, Ano. 2; No. 21:1374–75; Ano. 2; No. 23: 1738–39 and 1748.

RUELLAN, FRANCIS, and AROLDO DE AZEVEDO (1949). "Excusão a Região de Lorena e a Serra do Bocaina." *Anais de Associação dos Geógrafos Brasileiros*, Vol. 1, 1945–1946:19–39.

SCHEMAN, RONALD (1962). "Brazil's Career Judiciary." *Journal of the American Judicature Society*, Vol. 46, No. 7:134–40.

SCHMIDT, CARLOS BORGES (1943). "Aspectos da Vida Agrícola na Vale Paraitinga." *Sociologia*, No. 5:35:55.

——— (1946). *O Meio Rural: Segunda Edição*. São Paulo; Secretaria da Agricultura, Indústria e Comércio do Estado, Diretoria de Publicidade Agrícola.

——— (1949). "A Habitação Rural na Região do Paraitinga." *Boletim Paulista de Geografia*, No. 3, Oct., pp. 34–50.

——— (1950a). "Povamento ao longo de uma estrada Paulista." *Boletim Paulista de Geografia*, No. 6, Oct., pp. 44–45.

——— (1950b). "O Alto Vale do Paraíba." *Boletim Paulista de Geografia*, No. 4, Março, pp. 160–72.

——— (1951). "Rural Life in Brazil," in SMITH, T. LYNN, and ALEXANDER MARCHANT. *Brazil, Portrait of Half a Continent*.

SERVICE, ELMAN R. (1962). *Primitive Social Organization: An Evolutionary Perspective*. New York: Random House.

SETZER, JOSÉ (1946). "A Distribução normal das chuvas no Estado de São Paulo." *Revista Brasileira de Geografia*, Ano. 8, No. 1: 3–70.

Bibliography   283

SHIRLEY, ROBERT W. (1967). *The End of a Tradition: Culture Change and Development in the Município of Cunha, São Paulo, Brazil.* Ph.D. Thesis, Columbia University, New York City. Ann Arbor: University Microfilms.

SJOBERG, GIDEON (1952). " 'Folk' and 'Feudal' Societies." *American Journal of Sociology,* Vol. 58:231–39.

——— (1960). *The Pre-industrial City, Past and Present.* New York: The Free Press.

SKIDMORE, THOMAS E. (1967). *Politics in Brazil, 1930–1964: An Experiment in Democracy.* New York: Oxford University Press.

SMELSER, NEIL J. and SEYMOUR MARTIN LIPSET (1966). *Social Structure and Mobility in Economic Development.* Chicago: Aldine Publishing Company.

SMITH, T. LYNN (1963). *Brazil: People and Institutions.* Baton Rouge: Louisiana State University Press.

SMITH, T. LYNN, and ALEXANDER MARCHANT (1951). *Brazil: Portrait of Half a Continent.* New York: The Dryden Press.

SOUZA, BERNARDO JOSÉ DE (1961). *Dicionário da Terra e da Gente do Brasil.* Brasiliana: Grande Formato, Vol. 19. São Paulo: Companhia Editôria Nacional.

SPIX, JOHANN BAPTIST VON, and C. F. PHIL VON MARTIUS (1824). *Travels in Brazil in the Years 1817–1820.* London: Longman et al.

STADEN, HANS (1874). *The Captivity of Hans Stade of Hesse in A.D. 1547–1555 among the Wild Tribes of Eastern Brazil.* (Translated by Albert Tootal, annotated by Richard F. Burton.) London: The Hakluyt Society.

STEIN, STANLEY (1955). *"Brazilian Cotton Textiles Industry: 1850–1950,"* in KUZNETS, SIMON S., *Economic Growth: Brazil, India, Japan.*

——— (1957a). *Vassouras: A Brazilian Coffee County, 1850–1900.* Cambridge, Mass.: Harvard University Press.

——— (1957b). *The Brazilian Cotton Manufacture: Textile Enterprise in an Underdeveloped Area, 1850–1950.* Cambridge, Mass.: Harvard University Press.

TAUNAY, AFFONSO D'ESCRAGNOLLE (1939–1943). *História do Café no Brasil.* 15 vols. Rio de Janeiro: Edição do Departamento Nacional do Café.

———— (1945). *Pequena História do Café no Brasil.* Rio de Janeiro: Departamento Nacional do Café.

TAX, SOL (ed.) (1967). *Acculturation in the Americas.* (Proceedings and Selected Papers of the XXIXth International Congress of Americanists, 1949). Republished New York: Cooper Square Publishers, Inc.

TAYLOR, JAMES L. (1958). *A Portuguese-English Dictionary.* Stanford, Calif.: Stanford University Press.

TÔRRES, JOÃO CAMILLO DE OLIVEIRA (1965). *Estratificação Social no Brasil.* São Paulo: Difusão Européia do Livro.

WAGLEY, CHARLES (1949). Review of *Cunha,* by Emilio Willems. *American Anthropologist,* 51:306–308.

———— (1971). *An Introduction to Brazil,* Revised Edition. New York: Columbia University Press.

———— (1964). *Amazon Town: A Study of Man in the Tropics.* New York: Alfred A. Knopf.

WAGNER VIEIRA DA CUNHA, MARIO (1944). "O Povoamento do Município de Cunha." *Anais do IX Congresso Brasileiro de Geografia,* Vol. III:641–49.

———— (1963). *O Sistema Administrativo Brasileiro: 1930–1950.* Rio de Janeiro: Instituto Nacional de Estudos Pedagógicos, Ministério de Educação e Cultura.

WARNER, W. LLOYD (1960). *Social Class in America: The Evaluation of Status.* New York: Harper and Brothers, Torchbooks.

WEBER, MAX (1958). *From Max Weber: Essays in Sociology.* (Edited by H. H. Gerth and C. Wright Mills) New York: Oxford University Press, Galaxy Books.

WEREBE, MARIA JOSÉ GARCIA (1963). *Grandezas e Misérias do Ensino Brasileiro.* São Paulo: Difusão Européia do Livro.

WHITTEN, NORMAN E., JR. (1965). *Class, Kinship and Power in an Ecuadorian Town.* Stanford, California: Stanford University Press.

WILLEMS, EMILIO (1947). *Cunha: Tradição e Transição em uma Cultura Rural do Brasil.* São Paulo: Secretária da Agricultura do Estado.

———— (1949a). "Acculturative Aspects of the Feast of the Holy Ghost in Brazil." *American Anthropologist,* No. 51:400–408.

——— (1949b). "Caboclo Cultures in Southern Brazil," in TAX, SOL (ed.) *Acculturation in the Americas.*

——— (1953). "The Structure of the Brazilian Family." *Social Forces*, 31, No. 4:339–45.

——— (1955). "Protestantism as a Factor of Culture Change in Brazil." *Economic Development and Cultural Change*, 3, No. 4: 321–34.

——— (1961). *Uma Vila Brasileira: Tradição e Transição.* São Paulo: Difusão Européia do Livro.

——— (1967). *Followers of the New Faith: Culture Change and the Rise of Protestantism in Brazil and Chile.* Nashville, Tennessee: Vanderbilt University Press.

WILLIAMSON, JEFFREY G. (1965). "Regional Inequality and the Process of National Development." *Economic Development and Cultural Change*, Vol. 13, No. 4, Part II.

WOLF, ERIC R. (1957). "Closed Corporate Peasant Communities in Mesoamerica and Central Java." *Southwestern Journal of Anthropology*, 13:1–18.

——— (1966). *Peasants.* Englewood Cliffs, N.J.: Prentice Hall, Inc.

WYTHE, GEORGE (1955). "Brazil; Trends in Industrial Development," in S. S. KUZNETS, (ed.), *Economic Growth: Brazil, India, Japan.*

Index

Ab'Sáber, Aziz Nacib, 5
Action, social, 172-76
Adhemar de Barros, Dr., 64, 94, 101, 104, 109; interventor, 32
Advanced education, in Cunha, 223-26, 228
"Advertiser," the, 155
African community in Brazil, 73-74
Africans, 73-74 (*see also* Race in Cunha)
African slavery (*see* Slavery)
Agrarian Patriarchate (*see* Patriarchate, rural)
Agregado, 127
Agricultural station, in Cunha, 105, 107
Agriculture: caipira, 34-37 (*see also* Caipira); commercial (*see* Commerce, fazendeiro, and specific products, e.g., Corn, Cotton); decline, 65-67; education, 223; history, 19-20; politics, 100-101; production, 66; subsistence, 34-37; —cycle, 22; —decline, 67, —reversion no longer possible, 257
Agronomists: education, 233; lacking in Cunha, 255
Aguardente, *see* Pinga
Almanach, Administrativo, Commercial e Industrial da Provincia de São Paulo (title), 2, 15
Alta Paraíba (region), 4, 5, 6, 51; cotton production, 28
Altitude: of Cunha, 6; economic effects, 6, 8, 26

Alto de Cruzeiro (urban bairro), 166
Alves, Rodrigues (*see* Rodrigues Alves)
Amado, Jorge, 75 fn, 113 fn
Anderson, Nels, 69
Andreski, Stanislav, 112
Angra dos Reis, 2
Antibiotics, 169
Anticlericalism in Cunha, 245-46
Antunes, Antonio (pseud.), 102
Aparecida, Nossa Senhora da, 3, 21, 149
Appliances: market in Cunha, 153 (*see also* specific items, e.g., radios); stratification, 203-204
Araújo, Alceu Maynard, 34 fn, 36, 40, 41, 42, 89, 90, 173, 244, 261
Architecture in Cunha, 157, 163-66
Archives: municipal, burned, 101; state (*see* Arquivo do Estado de São Paulo)
Areias, 2, 21, 24, 25, 51, 144
Arensberg, Conrad M., 259
Aristocracy, imperial, 24 (*see also* Coffee barons, Coronelismo, Elite)
Armazem (general store) in Cunha, 154
Arming slaves, 74
Arquivo do Estado de São Paulo, 18
Assembléia de Deus (church), 234, 247-48 (*see also* Church, Pentecostal, Religion); foundation, 242-43; leader, 188
Assembly of God, *see* Assembléia de Deus

49-50; movement, 256-57; Paraíba Valley, 50-51; race, 208-11; rural, 142; rural exodus, 142-46; town growth, 147-48, 157-66
Populism in Cunha politics, 99, 101-104
Populist style politics, 92
Portuguese: elite, 73-75; settlement, 1, 14
Portuguese language (*see* Language)
Potatoes, 54, 66
Pottery in Cunha, 38
Poverty, 200-202; migration due to, 180
Power: authority, 113-14; Cunha (*see* Legal order); defined, 71; derived from authority, 71; derived from legal system, 72; force, decline, 114; force, primary, 113; influence, 196-99; land tenure, 113; use of, 83-84; wealth, 112-13
Prefeito: Clube, 173; Cunha, to *1932*, 80-81; Cunha, *1938–1958*, 98; Cunha, *1959* on, 99-104; official, 182, 184, 225
Prefeitura: burning, 101, 121; furnishing house plans, 164
Pre-Industrial City (title), 70
Pre-industrial education, 212-14, 220-21
Pre-industrial urbanism, 75-76
Prejudice: class, 208; color, 209
Pressure group politics, 92-93
Pressure groups, 63-64, 202
Prestige: authority and, 204; derived from power, 112; influence, 196-99; occupations, 204-208, 230; stratification, 111
Prestige economies, 204
Prices: food, 53-54, 65-67; government set, 60; houses, 166; land, 116; milk, 60
Priest, 182 (*see also* Vicar)
Privilege, 113
Production in Cunha, 66 (*see also* Agriculture)
"Produtos da sobremesa," 12
Professionals: Catholic church, 244; Cunha, 182, 185, 266, 267; Cunha, *1945–1966*, 149; education, 218-29, 232; legal order, 91; Methodist Church, 247
Promenading in Cunha, 176
Promises, political, in Brazil, 96
Promotor Público: Cunha, 90-91, 182, 184; office, 85
Propagandista, O, 155
Property: authority, 112-13; defended by judiciary, 114; defined, 103; race, 211; as resource, 202; standard of living, 202-204; stratification, 111-12
Prosperity, in coffee cycle, 27
Prosperous in Cunha, 200-201
Protection of industry, 48-49
Protestantism (*see also* Church, Religion): Brazilian, 238; Cunha, 239; missions (*see* Missions); Orthodox Catholicism, 244; pentecostals, 241-43
P.S.P., 104, 169 (*see also* Partido)
P.T.B., 92 (*see also* Partido)
Public finances in Cunha, 145-63; federal, 262, 263; municipal, 262, 264; state, 262, 263, 264
Public service: education, 216, 230; occupations, 187-88, 210, 266, 268; rural landowners attracted, 149

Quadros, Dr. Janio, 93, 104, 109
Quebra Cangalha, Serra da, 3, 4, 5, 21
Queluz, 21, 25
Quentão, 44

Race in Cunha (*see also* Slavery, Stratification): African, 16-19, 73-74; Indians, 10, 14; modern patterns, 208-11; Portuguese, 1, 10, 14, 73-75
Racism in the United States, 109 fn
Radios in Cunha, 108, 153, 265

"Sacred books," 213
Sagarana (title), 96 fn, 198 fn
Saint Vincent de Paul, society, 245
Salvador, Dr. Thales (pseud.), 80-
82, 83, 97, 98, 103, 209, 215
Sanitation (see Urban services)
Santa Casa (hospital), 170-71, 244-45
Santos, 2, 13, 21; exchange, 29
Santos, Joaquim Luis dos (pseud.),
139
São José dos Campos, 3, 21, 51
São Paulo city: location, 1, 2, 13,
21; population, 50, 51, 56, 144
São Paulo State (see also São Paulo
State Government) : history (see
Coffee, Constitutionalist Revolution); location, 11, 13; population, 50 (see also Population, Settlement patterns)
São Paulo State Government (see
also Legal order, Politics) : Cunha,
role, 102-10; development and,
255; donations to município, 105-
106; education (see Education,
Schools) ; escola normal, 225-26;
expenditures in Cunha, 262, 263,
264; highway costs, 262-63; lack
of investment in rural zones, 107;
politics and Cunha, 102-10; receipts in Cunha, 262, 263, 264;
roads, 106, 122-23, 262-63; state
police (see Fôrça Pública) ; urban
services, 105, 166-76 (see also
Urban services)
Sapé, 37, 164
Sawmill in Cunha, 151
Scale, standard of living, 265-66
Scheman, Ronald, 88
Schmidt, Carlos Borges, 34 fn, 261
Schools (see also Education, Escola
Normal, Ginásio, School teachers) : Catholic Church, 245; construction, 103, 105, 215, 217; defined, 212; development, 214-26;
director, 182; history, 215-16; industrial society, 213; Methodist

church, 247; pre-industrial society,
212-13; professionalization, 225-
26; rural, 216-17, 221-23; struc-
tural change, 219-20
School teachers, 184, 189 (see also
Education, Schools) ; demand,
220; methods, 221; number, 215-
16, 217; pay, 223; training, 221-
22; woman's status, 223-24
Sêca, 8, 63
Secondary education and above in
Cunha, 227 (see also Education)
Secondary school (see Ginásio)
Sêcos e Molhados, 154
Secretário de Agricultura do Estado
de São Paulo, 63, 65
Sede (see Town)
Semiemployment, 189
Serra do Mar, 2, 5, 21, 61, 151
Sertão, 8, 117, 121
Service occupations, 187-88
Services: commercial in Cunha, 154
Services: urban in Cunha, 166-76
(see also Urban services)
Serviço Nacional de Pesquisas Agro-
nômicas (S.N.P.A.), 6
Sesmarias, 16, 22, 46
Setzer, José, 8
Settlement patterns (see also Land
tenure) : caipira, 34-35, 38-39;
Cunha, 15-22; neighborhoods, 40-
41; research, 261; Southern Bra-
zil, 14
Sewage network, 106, 168
Sewing machines in Cunha, 153, 265
Sex and education, 213, 219, 228-29
Sharecroppers (see Rural labor)
Shop owners, 183, 210, 266, 268
Shops in Cunha, 154
Showers, electric in Cunha, 265
Silos, 63
Simon, Nilo (pseud.), 99-104
Simonsen, Roberto C., 73
Simple gradation in stratification, 112
Sitiante: caipira, 193-94, 256; de-
fined, 17, 18 fn, 192; education,

Spiritualists in Cunha)
Sweet potato, 36
Swidden agriculture (see Agriculture, subsistence)
"Switzerland of Brazil," 3
Syrians (see Lebanese)

Tailors in Cunha, 154
Taubeté, 3, 15, 21, 24, 25, 51, 98, 144
Taunay, Affonso D'Escragnolle, 12, 24, 25, 26
Taxation, 262 (see also Public finance in Cunha) : base, 106; collection, 102; collector, federal, 182; collector, state, 182, 184; travel, 122
Teachers (see School teachers)
Teaching (see Education, Schools, School teachers)
Telephone service in Cunha, 167, 189, 265
Television, in Cunha, 108, 265
Tepoztlán, 33, 260
"Threat" system and power, 114
Tiles, roof, 163
Tobacco, 37, 54, 66
Topographer, 182
Tôrres, João Camillo de Oliveira, 1
Town of Cunha: bairro center, town as, 195; bairros, urban, 162; band, 249; center, 165-66; coffee cycle, 26; commerce, 153-57 (see also Commerce) ; Constitutionalist Revolution, 31-32; description, 5; education (see Education, Schools) ; foundation around Matriz, 235-36; function, 147-48, 252; growth, 147-48, 157-66; —and education, 214; location, 4, 5, 21; map, 1945, 158-59; map, 1966, 160-61; market failure, 56; Methodist church, 240-41; metropolitan integration, 255; movimento, 172-76; occupations (see Occupations) ; outpost, governmental, 20; predictions, 252; religion (see Church) ; shops, 154;

urban quality, 69-70; urban stimulation by road, 20; war, 31-32
Town, Indonesian, 147
Towns, role, 75-76
Trade (see Commerce)
Tradition, end, 252-53
Transportation (see also Roads) : Cunha, 121-26; development, 51; geography, 2, 6, 8, 61 fn; milk distribution, 60-61
Trials, legal, 118; power of Juiz, 89; records, 85
"Troubles," time of, 79-80
Trucks in Cunha, 123-24
Tuberão de Terra, 117
Tweed, "Boss," 96
"Two Brazils," 1

Uma Vila Brasileira (title), 260
United States: aid, 221; cotton, 27-29
University education (see also advanced education), few in Cunha, 223
Upper class (see Elite)
Urban education in rural zones, 217
Urban form of Cunha, 165-66
Urbanism, elite, 75-76; industrial (see Industrial urbanism, Industry) ; pre-industrial (see Pre-industrial urbanism)
Urbanization: commerce, 153; Cunha, 146; literacy, 232-33; school, 212-14
Urban labor (see Labor)
Urban law (see Legal order)
Urban life: stimulated in gold rush, 20, 22; style, 203-204
Urban migration, 142-46 (see Rural exodus)
Urban occupations (see Occupations)
Urban quality of Brazilian towns, 69, 260
Urban-rural dichotomy in Cunha, 20
Urban-rural relations, 44-47
Urban services (see also Dental care,